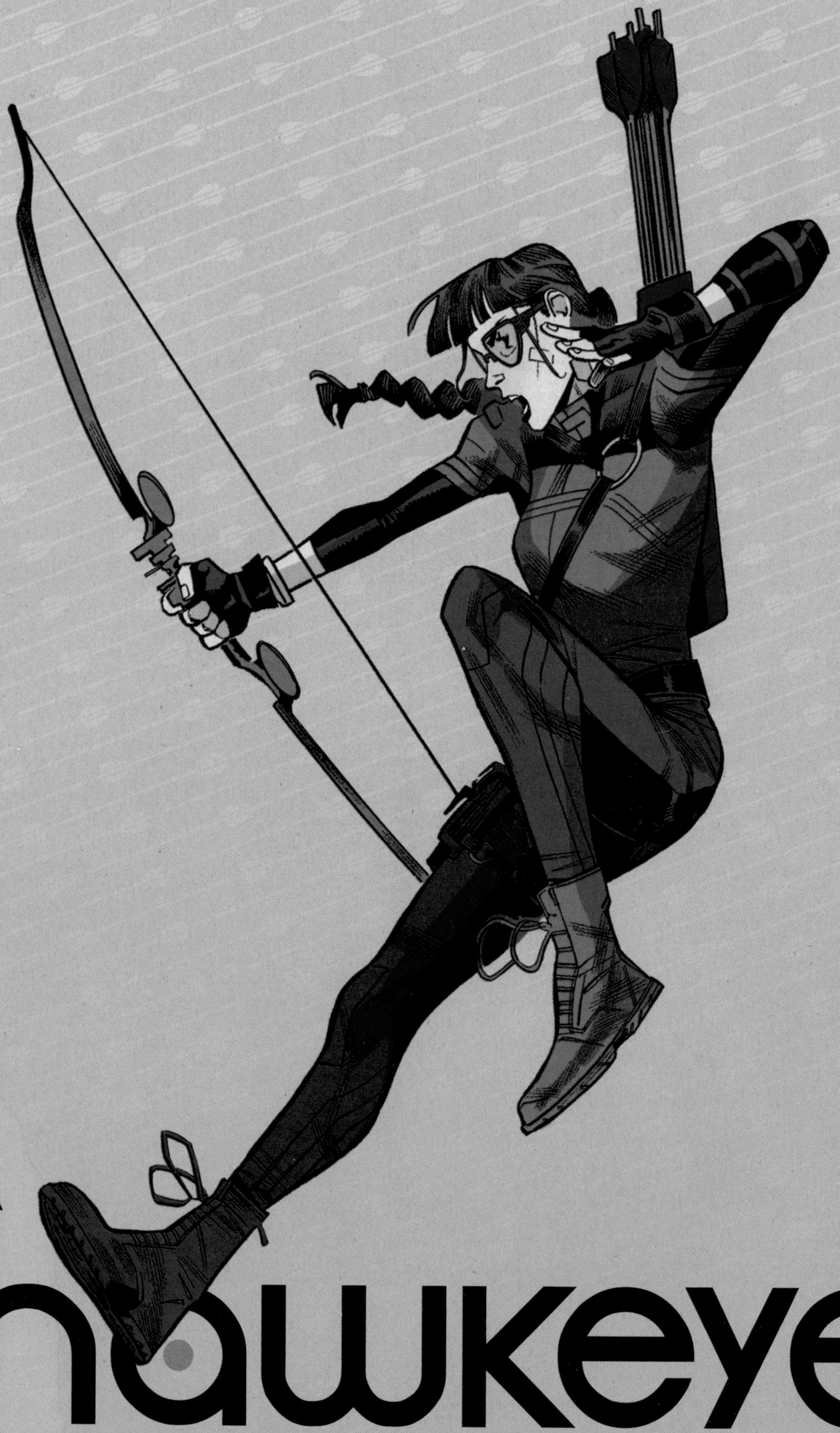

hawkeye

kate bishop

Kate Bishop: Private investigator. Dog lover.
Former Young and West Coast Avenger.
Best Hawkeye.
For all investigatory and/or arrow-related needs, please reach out to...

haw

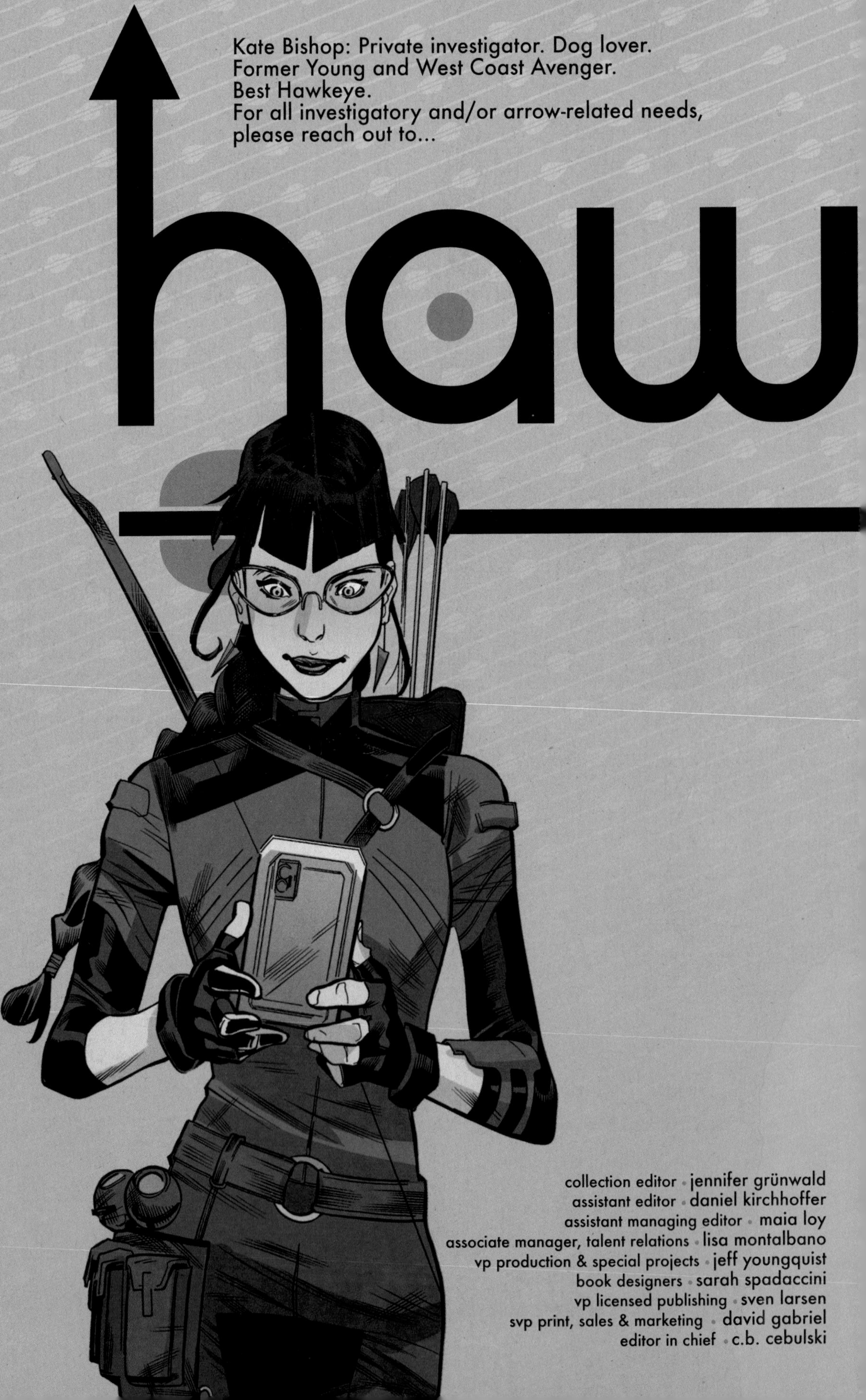

collection editor • jennifer grünwald
assistant editor • daniel kirchhoffer
assistant managing editor • maia loy
associate manager, talent relations • lisa montalbano
vp production & special projects • jeff youngquist
book designers • sarah spadaccini
vp licensed publishing • sven larsen
svp print, sales & marketing • david gabriel
editor in chief • c.b. cebulski

keye
— kate bishop -

Writer
Marieke Nijkamp

Penciler
Enid Balám

Inkers
Oren Junior
with Roberto Poggi (#5)

Color Artists
Brittany Peer
with Cris Peter (#2)
& Rachelle Rosenberg (#5)

Letterer
VC's Joe Caramagna

Cover Art
Jahnoy Lindsay

Editor
Caitlin O'Connell

Senior Editor
Lauren Bisom

HAWKEYE: KATE BISHOP. Contains material originally published in magazine form as HAWKEYE: KATE BISHOP (2021) #1-5. First printing 2022. ISBN 978-1-302-93299-2. Published by MARVEL WORLDWIDE, INC., a subsidiary of MARVEL ENTERTAINMENT, LLC. OFFICE OF PUBLICATION: 1290 Avenue of the Americas, New York, NY 10104. © 2022 MARVEL No similarity between any of the names, characters, persons, and/or institutions in this book with those of any living or dead person or institution is intended, and any such similarity which may exist is purely coincidental. **Printed in Canada.** KEVIN FEIGE, Chief Creative Officer; DAN BUCKLEY, President, Marvel Entertainment; JOE QUESADA, EVP & Creative Director; DAVID BOGART, Associate Publisher & SVP of Talent Affairs; TOM BREVOORT, VP, Executive Editor; NICK LOWE, Executive Editor, VP of Content, Digital Publishing; DAVID GABRIEL, VP of Print & Digital Publishing; MARK ANNUNZIATO, VP of Planning & Forecasting; JEFF YOUNGQUIST, VP of Production & Special Projects; ALEX MORALES, Director of Publishing Operations; DAN EDINGTON, Director of Editorial Operations; RICKEY PURDIN, Director of Talent Relations; JENNIFER GRÜNWALD, Director of Production & Special Projects; SUSAN CRESPI, Production Manager; STAN LEE, Chairman Emeritus. For information regarding advertising in Marvel Comics or on Marvel.com, please contact Vit DeBellis, Custom Solutions & Integrated Advertising Manager, at vdebellis@marvel.com. For Marvel subscription inquiries, please call 888-511-5480. **Manufactured between 2/25/2022 and 3/29/2022 by SOLISCO PRINTERS, SCOTT, QC, CANADA.**

10 9 8 7 6 5 4 3 2 1

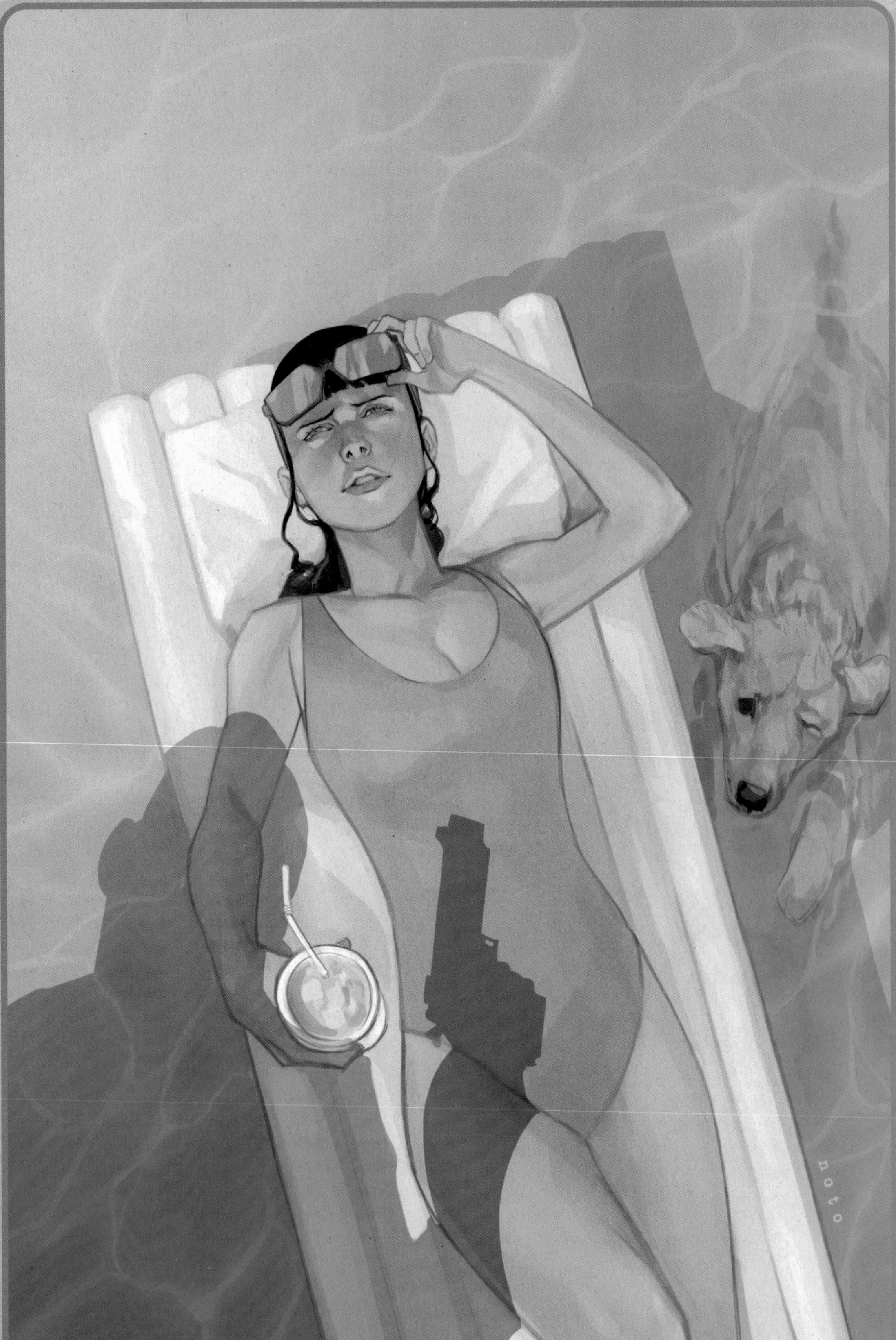
noto

#1 VARIANT
BY **PHIL NOTO**

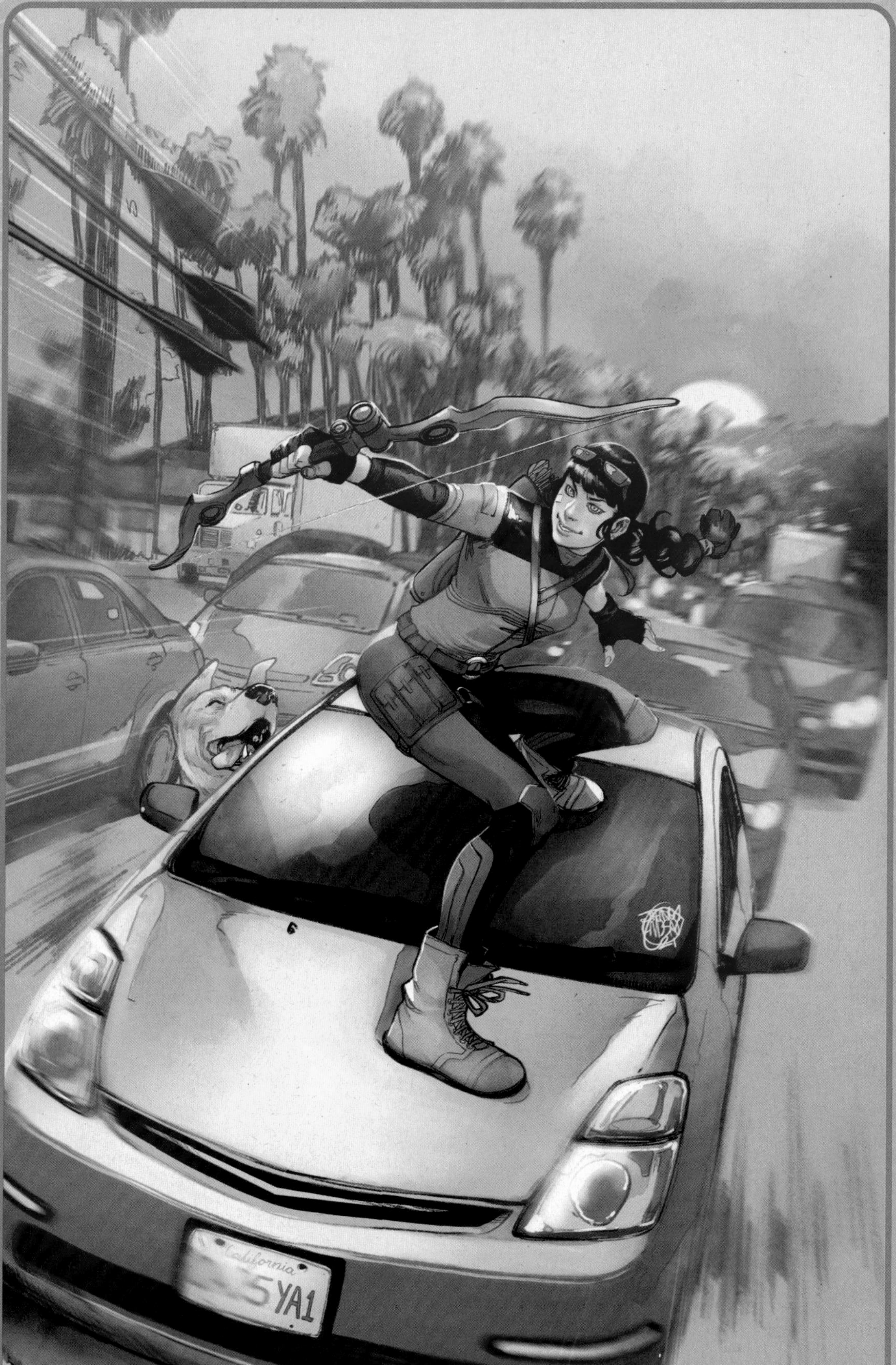
California
YA1

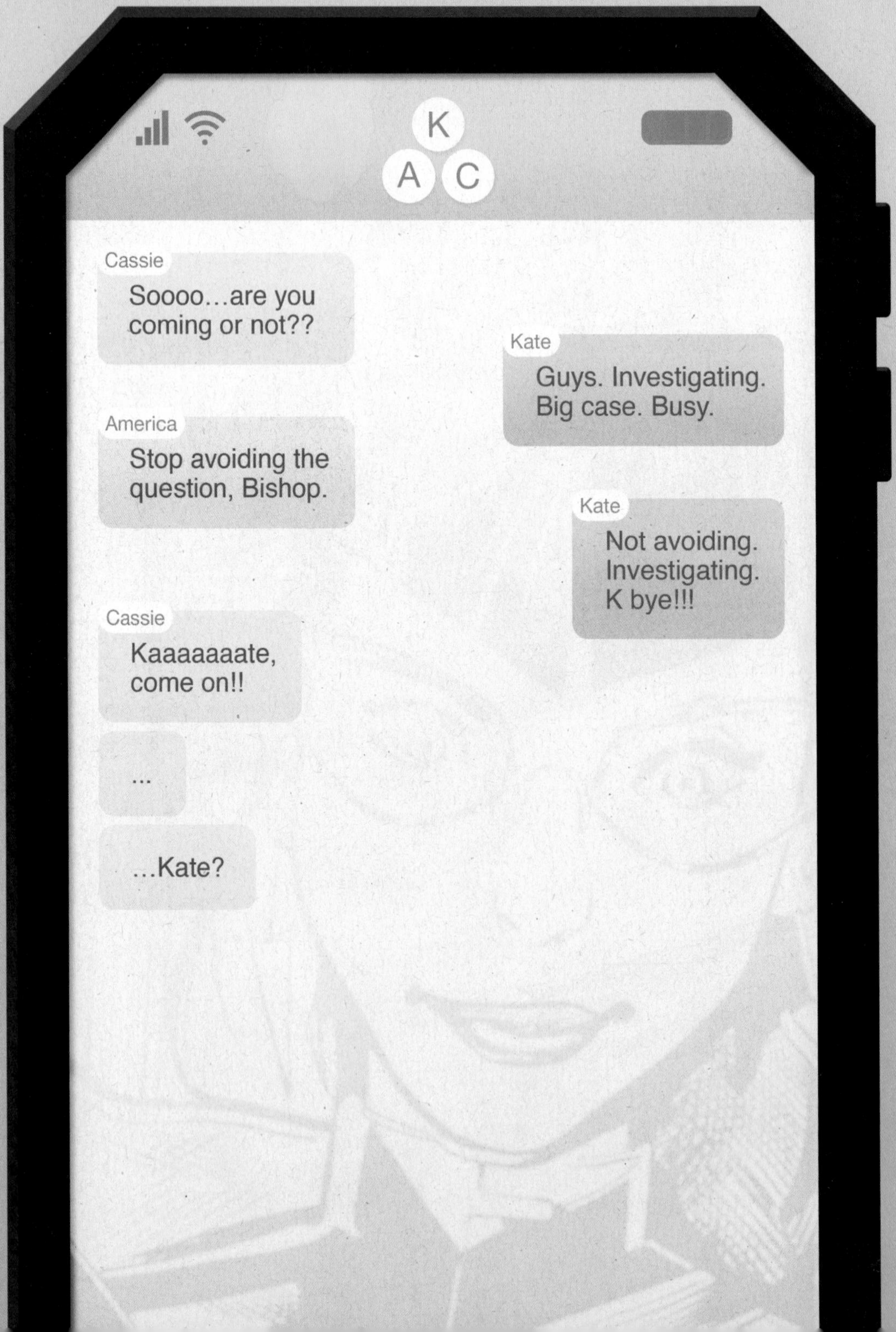
K
A C
Cassie
Soooo...are you coming or not??
Kate
Guys. Investigating. Big case. Busy.
America
Stop avoiding the question, Bishop.
Kate
Not avoiding. Investigating. K bye!!!
Cassie
Kaaaaaaate, come on!!
...
...Kate?

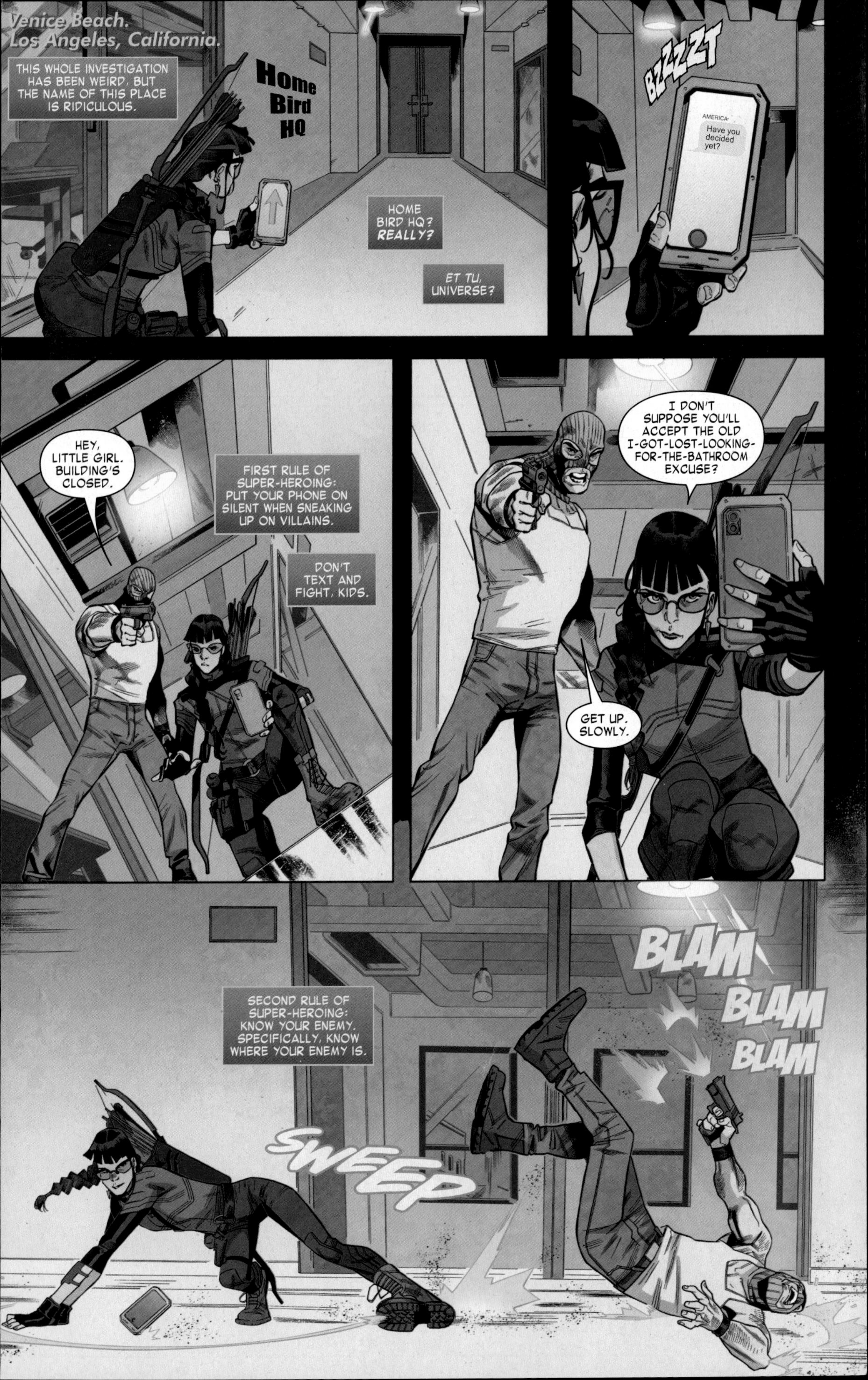
Venice Beach.
Los Angeles, California.
THIS WHOLE INVESTIGATION HAS BEEN WEIRD, BUT THE NAME OF THIS PLACE IS RIDICULOUS.
Home Bird HQ
HOME BIRD HQ? REALLY?
ET TU, UNIVERSE?
BZZZZT
AMERICA
Have you decided yet?
HEY, LITTLE GIRL. BUILDING'S CLOSED.
FIRST RULE OF SUPER-HEROING: PUT YOUR PHONE ON SILENT WHEN SNEAKING UP ON VILLAINS.
DON'T TEXT AND FIGHT, KIDS.
I DON'T SUPPOSE YOU'LL ACCEPT THE OLD I-GOT-LOST-LOOKING-FOR-THE-BATHROOM EXCUSE?
GET UP. SLOWLY.
BLAM
BLAM
BLAM
SECOND RULE OF SUPER-HEROING: KNOW YOUR ENEMY. SPECIFICALLY, KNOW WHERE YOUR ENEMY IS.
SWEEP

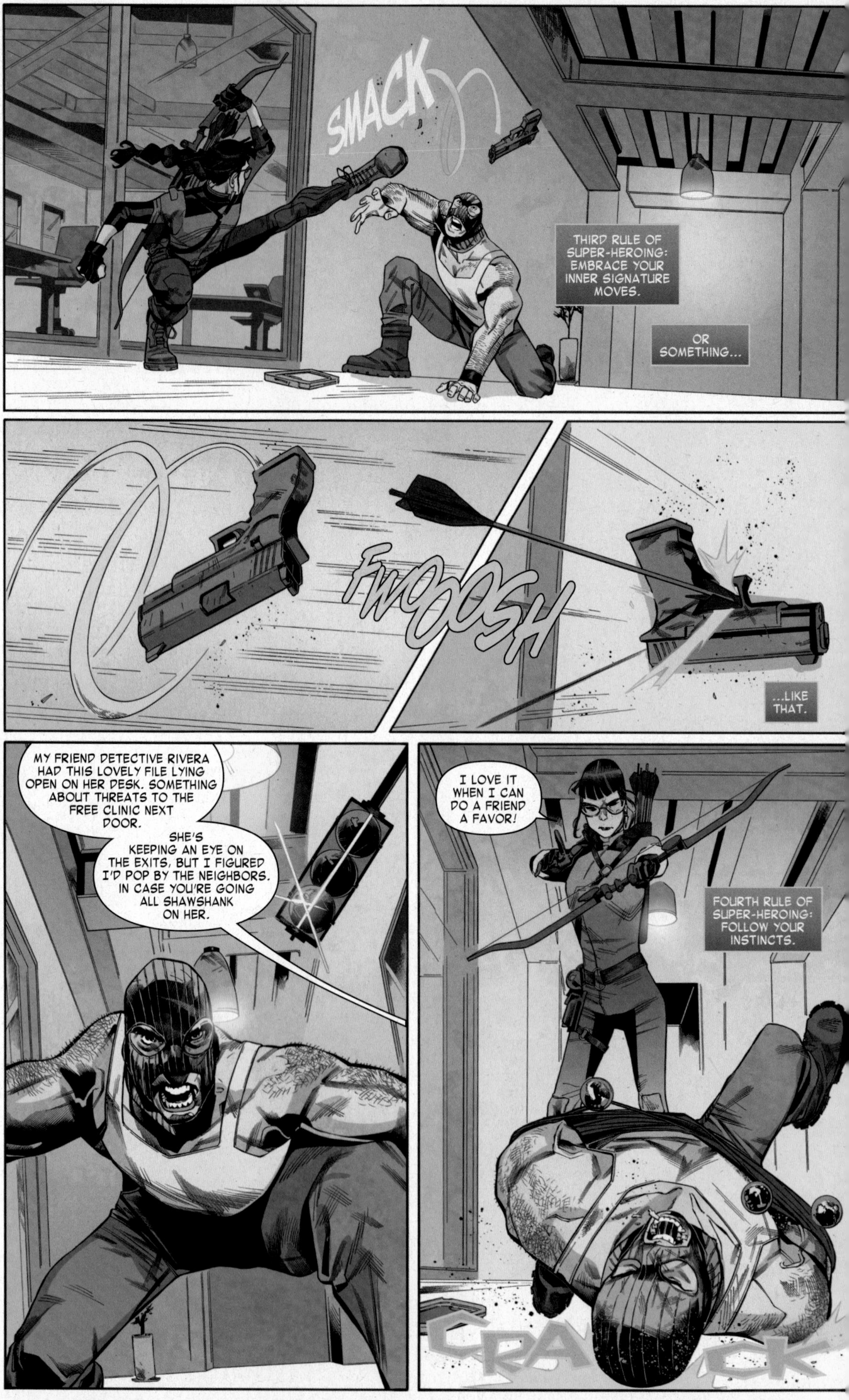
SMACK
THIRD RULE OF SUPER-HEROING: EMBRACE YOUR INNER SIGNATURE MOVES.
OR SOMETHING...
FWOOOSH
...LIKE THAT.
MY FRIEND DETECTIVE RIVERA HAD THIS LOVELY FILE LYING OPEN ON HER DESK. SOMETHING ABOUT THREATS TO THE FREE CLINIC NEXT DOOR.
SHE'S KEEPING AN EYE ON THE EXITS, BUT I FIGURED I'D POP BY THE NEIGHBORS. IN CASE YOU'RE GOING ALL SHAWSHANK ON HER.
I LOVE IT WHEN I CAN DO A FRIEND A FAVOR!
FOURTH RULE OF SUPER-HEROING: FOLLOW YOUR INSTINCTS.

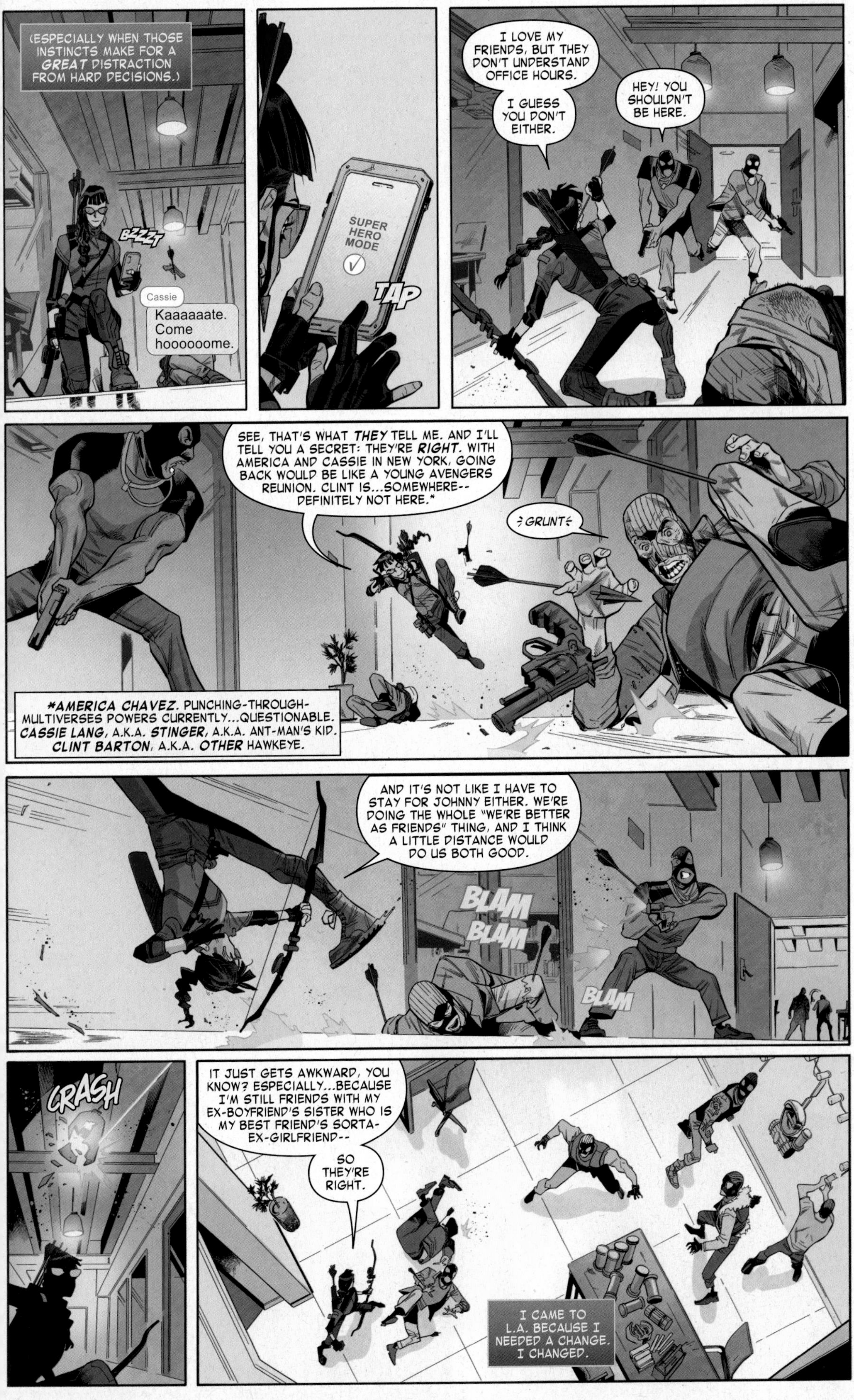
(ESPECIALLY WHEN THOSE INSTINCTS MAKE FOR A GREAT DISTRACTION FROM HARD DECISIONS.)
BZZZT
Cassie
Kaaaaaate. Come hoooooome.
SUPER HERO MODE
TAP
I LOVE MY FRIENDS, BUT THEY DON'T UNDERSTAND OFFICE HOURS.
I GUESS YOU DON'T EITHER.
HEY! YOU SHOULDN'T BE HERE.
SEE, THAT'S WHAT THEY TELL ME. AND I'LL TELL YOU A SECRET: THEY'RE RIGHT. WITH AMERICA AND CASSIE IN NEW YORK, GOING BACK WOULD BE LIKE A YOUNG AVENGERS REUNION. CLINT IS...SOMEWHERE-- DEFINITELY NOT HERE.*
GRUNT
*AMERICA CHAVEZ. PUNCHING-THROUGH-MULTIVERSES POWERS CURRENTLY...QUESTIONABLE. CASSIE LANG, A.K.A. STINGER, A.K.A. ANT-MAN'S KID. CLINT BARTON, A.K.A. OTHER HAWKEYE.
AND IT'S NOT LIKE I HAVE TO STAY FOR JOHNNY EITHER. WE'RE DOING THE WHOLE "WE'RE BETTER AS FRIENDS" THING, AND I THINK A LITTLE DISTANCE WOULD DO US BOTH GOOD.
BLAM
BLAM
BLAM
CRASH
IT JUST GETS AWKWARD, YOU KNOW? ESPECIALLY...BECAUSE I'M STILL FRIENDS WITH MY EX-BOYFRIEND'S SISTER WHO IS MY BEST FRIEND'S SORTA-EX-GIRLFRIEND--
SO THEY'RE RIGHT.
I CAME TO L.A. BECAUSE I NEEDED A CHANGE. I CHANGED.

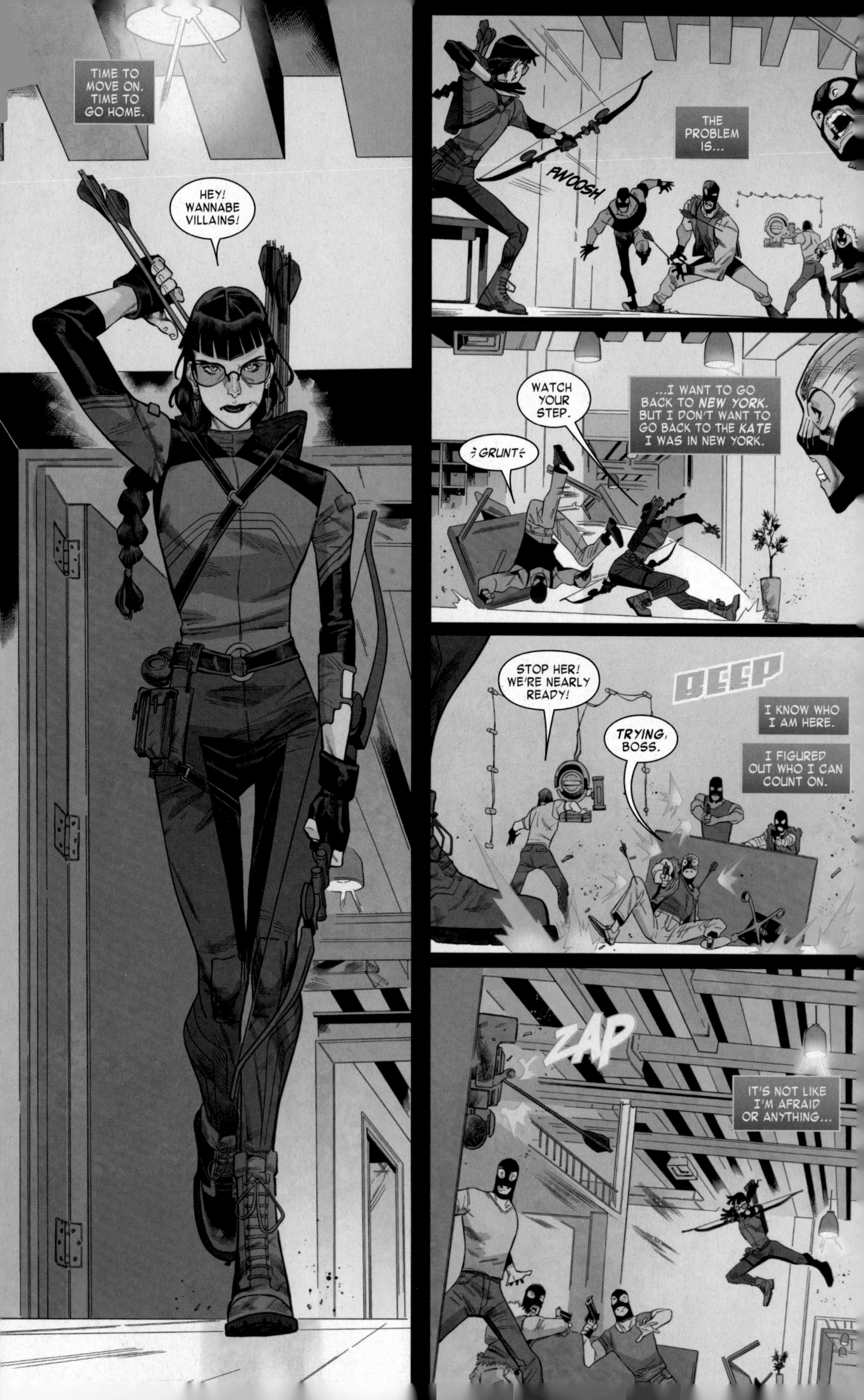
TIME TO MOVE ON. TIME TO GO HOME.
HEY! WANNABE VILLAINS!
THE PROBLEM IS...
FWOOSH
WATCH YOUR STEP.
...I WANT TO GO BACK TO NEW YORK. BUT I DON'T WANT TO GO BACK TO THE KATE I WAS IN NEW YORK.
GRUNT
STOP HER! WE'RE NEARLY READY!
BEEP
I KNOW WHO I AM HERE.
TRYING, BOSS.
I FIGURED OUT WHO I CAN COUNT ON.
ZAP
IT'S NOT LIKE I'M AFRAID OR ANYTHING...

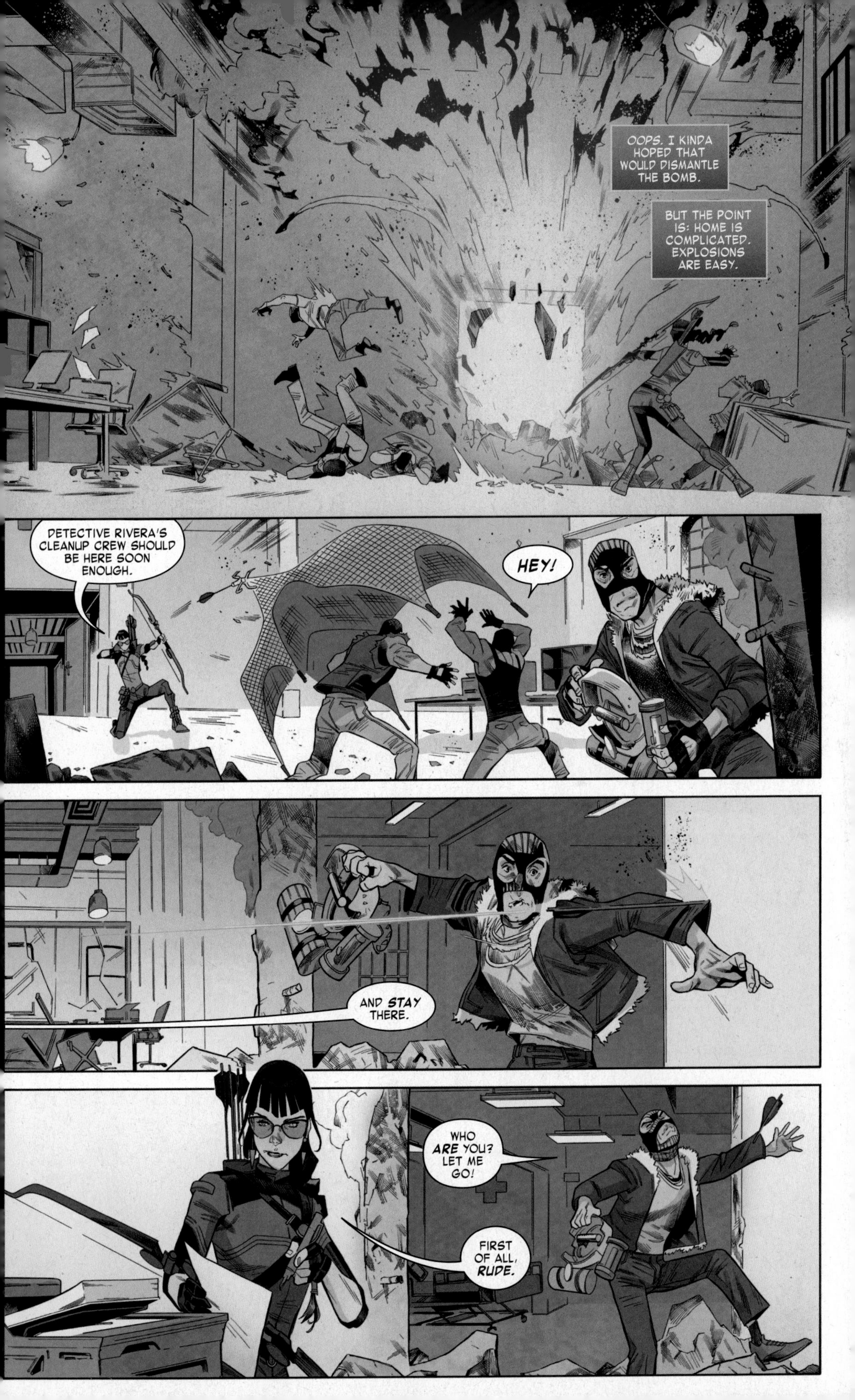
OOPS. I KINDA HOPED THAT WOULD DISMANTLE THE BOMB.
BUT THE POINT IS: HOME IS COMPLICATED. EXPLOSIONS ARE EASY.
DETECTIVE RIVERA'S CLEANUP CREW SHOULD BE HERE SOON ENOUGH.
HEY!
AND STAY THERE.
WHO ARE YOU? LET ME GO!
FIRST OF ALL, RUDE.

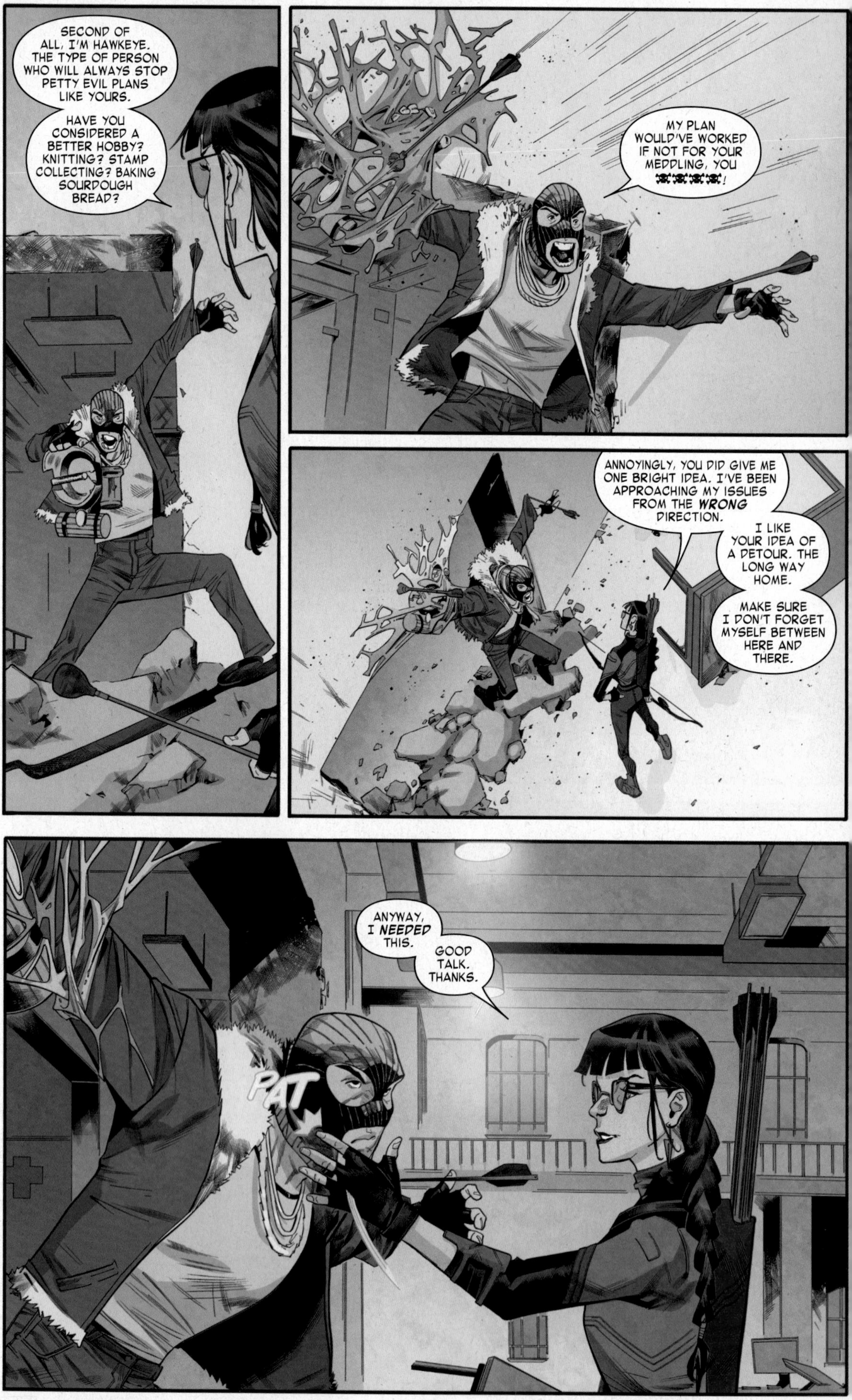
SECOND OF ALL, I'M HAWKEYE. THE TYPE OF PERSON WHO WILL ALWAYS STOP PETTY EVIL PLANS LIKE YOURS.
HAVE YOU CONSIDERED A BETTER HOBBY? KNITTING? STAMP COLLECTING? BAKING SOURDOUGH BREAD?
MY PLAN WOULD'VE WORKED IF NOT FOR YOUR MEDDLING, YOU ☠☠☠☠!
ANNOYINGLY, YOU DID GIVE ME ONE BRIGHT IDEA. I'VE BEEN APPROACHING MY ISSUES FROM THE WRONG DIRECTION.
I LIKE YOUR IDEA OF A DETOUR. THE LONG WAY HOME.
MAKE SURE I DON'T FORGET MYSELF BETWEEN HERE AND THERE.
ANYWAY, I NEEDED THIS.
GOOD TALK. THANKS.
PAT

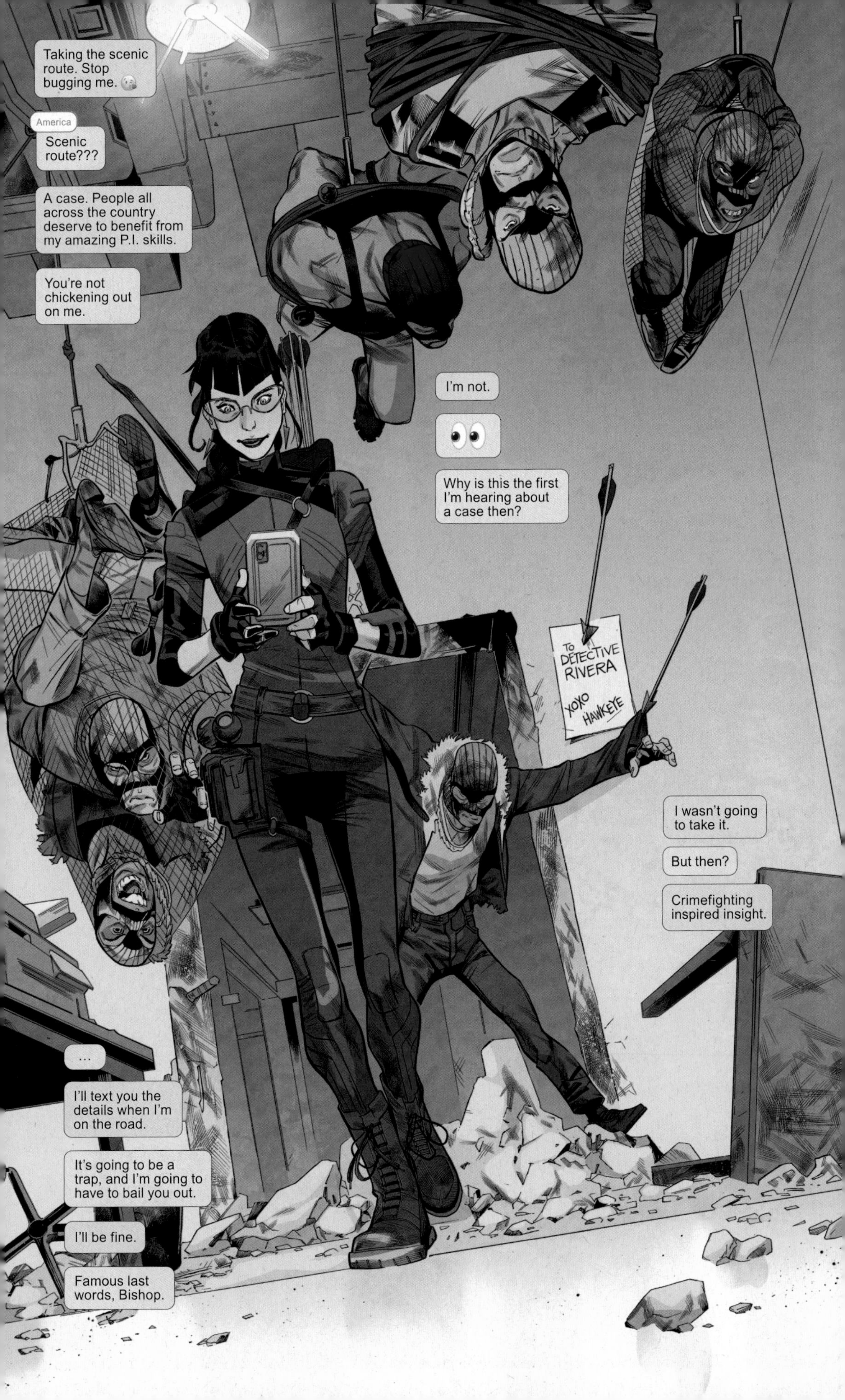
Taking the scenic route. Stop bugging me.
America
Scenic route???
A case. People all across the country deserve to benefit from my amazing P.I. skills.
You're not chickening out on me.
I'm not.
Why is this the first I'm hearing about a case then?
TO DETECTIVE RIVERA
XOXO HAWKEYE
I wasn't going to take it.
But then?
Crimefighting inspired insight.
...
I'll text you the details when I'm on the road.
It's going to be a trap, and I'm going to have to bail you out.
I'll be fine.
Famous last words, Bishop.

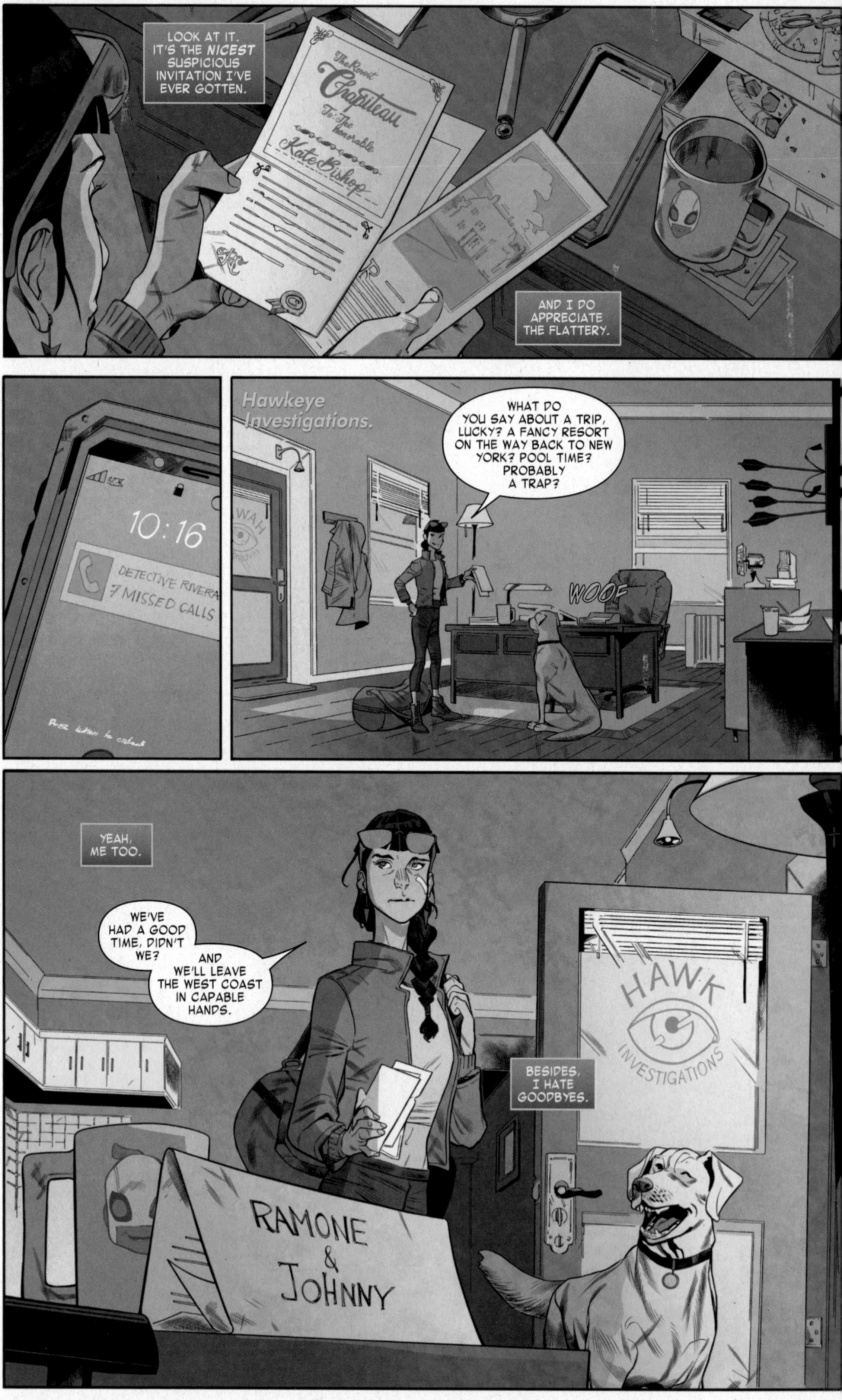
LOOK AT IT. IT'S THE *NICEST* SUSPICIOUS INVITATION I'VE EVER GOTTEN.
The Resort Chapiteau
To: The Honorable
Kate Bishop
AND I DO APPRECIATE THE FLATTERY.
10:16
DETECTIVE RIVERA
7 MISSED CALLS
Hawkeye Investigations.
WHAT DO YOU SAY ABOUT A TRIP, LUCKY? A FANCY RESORT ON THE WAY BACK TO NEW YORK? POOL TIME? PROBABLY A TRAP?
WOOF
YEAH, ME TOO.
WE'VE HAD A GOOD TIME, DIDN'T WE?
AND WE'LL LEAVE THE WEST COAST IN CAPABLE HANDS.
HAWK INVESTIGATIONS
BESIDES, I HATE GOODBYES.
RAMONE & JOHNNY

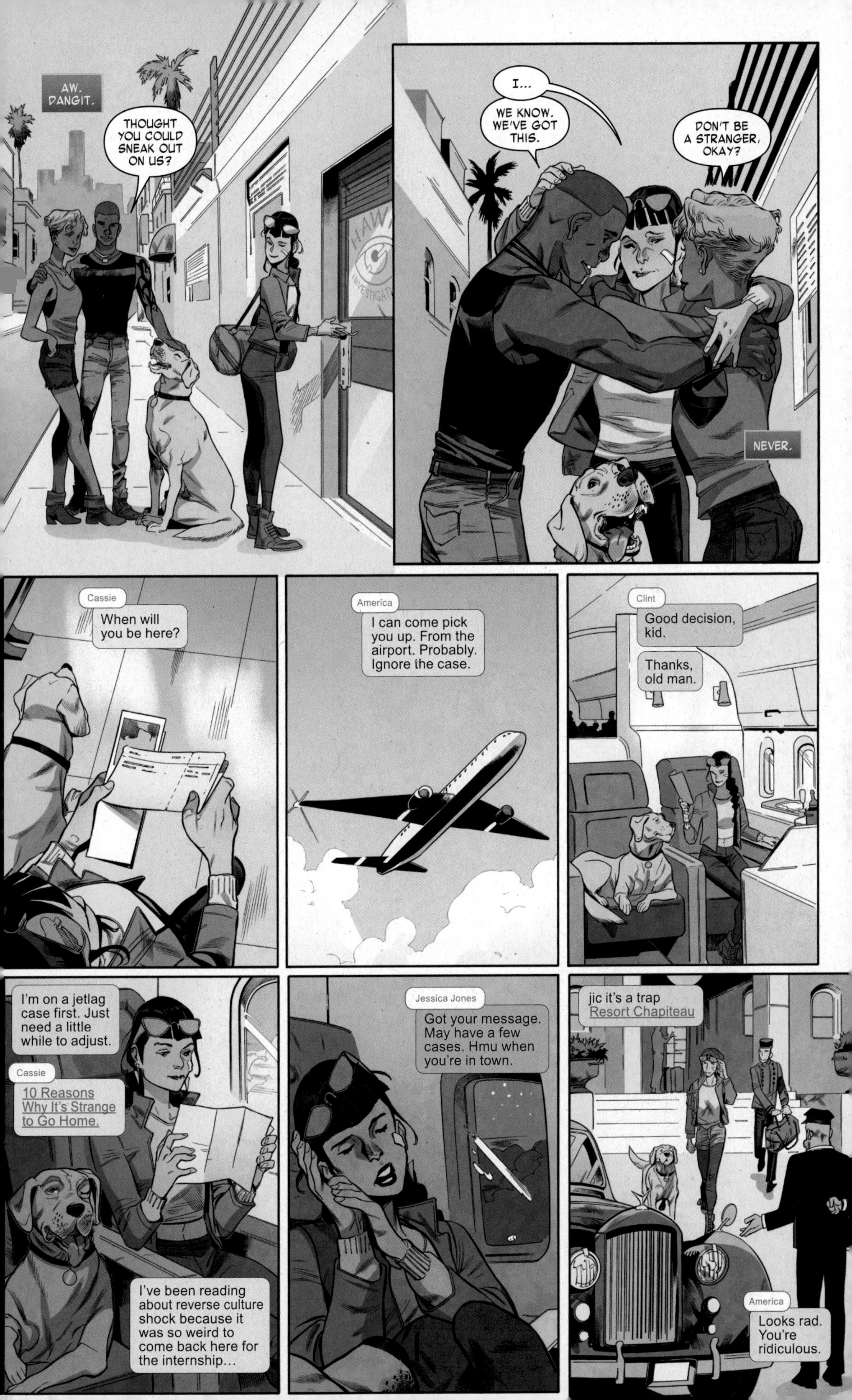
AW. DANGIT.
THOUGHT YOU COULD SNEAK OUT ON US?
I...
WE KNOW. WE'VE GOT THIS.
DON'T BE A STRANGER, OKAY?
NEVER.
Cassie
When will you be here?
America
I can come pick you up. From the airport. Probably. Ignore the case.
Clint
Good decision, kid.
Thanks, old man.
I'm on a jetlag case first. Just need a little while to adjust.
Cassie
10 Reasons Why It's Strange to Go Home.
I've been reading about reverse culture shock because it was so weird to come back here for the internship...
Jessica Jones
Got your message. May have a few cases. Hmu when you're in town.
jic it's a trap
Resort Chapiteau
America
Looks rad. You're ridiculous.

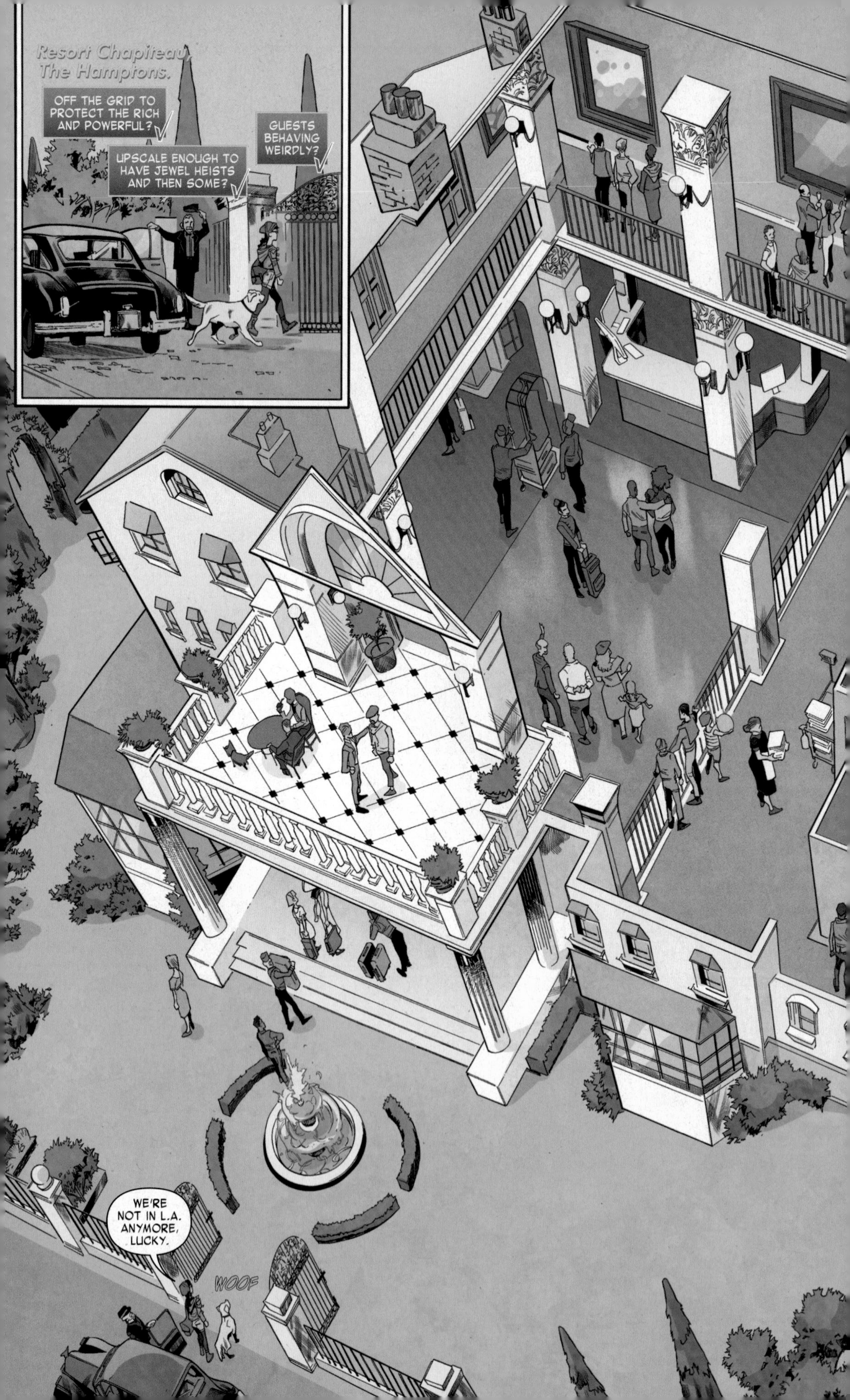
Resort Chapiteau, The Hamptons.
OFF THE GRID TO PROTECT THE RICH AND POWERFUL?
UPSCALE ENOUGH TO HAVE JEWEL HEISTS AND THEN SOME?
GUESTS BEHAVING WEIRDLY?
WE'RE NOT IN L.A. ANYMORE, LUCKY.
WOOF

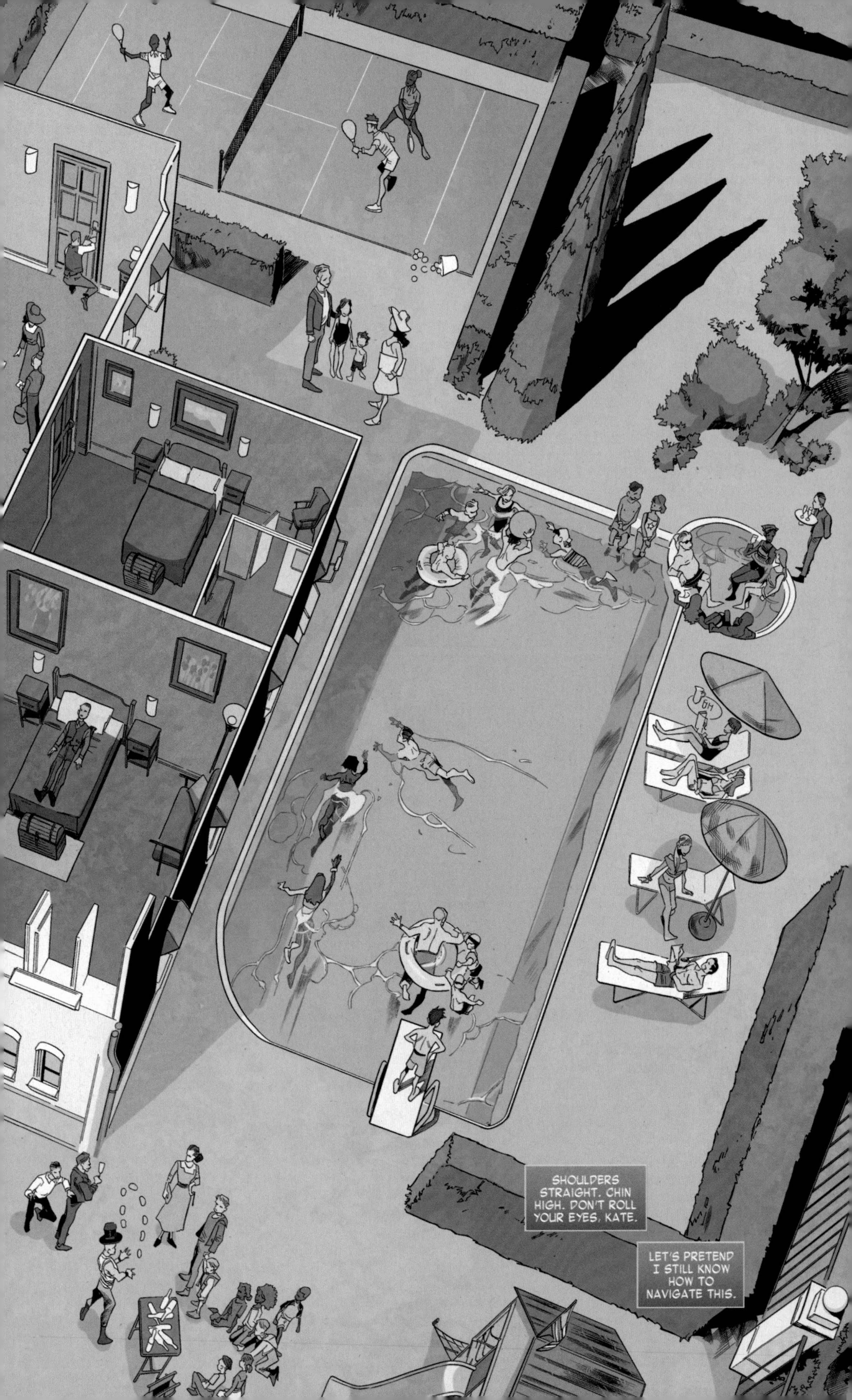
SHOULDERS STRAIGHT. CHIN HIGH. DON'T ROLL YOUR EYES, KATE.
LET'S PRETEND I STILL KNOW HOW TO NAVIGATE THIS.

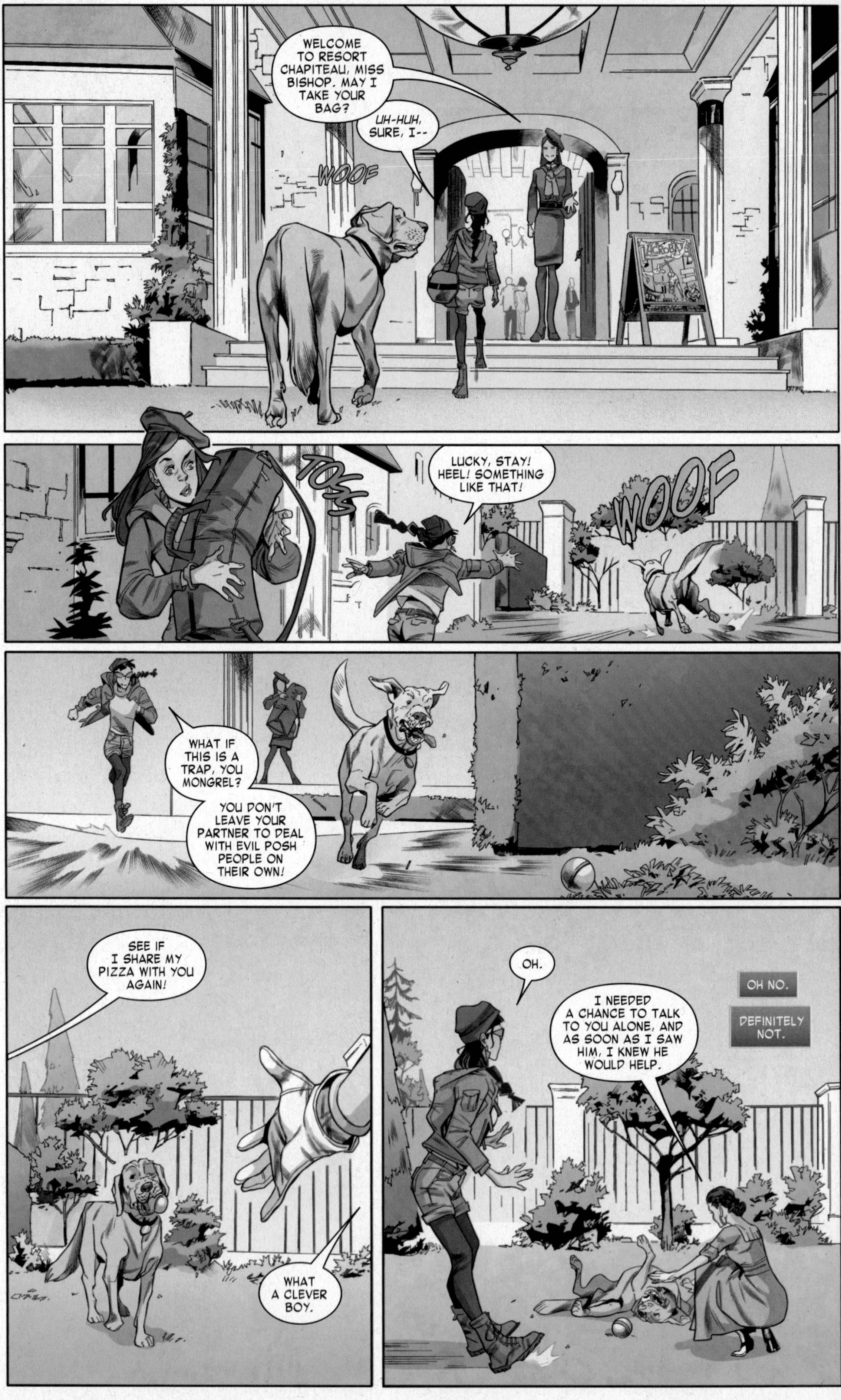

WELCOME TO RESORT CHAPITEAU, MISS BISHOP. MAY I TAKE YOUR BAG?
UH-HUH, SURE, I--
WOOF
TOSS
LUCKY, STAY! HEEL! SOMETHING LIKE THAT!
WOOF
WHAT IF THIS IS A TRAP, YOU MONGREL?
YOU DON'T LEAVE YOUR PARTNER TO DEAL WITH EVIL POSH PEOPLE ON THEIR OWN!
SEE IF I SHARE MY PIZZA WITH YOU AGAIN!
WHAT A CLEVER BOY.
OH.
I NEEDED A CHANCE TO TALK TO YOU ALONE, AND AS SOON AS I SAW HIM, I KNEW HE WOULD HELP.
OH NO.
DEFINITELY NOT.

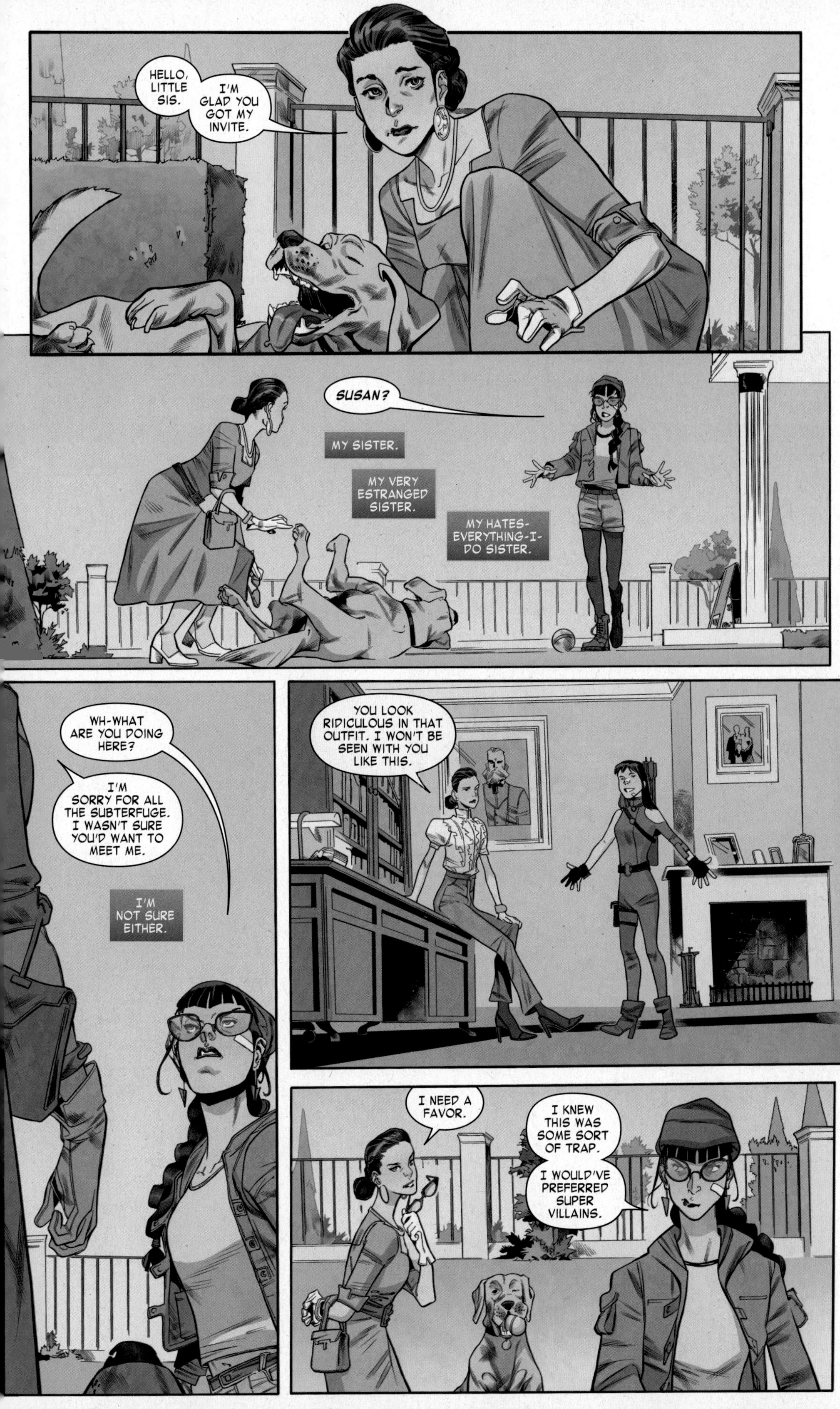
HELLO, LITTLE SIS.
I'M GLAD YOU GOT MY INVITE.
SUSAN?
MY SISTER.
MY VERY ESTRANGED SISTER.
MY HATES-EVERYTHING-I-DO SISTER.
WH-WHAT ARE YOU DOING HERE?
I'M SORRY FOR ALL THE SUBTERFUGE. I WASN'T SURE YOU'D WANT TO MEET ME.
I'M NOT SURE EITHER.
YOU LOOK RIDICULOUS IN THAT OUTFIT. I WON'T BE SEEN WITH YOU LIKE THIS.
I NEED A FAVOR.
I KNEW THIS WAS SOME SORT OF TRAP.
I WOULD'VE PREFERRED SUPER VILLAINS.

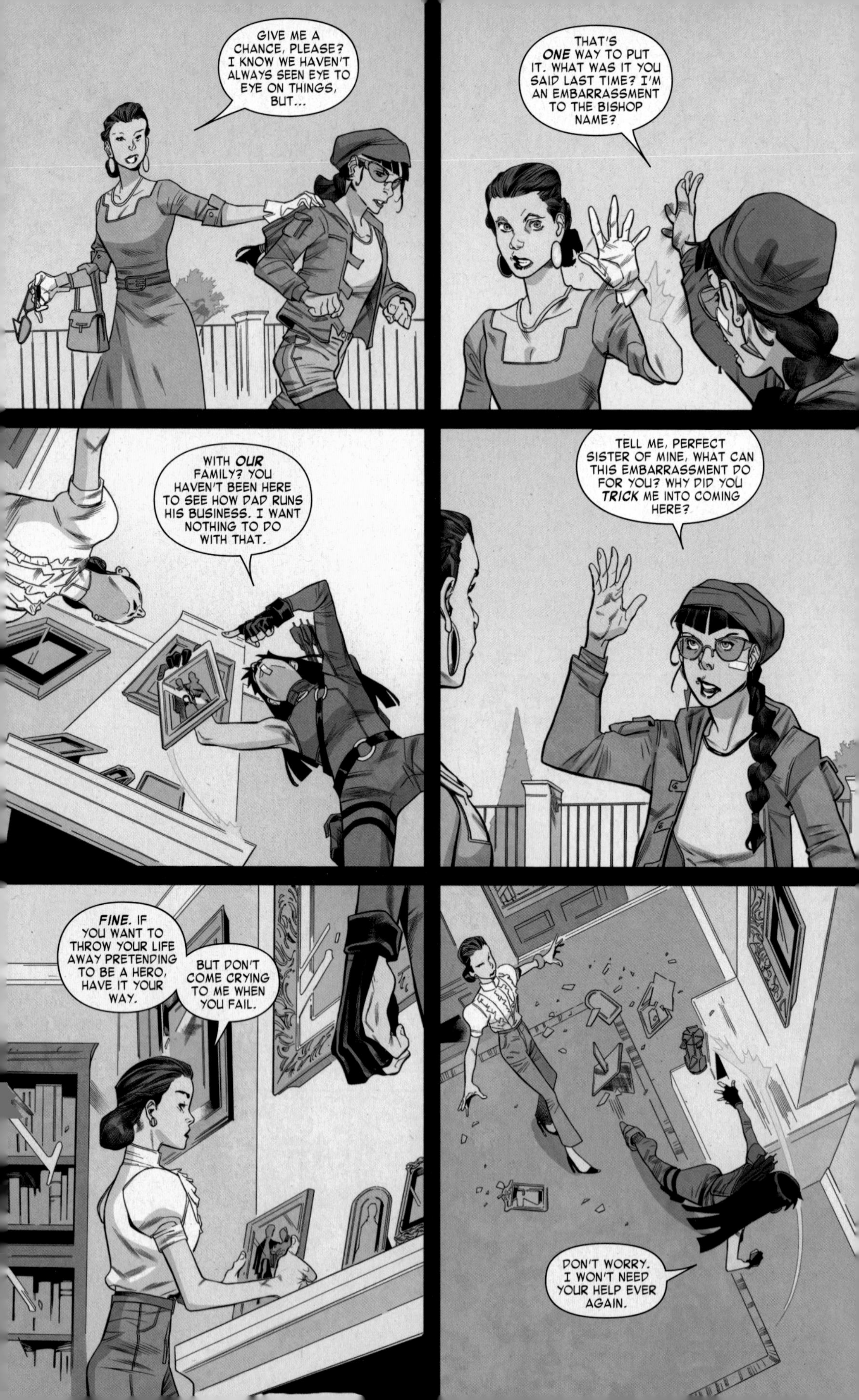
GIVE ME A CHANCE, PLEASE? I KNOW WE HAVEN'T ALWAYS SEEN EYE TO EYE ON THINGS, BUT...
THAT'S *ONE* WAY TO PUT IT. WHAT WAS IT YOU SAID LAST TIME? I'M AN EMBARRASSMENT TO THE BISHOP NAME?
WITH *OUR* FAMILY? YOU HAVEN'T BEEN HERE TO SEE HOW DAD RUNS HIS BUSINESS. I WANT NOTHING TO DO WITH THAT.
TELL ME, PERFECT SISTER OF MINE, WHAT CAN THIS EMBARRASSMENT DO FOR YOU? WHY DID YOU *TRICK* ME INTO COMING HERE?
FINE. IF YOU WANT TO THROW YOUR LIFE AWAY PRETENDING TO BE A HERO, HAVE IT YOUR WAY.
BUT DON'T COME CRYING TO ME WHEN YOU FAIL.
DON'T WORRY. I WON'T NEED YOUR HELP EVER AGAIN.

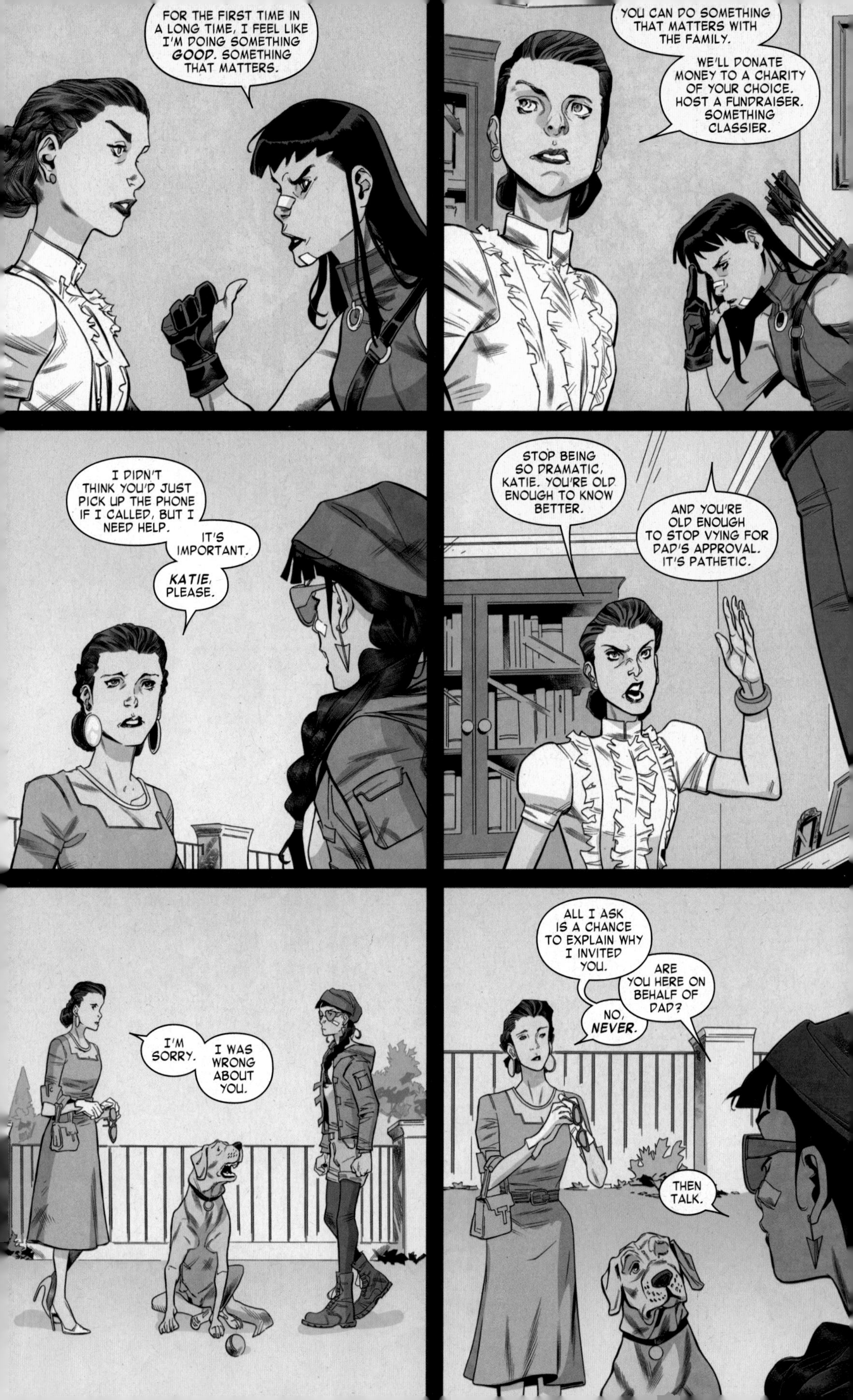
FOR THE FIRST TIME IN A LONG TIME, I FEEL LIKE I'M DOING SOMETHING **GOOD**. SOMETHING THAT MATTERS.
YOU CAN DO SOMETHING THAT MATTERS WITH THE FAMILY.
WE'LL DONATE MONEY TO A CHARITY OF YOUR CHOICE. HOST A FUNDRAISER. SOMETHING CLASSIER.
I DIDN'T THINK YOU'D JUST PICK UP THE PHONE IF I CALLED, BUT I NEED HELP.
IT'S IMPORTANT.
KATIE, PLEASE.
STOP BEING SO DRAMATIC, KATIE. YOU'RE OLD ENOUGH TO KNOW BETTER.
AND YOU'RE OLD ENOUGH TO STOP VYING FOR DAD'S APPROVAL. IT'S PATHETIC.
I'M SORRY.
I WAS WRONG ABOUT YOU.
ALL I ASK IS A CHANCE TO EXPLAIN WHY I INVITED YOU.
ARE YOU HERE ON BEHALF OF DAD?
NO, **NEVER**.
THEN TALK.

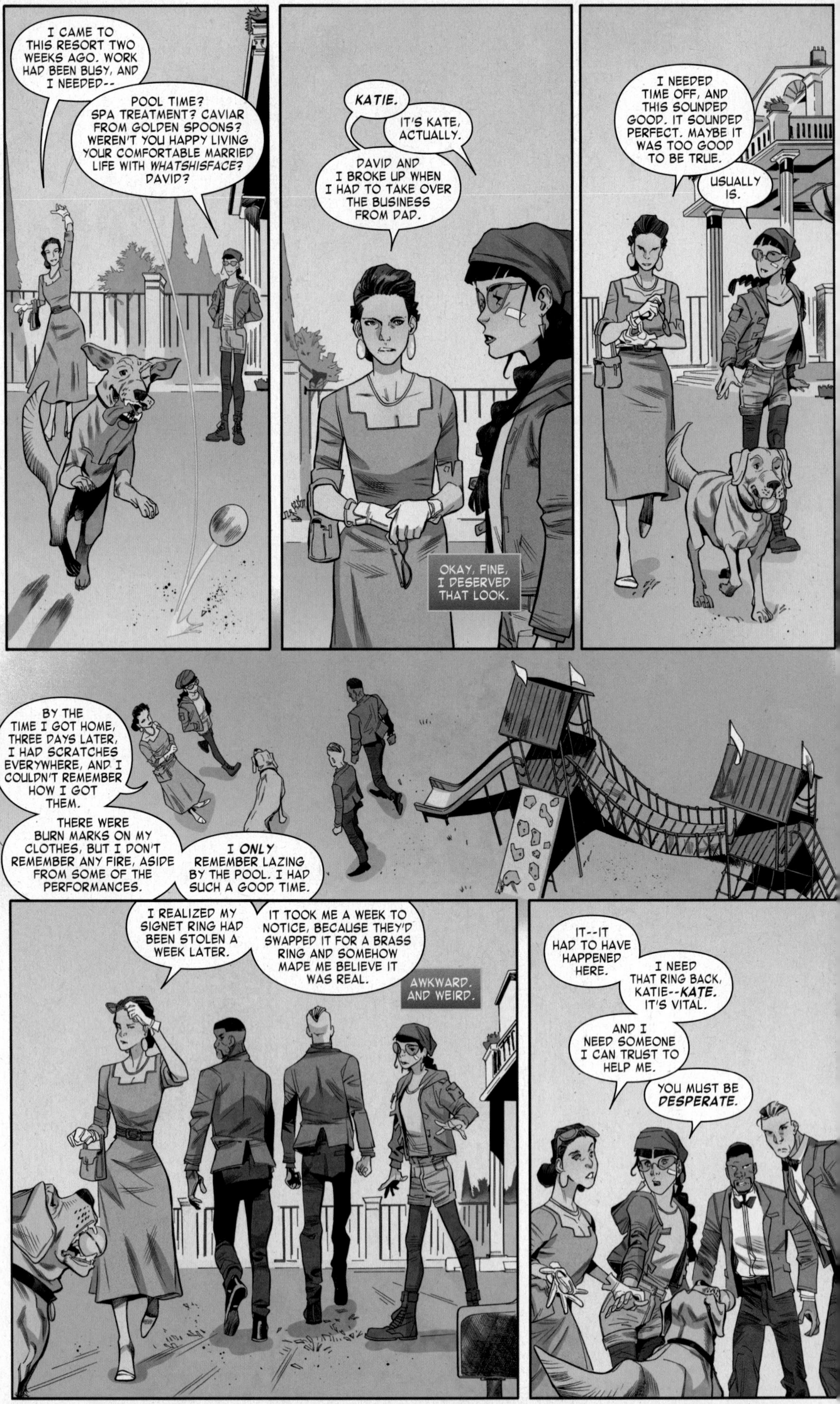

I CAME TO THIS RESORT TWO WEEKS AGO. WORK HAD BEEN BUSY, AND I NEEDED--
POOL TIME? SPA TREATMENT? CAVIAR FROM GOLDEN SPOONS? WEREN'T YOU HAPPY LIVING YOUR COMFORTABLE MARRIED LIFE WITH WHATSHISFACE? DAVID?
KATIE.
IT'S KATE, ACTUALLY.
DAVID AND I BROKE UP WHEN I HAD TO TAKE OVER THE BUSINESS FROM DAD.
OKAY, FINE, I DESERVED THAT LOOK.
I NEEDED TIME OFF, AND THIS SOUNDED GOOD. IT SOUNDED PERFECT. MAYBE IT WAS TOO GOOD TO BE TRUE.
USUALLY IS.
BY THE TIME I GOT HOME, THREE DAYS LATER, I HAD SCRATCHES EVERYWHERE, AND I COULDN'T REMEMBER HOW I GOT THEM.
THERE WERE BURN MARKS ON MY CLOTHES, BUT I DON'T REMEMBER ANY FIRE, ASIDE FROM SOME OF THE PERFORMANCES.
I ONLY REMEMBER LAZING BY THE POOL. I HAD SUCH A GOOD TIME.
I REALIZED MY SIGNET RING HAD BEEN STOLEN A WEEK LATER.
IT TOOK ME A WEEK TO NOTICE, BECAUSE THEY'D SWAPPED IT FOR A BRASS RING AND SOMEHOW MADE ME BELIEVE IT WAS REAL.
AWKWARD. AND WEIRD.
IT--IT HAD TO HAVE HAPPENED HERE.
I NEED THAT RING BACK, KATIE--KATE. IT'S VITAL.
AND I NEED SOMEONE I CAN TRUST TO HELP ME.
YOU MUST BE DESPERATE.

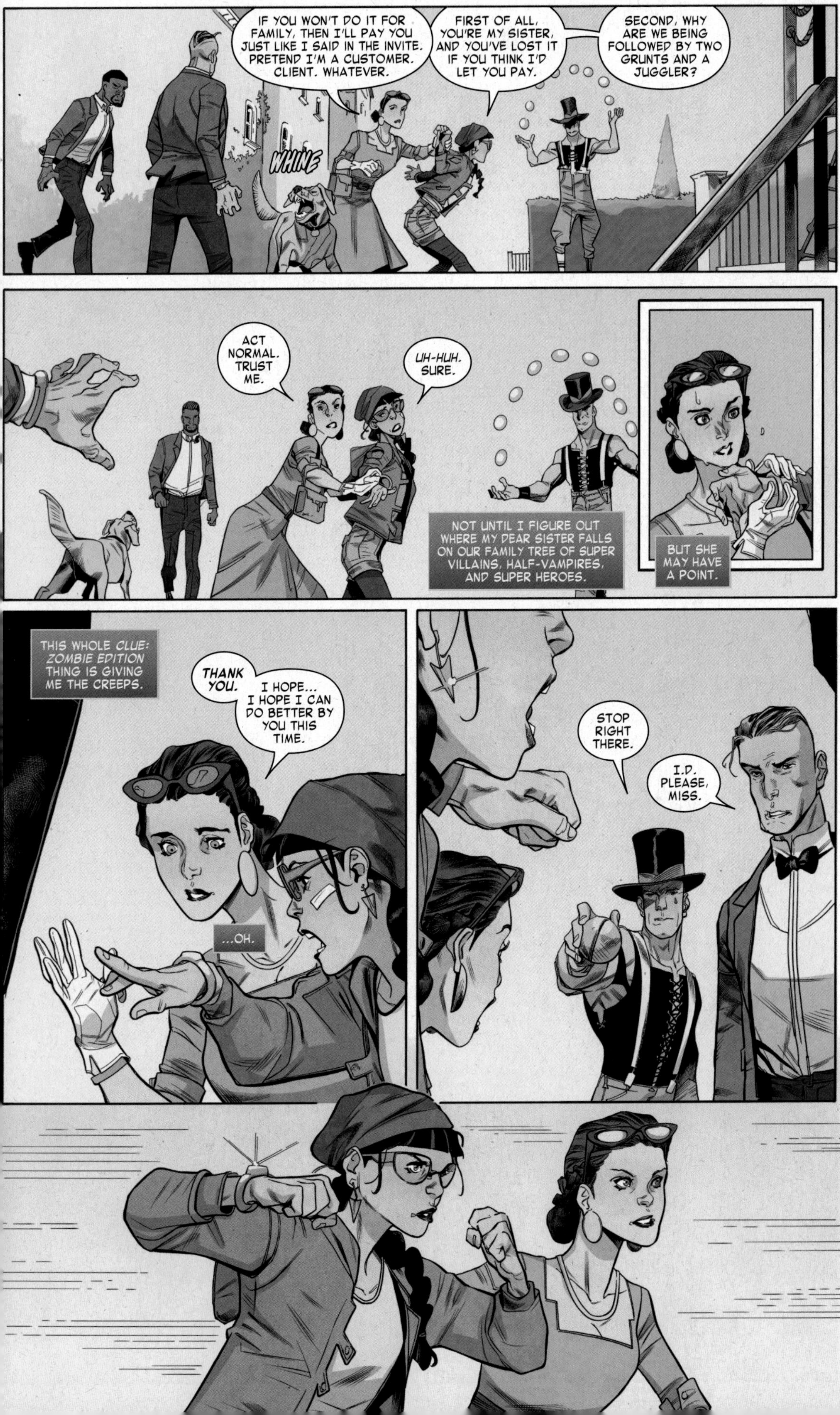
IF YOU WON'T DO IT FOR FAMILY, THEN I'LL PAY YOU JUST LIKE I SAID IN THE INVITE. PRETEND I'M A CUSTOMER. CLIENT. WHATEVER.
FIRST OF ALL, YOU'RE MY SISTER, AND YOU'VE LOST IT IF YOU THINK I'D LET YOU PAY.
SECOND, WHY ARE WE BEING FOLLOWED BY TWO GRUNTS AND A JUGGLER?
WHINE
ACT NORMAL. TRUST ME.
UH-HUH. SURE.
NOT UNTIL I FIGURE OUT WHERE MY DEAR SISTER FALLS ON OUR FAMILY TREE OF SUPER VILLAINS, HALF-VAMPIRES, AND SUPER HEROES.
BUT SHE MAY HAVE A POINT.
THIS WHOLE CLUE: ZOMBIE EDITION THING IS GIVING ME THE CREEPS.
THANK YOU.
I HOPE... I HOPE I CAN DO BETTER BY YOU THIS TIME.
...OH.
STOP RIGHT THERE.
I.D. PLEASE, MISS.

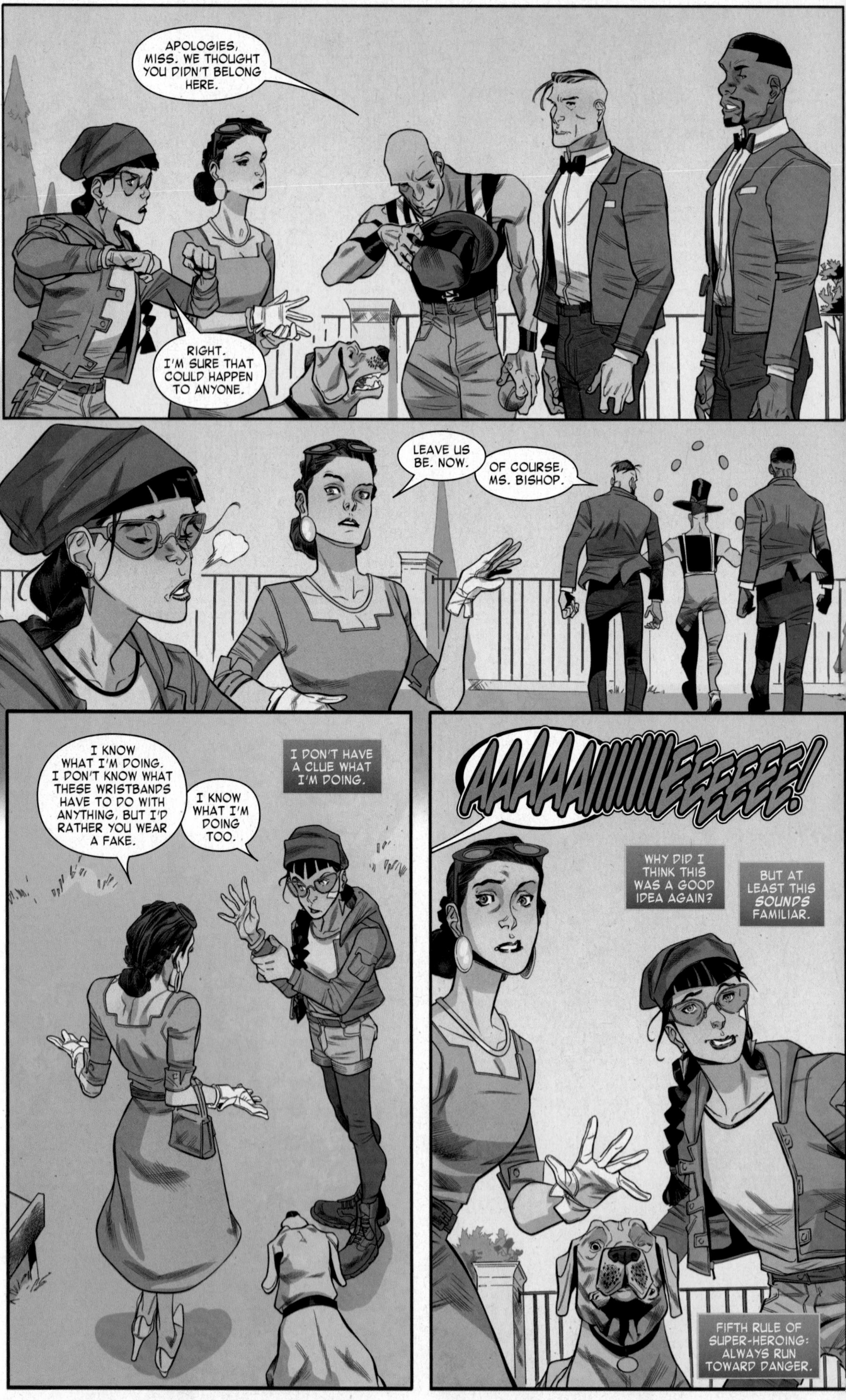
APOLOGIES, MISS. WE THOUGHT YOU DIDN'T BELONG HERE.
RIGHT. I'M SURE THAT COULD HAPPEN TO ANYONE.
LEAVE US BE. NOW.
OF COURSE, MS. BISHOP.
I KNOW WHAT I'M DOING. I DON'T KNOW WHAT THESE WRISTBANDS HAVE TO DO WITH ANYTHING, BUT I'D RATHER YOU WEAR A FAKE.
I KNOW WHAT I'M DOING TOO.
I DON'T HAVE A CLUE WHAT I'M DOING.
AAAAAIIIIIIIEEEEEE!
WHY DID I THINK THIS WAS A GOOD IDEA AGAIN?
BUT AT LEAST THIS *SOUNDS* FAMILIAR.
FIFTH RULE OF SUPER-HEROING: ALWAYS RUN TOWARD DANGER.

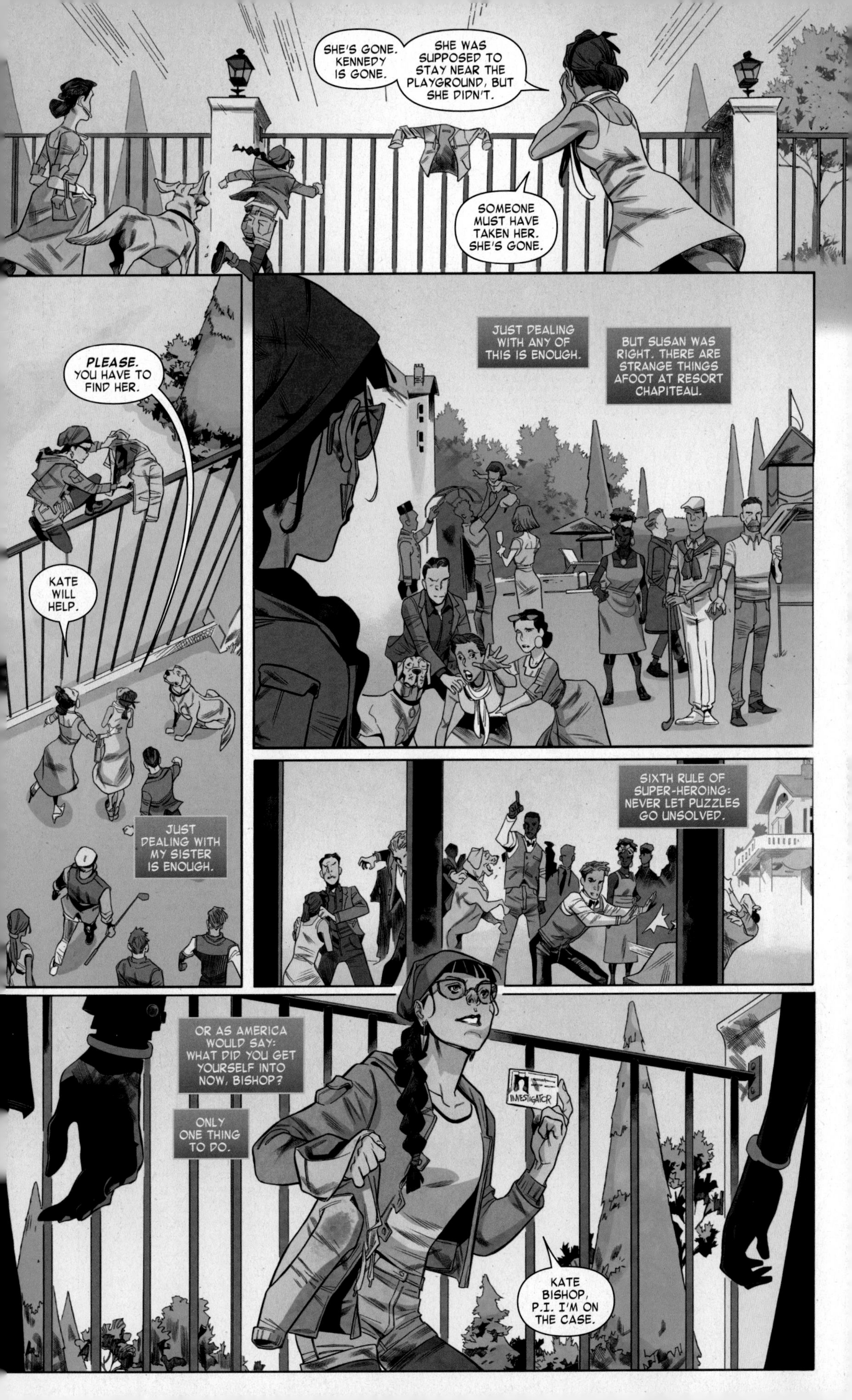
SHE'S GONE. KENNEDY IS GONE.
SHE WAS SUPPOSED TO STAY NEAR THE PLAYGROUND, BUT SHE DIDN'T.
SOMEONE MUST HAVE TAKEN HER. SHE'S GONE.
PLEASE. YOU HAVE TO FIND HER.
KATE WILL HELP.
JUST DEALING WITH MY SISTER IS ENOUGH.
JUST DEALING WITH ANY OF THIS IS ENOUGH.
BUT SUSAN WAS RIGHT. THERE ARE STRANGE THINGS AFOOT AT RESORT CHAPITEAU.
SIXTH RULE OF SUPER-HEROING: NEVER LET PUZZLES GO UNSOLVED.
OR AS AMERICA WOULD SAY: WHAT DID YOU GET YOURSELF INTO NOW, BISHOP?
ONLY ONE THING TO DO.
INVESTIGATOR
KATE BISHOP, P.I. I'M ON THE CASE.

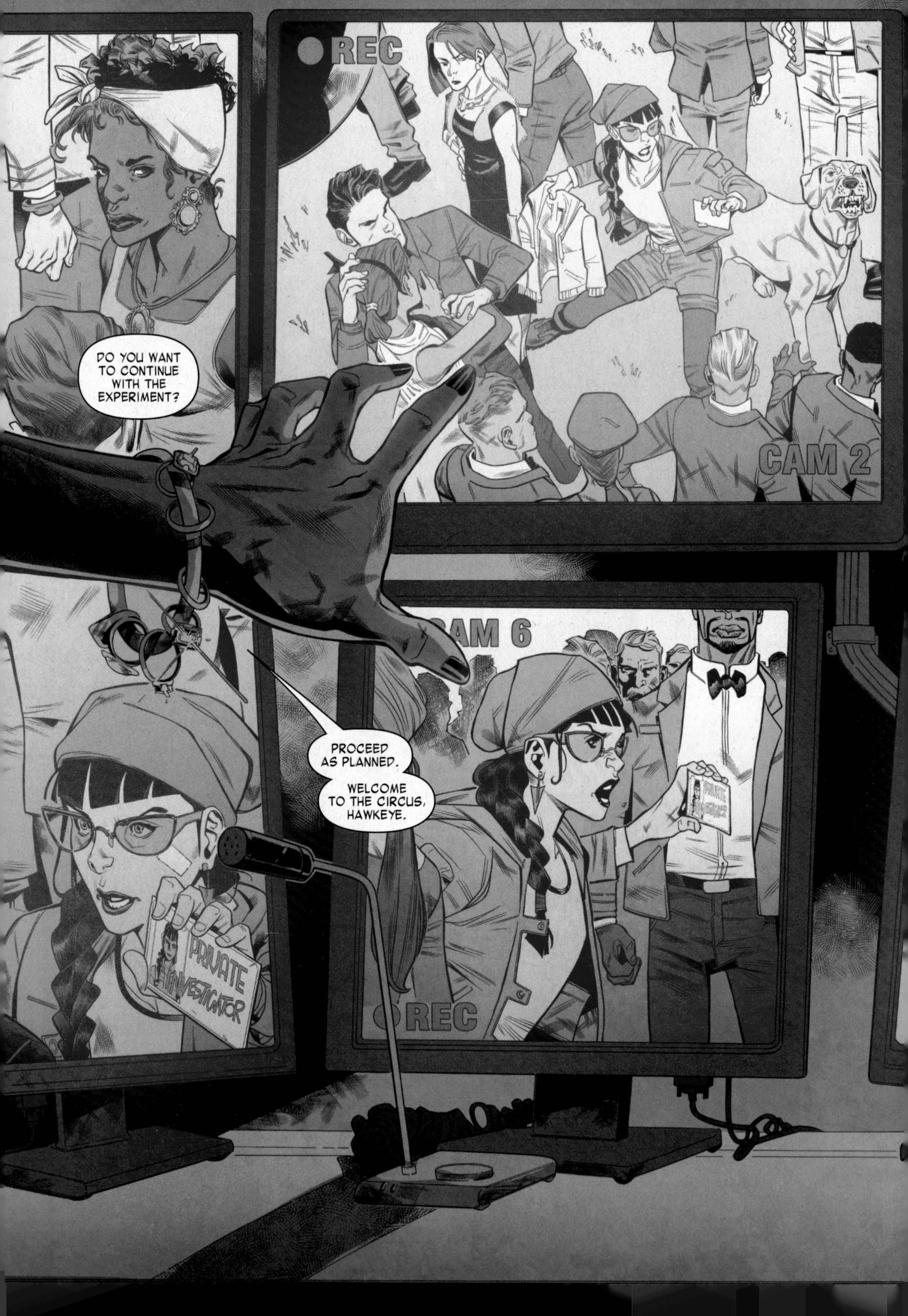
REC
DO YOU WANT TO CONTINUE WITH THE EXPERIMENT?
CAM 2
CAM 6
PROCEED AS PLANNED.
WELCOME TO THE CIRCUS, HAWKEYE.
PRIVATE INVESTIGATOR
REC

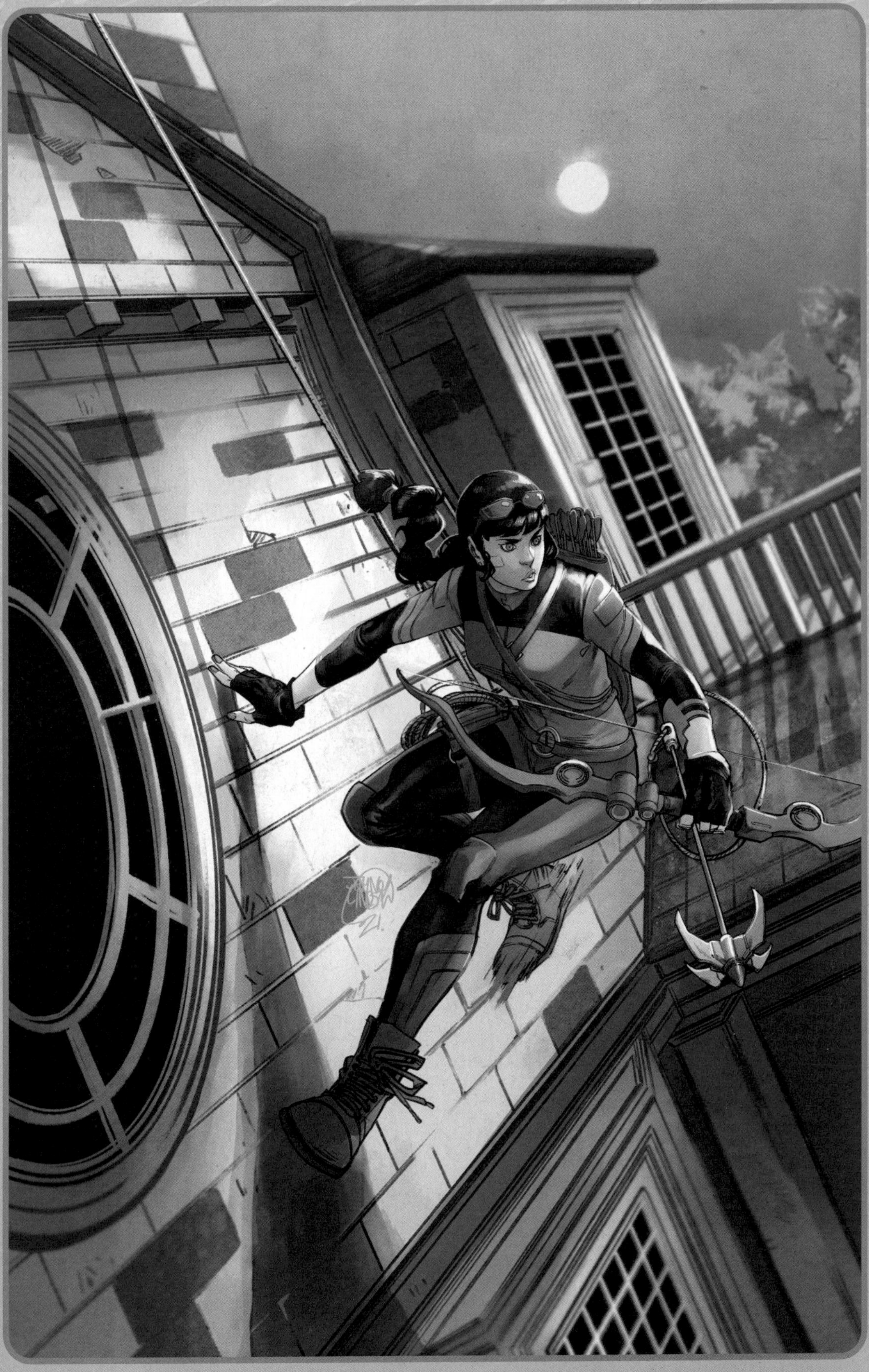

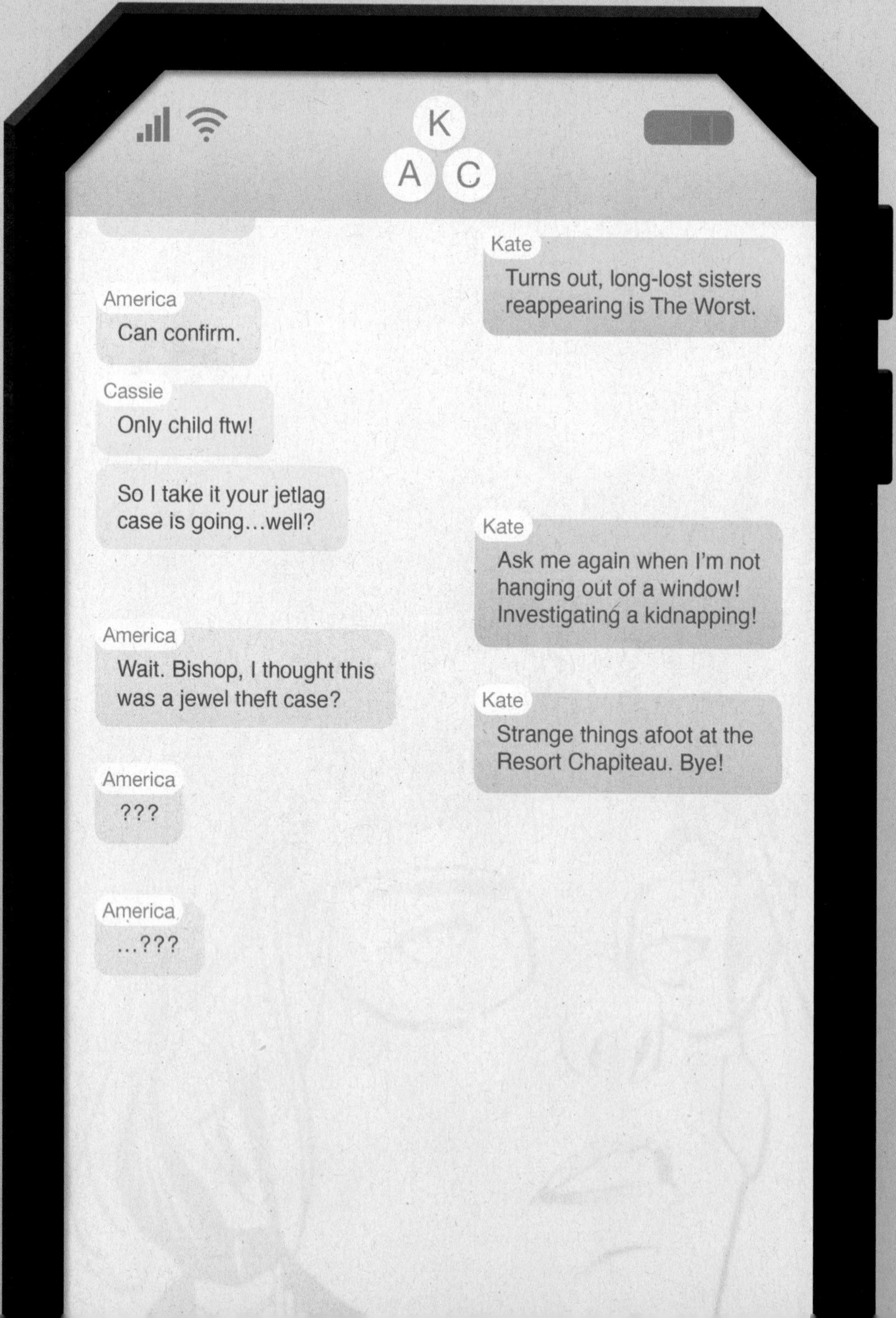
K
A
C
Kate
Turns out, long-lost sisters reappearing is The Worst.
America
Can confirm.
Cassie
Only child ftw!
So I take it your jetlag case is going…well?
Kate
Ask me again when I'm not hanging out of a window! Investigating a kidnapping!
America
Wait. Bishop, I thought this was a jewel theft case?
Kate
Strange things afoot at the Resort Chapiteau. Bye!
America
???
America
…???

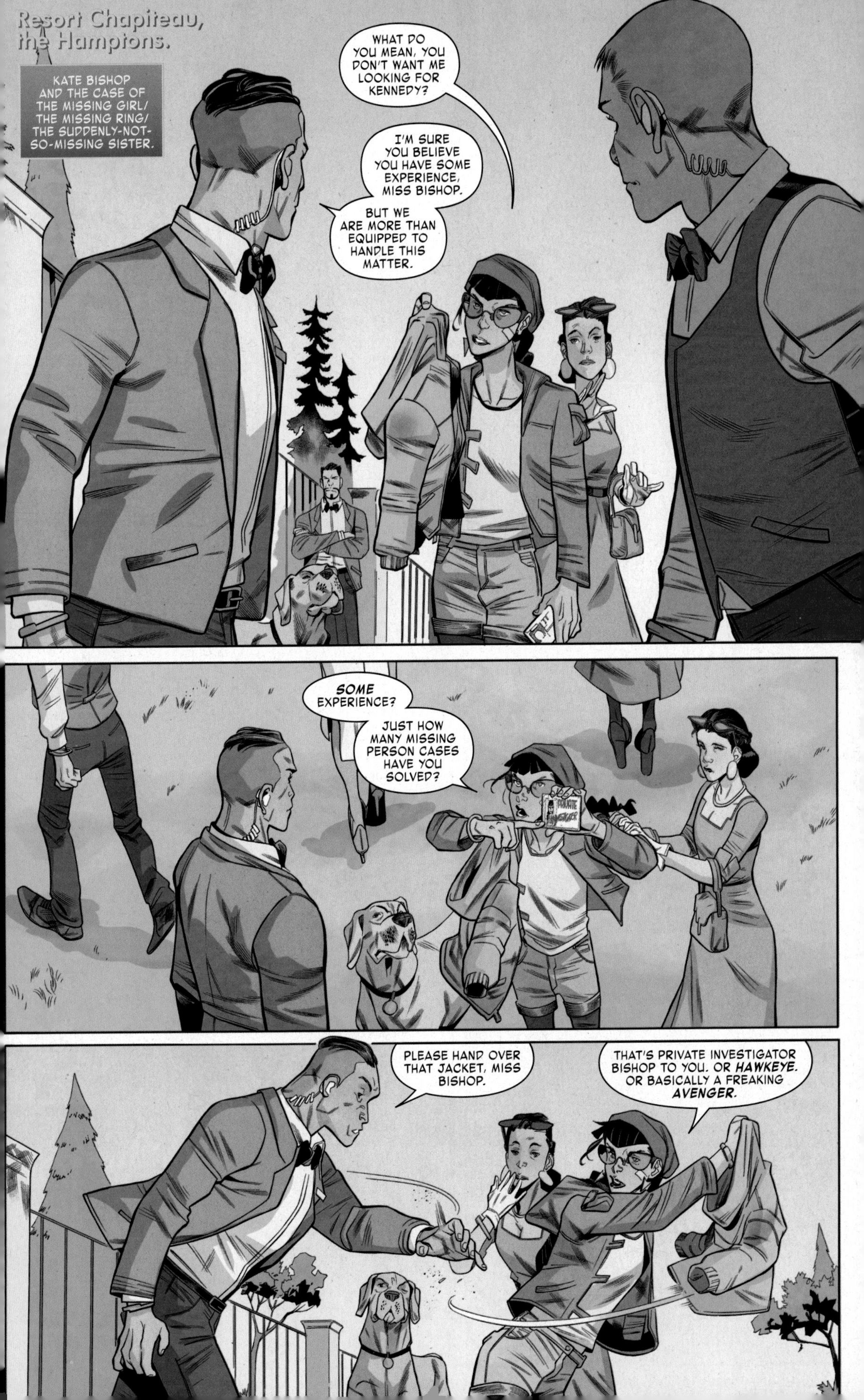
Resort Chapiteau, the Hamptons.
KATE BISHOP AND THE CASE OF THE MISSING GIRL/ THE MISSING RING/ THE SUDDENLY-NOT-SO-MISSING SISTER.
WHAT DO YOU MEAN, YOU DON'T WANT ME LOOKING FOR KENNEDY?
I'M SURE YOU BELIEVE YOU HAVE SOME EXPERIENCE, MISS BISHOP.
BUT WE ARE MORE THAN EQUIPPED TO HANDLE THIS MATTER.
SOME EXPERIENCE?
JUST HOW MANY MISSING PERSON CASES HAVE YOU SOLVED?
PLEASE HAND OVER THAT JACKET, MISS BISHOP.
THAT'S PRIVATE INVESTIGATOR BISHOP TO YOU. OR HAWKEYE. OR BASICALLY A FREAKING AVENGER.

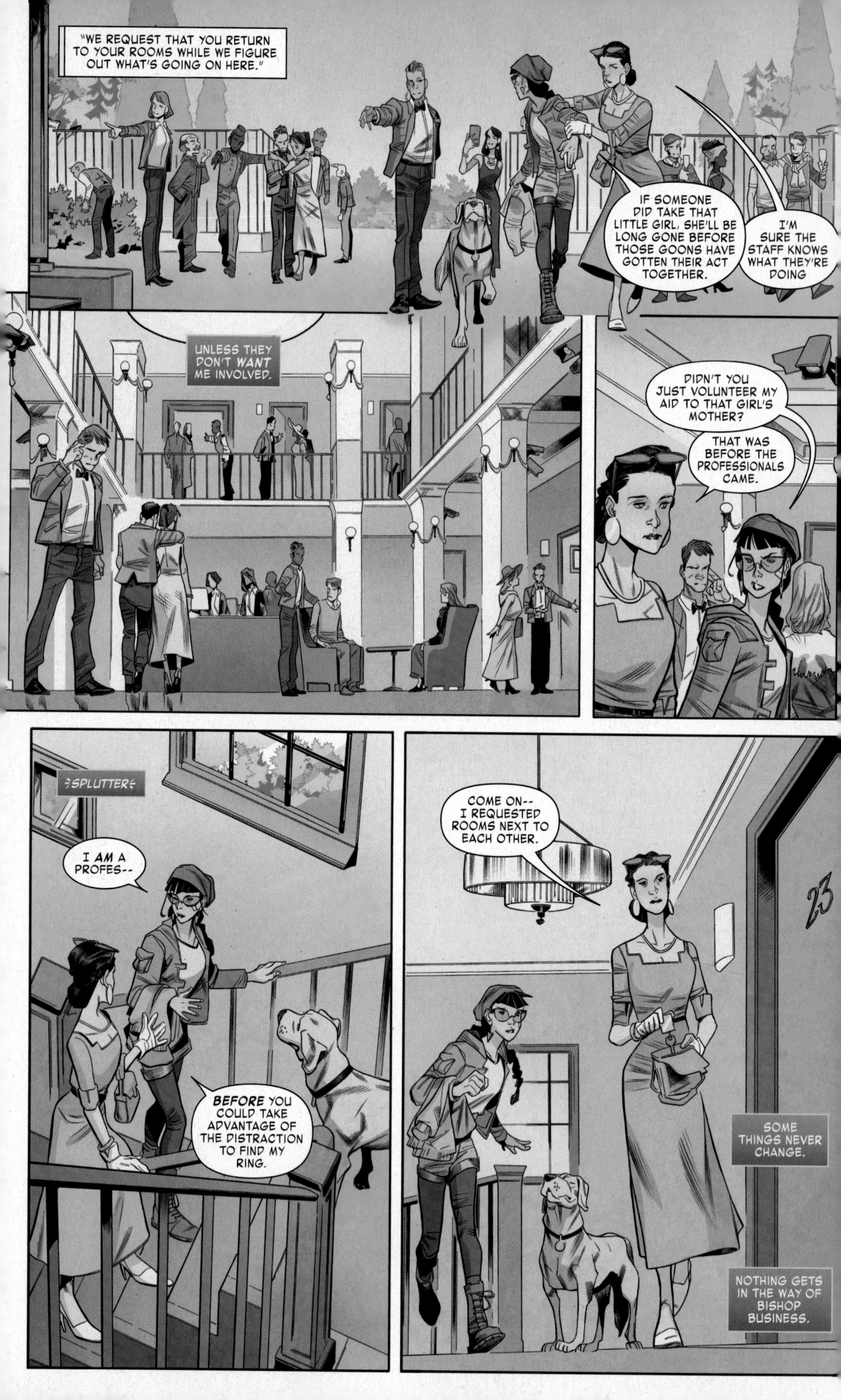
"WE REQUEST THAT YOU RETURN TO YOUR ROOMS WHILE WE FIGURE OUT WHAT'S GOING ON HERE."
IF SOMEONE DID TAKE THAT LITTLE GIRL, SHE'LL BE LONG GONE BEFORE THOSE GOONS HAVE GOTTEN THEIR ACT TOGETHER.
I'M SURE THE STAFF KNOWS WHAT THEY'RE DOING
UNLESS THEY DON'T *WANT* ME INVOLVED.
DIDN'T YOU JUST VOLUNTEER MY AID TO THAT GIRL'S MOTHER?
THAT WAS BEFORE THE PROFESSIONALS CAME.
SPLUTTER
I *AM* A PROFES--
BEFORE YOU COULD TAKE ADVANTAGE OF THE DISTRACTION TO FIND MY RING.
COME ON-- I REQUESTED ROOMS NEXT TO EACH OTHER.
23
SOME THINGS NEVER CHANGE.
NOTHING GETS IN THE WAY OF BISHOP BUSINESS.

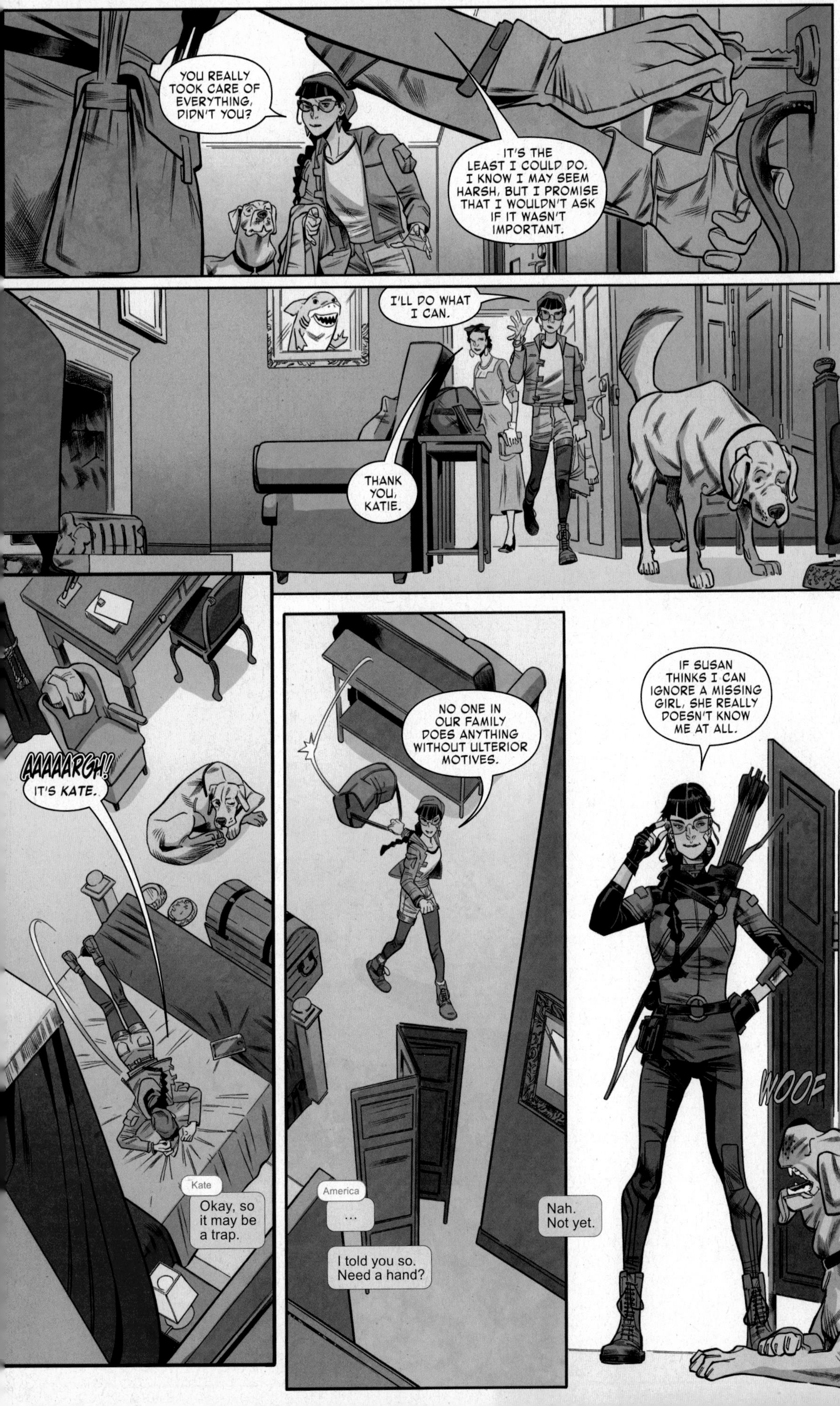
YOU REALLY TOOK CARE OF EVERYTHING, DIDN'T YOU?
IT'S THE LEAST I COULD DO. I KNOW I MAY SEEM HARSH, BUT I PROMISE THAT I WOULDN'T ASK IF IT WASN'T IMPORTANT.
I'LL DO WHAT I CAN.
THANK YOU, KATIE.
AAAAARGH!
IT'S KATE.
Kate
Okay, so it may be a trap.
NO ONE IN OUR FAMILY DOES ANYTHING WITHOUT ULTERIOR MOTIVES.
America
...
I told you so. Need a hand?
Nah. Not yet.
IF SUSAN THINKS I CAN IGNORE A MISSING GIRL, SHE REALLY DOESN'T KNOW ME AT ALL.
WOOF

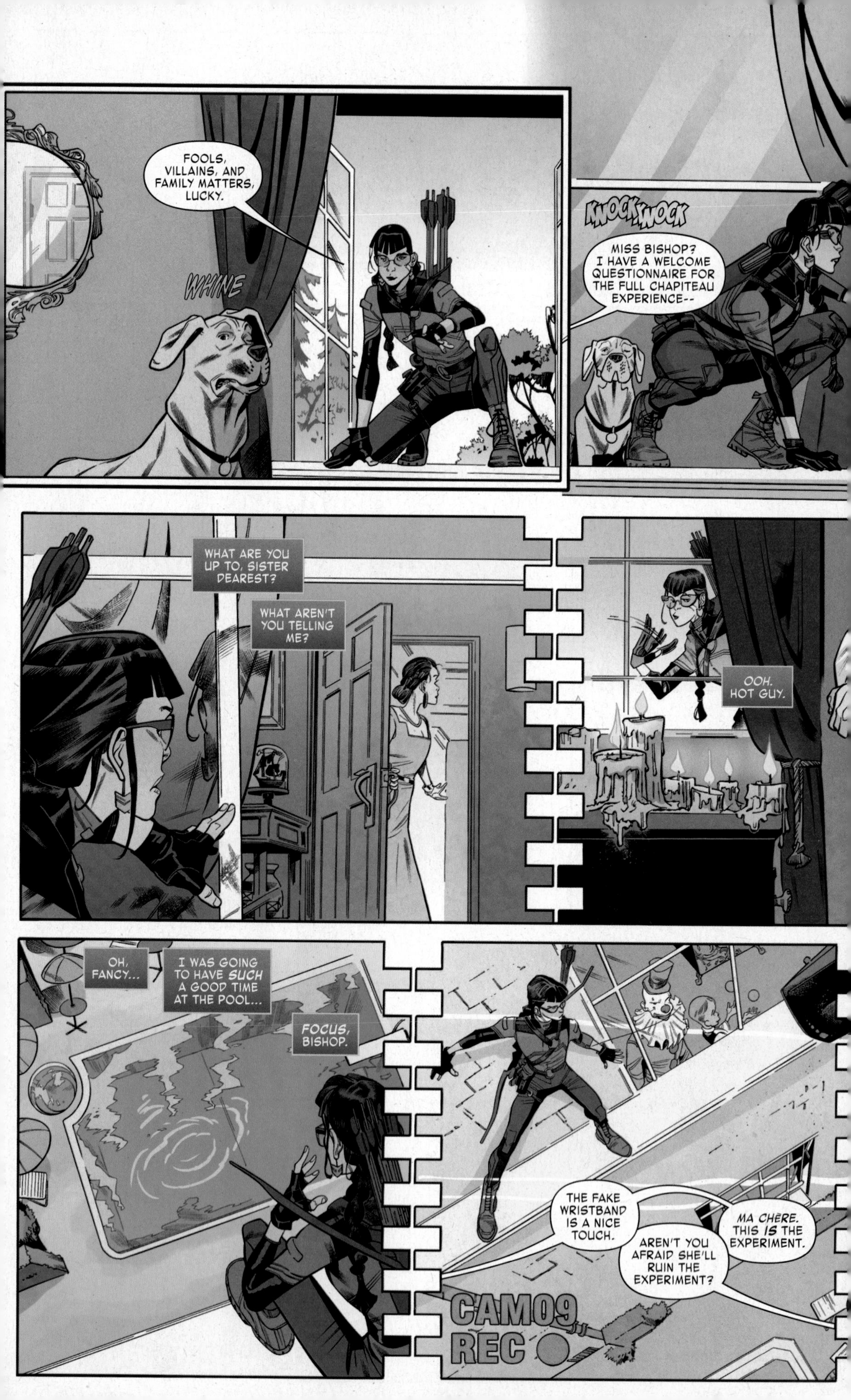
FOOLS, VILLAINS, AND FAMILY MATTERS, LUCKY.
WHINE
KNOCK KNOCK
MISS BISHOP? I HAVE A WELCOME QUESTIONNAIRE FOR THE FULL CHAPITEAU EXPERIENCE--
WHAT ARE YOU UP TO, SISTER DEAREST?
WHAT AREN'T YOU TELLING ME?
OOH. HOT GUY.
OH, FANCY...
I WAS GOING TO HAVE SUCH A GOOD TIME AT THE POOL...
FOCUS, BISHOP.
THE FAKE WRISTBAND IS A NICE TOUCH.
AREN'T YOU AFRAID SHE'LL RUIN THE EXPERIMENT?
MA CHÈRE. THIS IS THE EXPERIMENT.
CAM09
REC

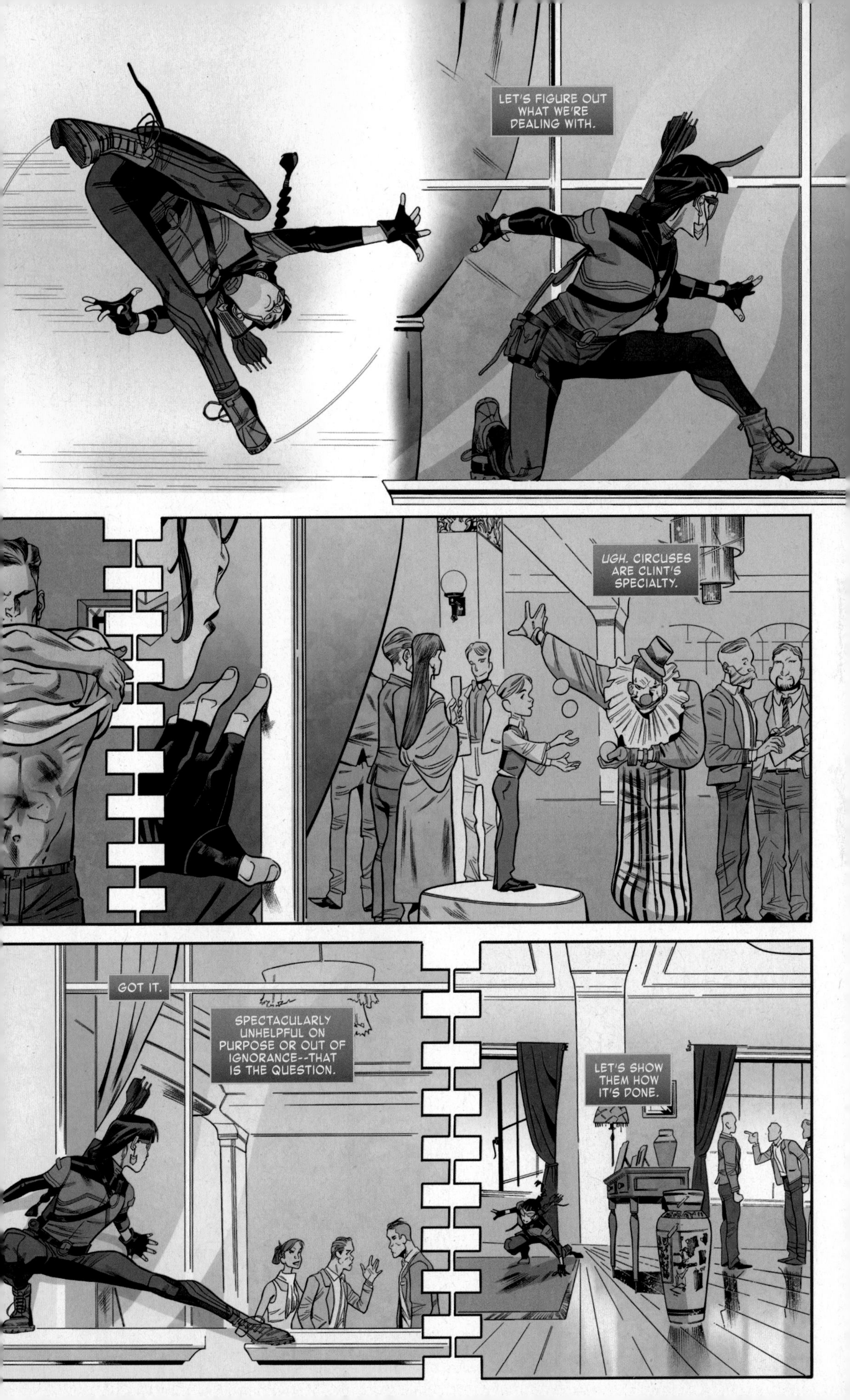
LET'S FIGURE OUT WHAT WE'RE DEALING WITH.
UGH. CIRCUSES ARE CLINT'S SPECIALTY.
GOT IT.
SPECTACULARLY UNHELPFUL ON PURPOSE OR OUT OF IGNORANCE--THAT IS THE QUESTION.
LET'S SHOW THEM HOW IT'S DONE.

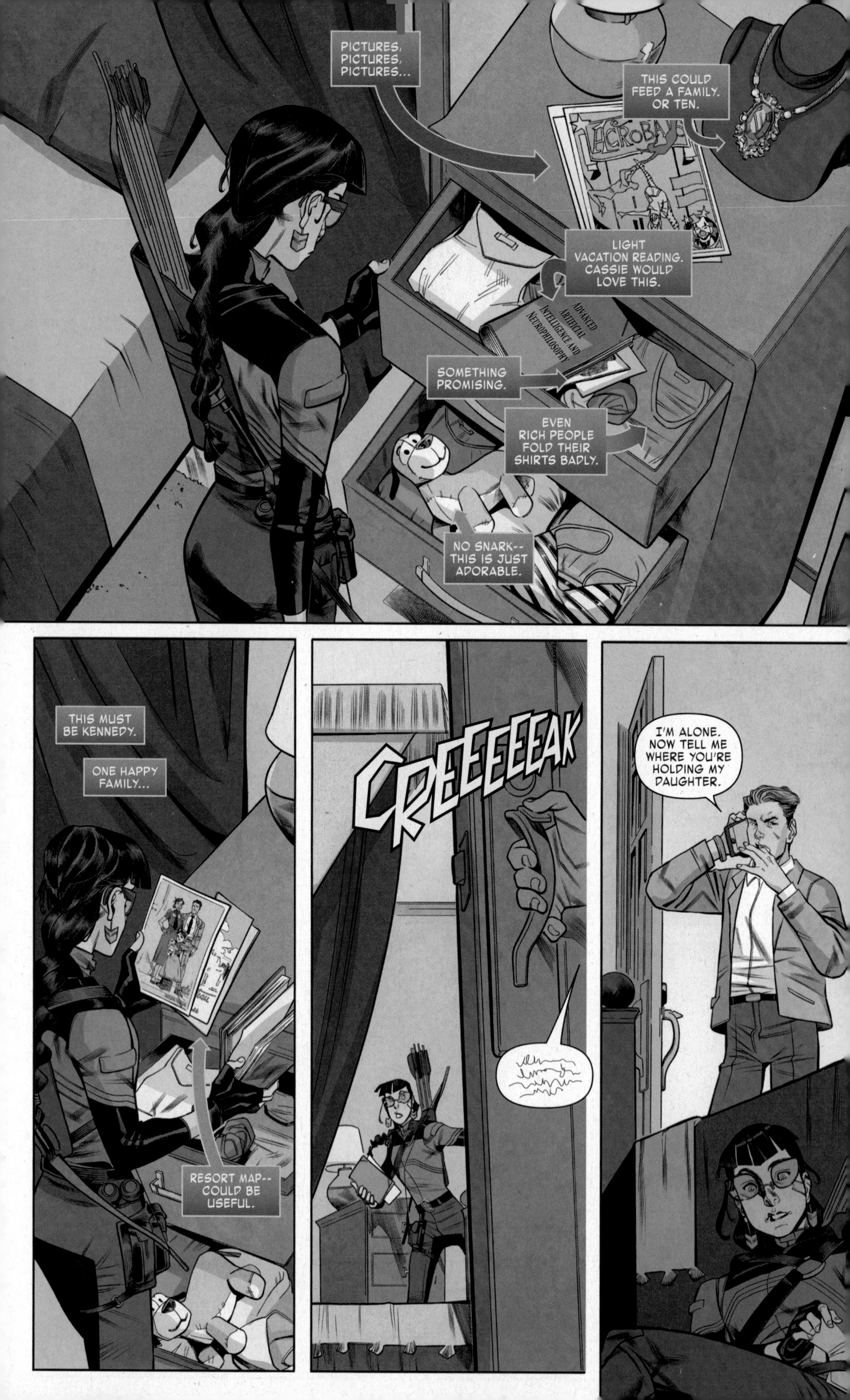
PICTURES, PICTURES, PICTURES...
THIS COULD FEED A FAMILY. OR TEN.
ADVANCED ARTIFICIAL INTELLIGENCE AND NEUROPHILOSOPHY
LIGHT VACATION READING. CASSIE WOULD LOVE THIS.
SOMETHING PROMISING.
EVEN RICH PEOPLE FOLD THEIR SHIRTS BADLY.
NO SNARK-- THIS IS JUST ADORABLE.
THIS MUST BE KENNEDY.
ONE HAPPY FAMILY...
RESORT MAP-- COULD BE USEFUL.
CREEEEEAK
I'M ALONE. NOW TELL ME WHERE YOU'RE HOLDING MY DAUGHTER.

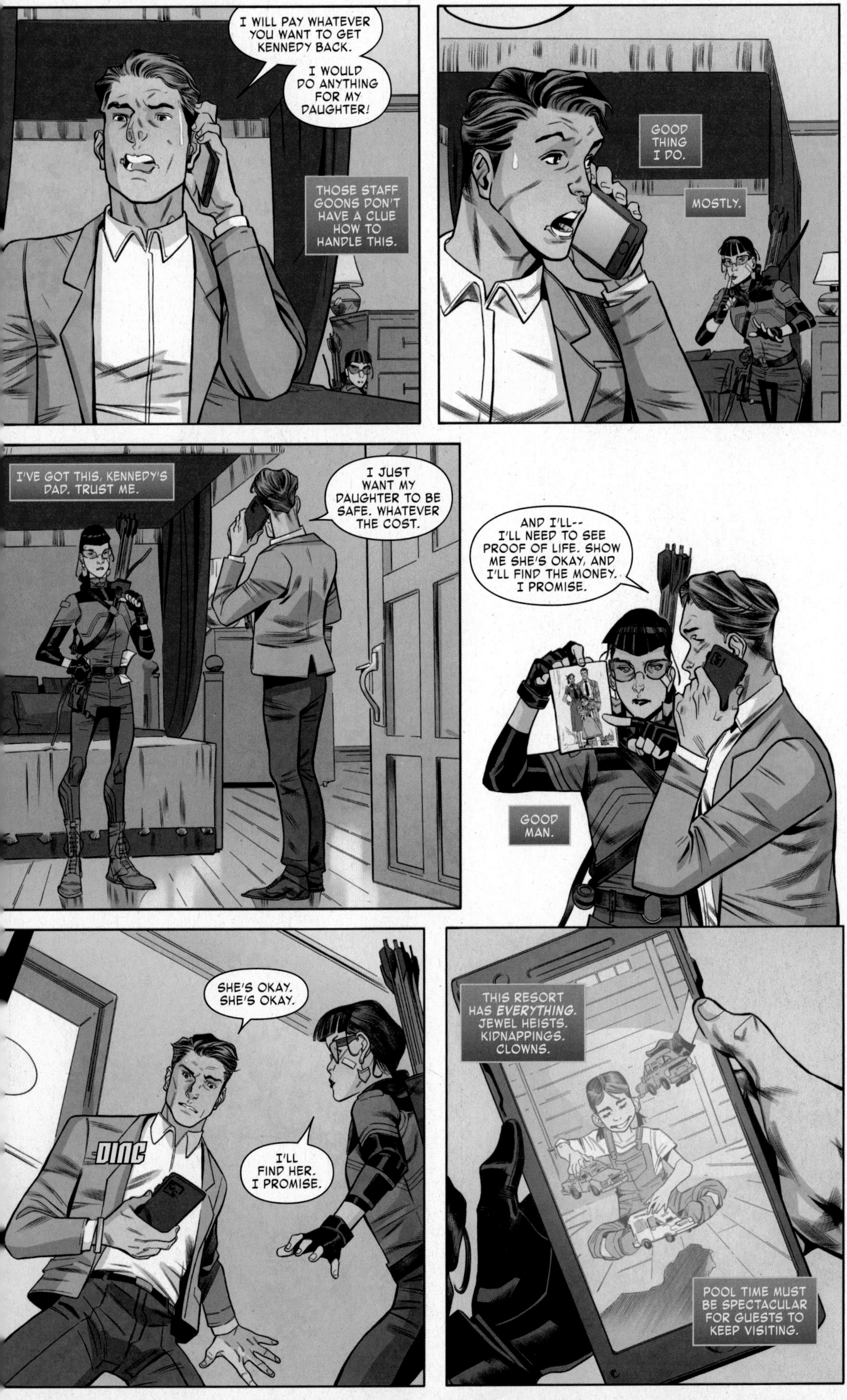
I WILL PAY WHATEVER YOU WANT TO GET KENNEDY BACK.
I WOULD DO ANYTHING FOR MY DAUGHTER!
THOSE STAFF GOONS DON'T HAVE A CLUE HOW TO HANDLE THIS.
GOOD THING I DO.
MOSTLY.
I'VE GOT THIS, KENNEDY'S DAD. TRUST ME.
I JUST WANT MY DAUGHTER TO BE SAFE. WHATEVER THE COST.
AND I'LL-- I'LL NEED TO SEE PROOF OF LIFE. SHOW ME SHE'S OKAY, AND I'LL FIND THE MONEY. I PROMISE.
GOOD MAN.
SHE'S OKAY. SHE'S OKAY.
DING
I'LL FIND HER. I PROMISE.
THIS RESORT HAS EVERYTHING. JEWEL HEISTS. KIDNAPPINGS. CLOWNS.
POOL TIME MUST BE SPECTACULAR FOR GUESTS TO KEEP VISITING.

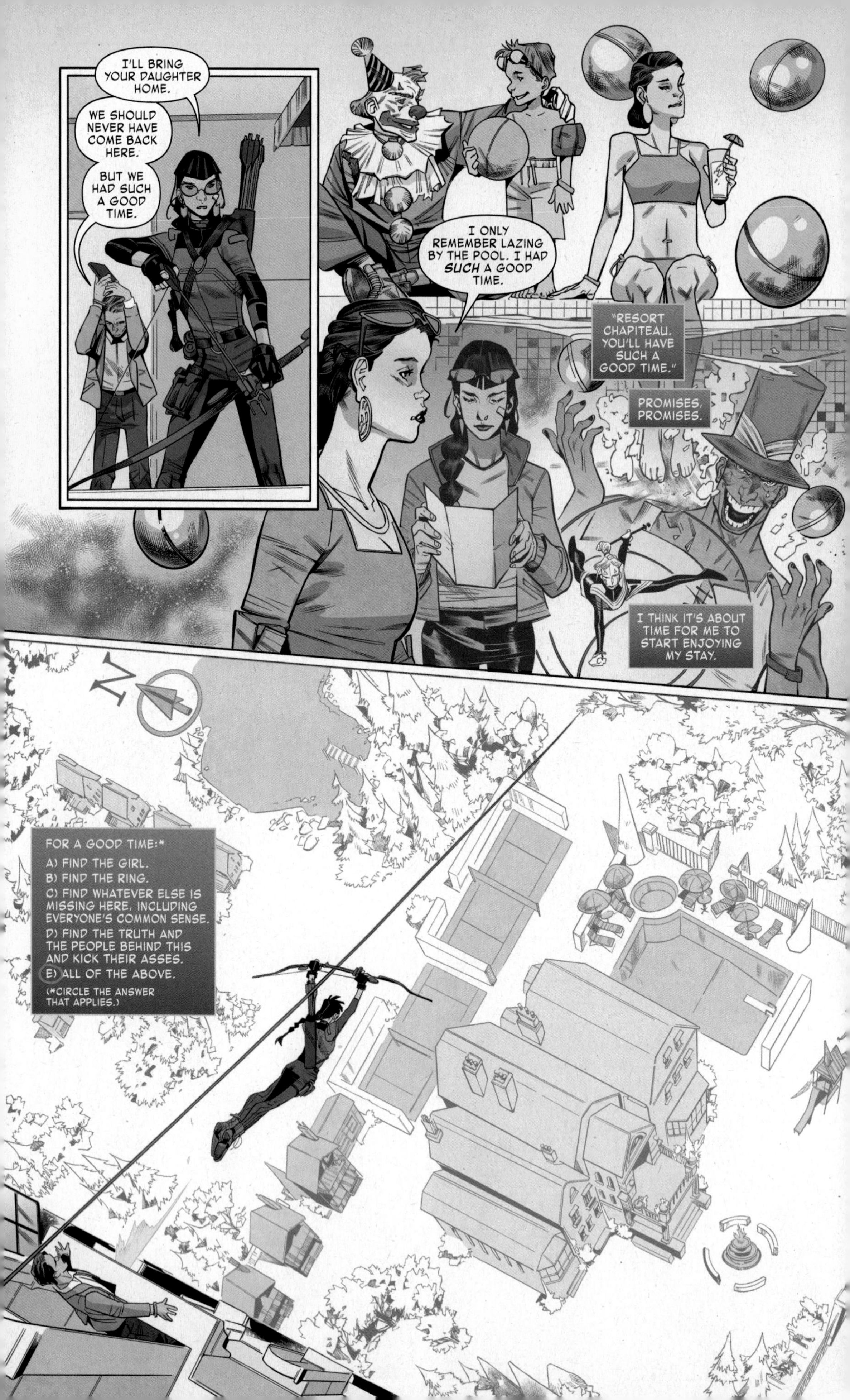
I'LL BRING YOUR DAUGHTER HOME.
WE SHOULD NEVER HAVE COME BACK HERE.
BUT WE HAD SUCH A GOOD TIME.
I ONLY REMEMBER LAZING BY THE POOL. I HAD SUCH A GOOD TIME.
"RESORT CHAPITEAU. YOU'LL HAVE SUCH A GOOD TIME."
PROMISES, PROMISES.
I THINK IT'S ABOUT TIME FOR ME TO START ENJOYING MY STAY.
N
FOR A GOOD TIME:*
A) FIND THE GIRL.
B) FIND THE RING.
C) FIND WHATEVER ELSE IS MISSING HERE, INCLUDING EVERYONE'S COMMON SENSE.
D) FIND THE TRUTH AND THE PEOPLE BEHIND THIS AND KICK THEIR ASSES.
E) ALL OF THE ABOVE.
(*CIRCLE THE ANSWER THAT APPLIES.)

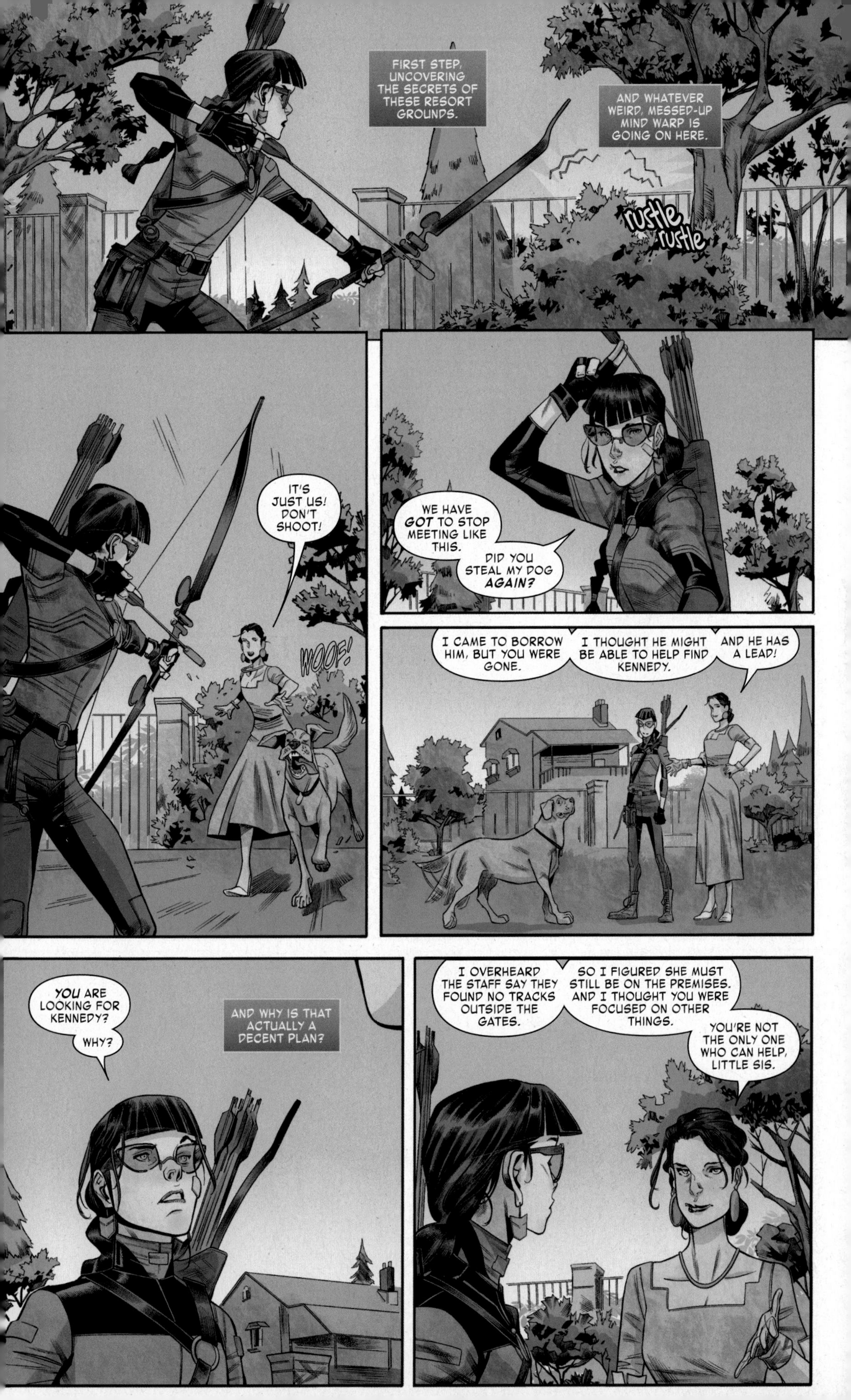
FIRST STEP, UNCOVERING THE SECRETS OF THESE RESORT GROUNDS.
AND WHATEVER WEIRD, MESSED-UP MIND WARP IS GOING ON HERE.
rustle rustle
IT'S JUST US! DON'T SHOOT!
WOOF!
WE HAVE GOT TO STOP MEETING LIKE THIS.
DID YOU STEAL MY DOG AGAIN?
I CAME TO BORROW HIM, BUT YOU WERE GONE.
I THOUGHT HE MIGHT BE ABLE TO HELP FIND KENNEDY.
AND HE HAS A LEAD!
YOU ARE LOOKING FOR KENNEDY?
WHY?
AND WHY IS THAT ACTUALLY A DECENT PLAN?
I OVERHEARD THE STAFF SAY THEY FOUND NO TRACKS OUTSIDE THE GATES.
SO I FIGURED SHE MUST STILL BE ON THE PREMISES. AND I THOUGHT YOU WERE FOCUSED ON OTHER THINGS.
YOU'RE NOT THE ONLY ONE WHO CAN HELP, LITTLE SIS.

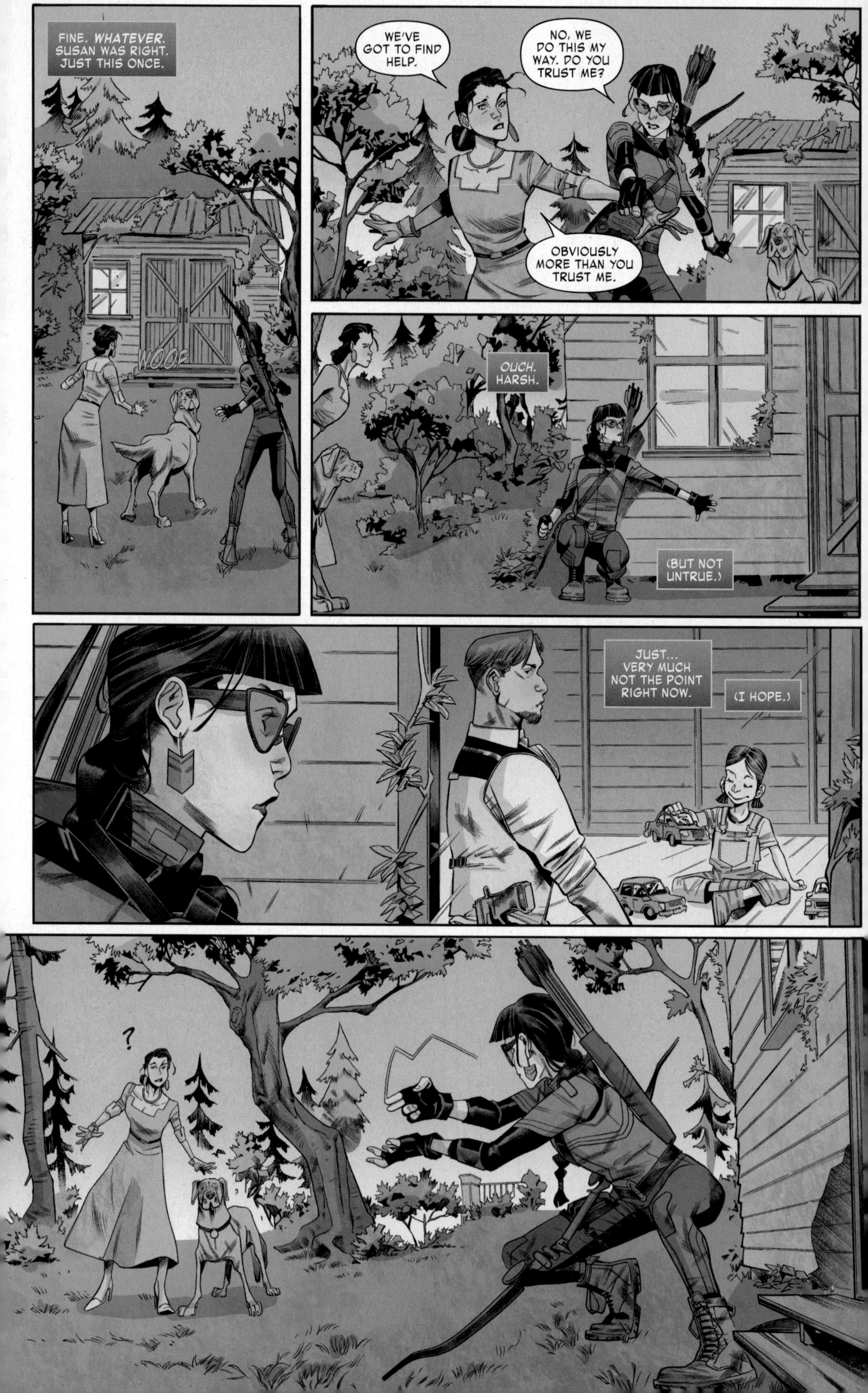
FINE. *WHATEVER.* SUSAN WAS RIGHT. JUST THIS ONCE.
WOOF
WE'VE GOT TO FIND HELP.
NO, WE DO THIS MY WAY. DO YOU TRUST ME?
OBVIOUSLY MORE THAN YOU TRUST ME.
OUCH. HARSH.
(BUT NOT UNTRUE.)
JUST... VERY MUCH NOT THE POINT RIGHT NOW.
(I HOPE.)
?

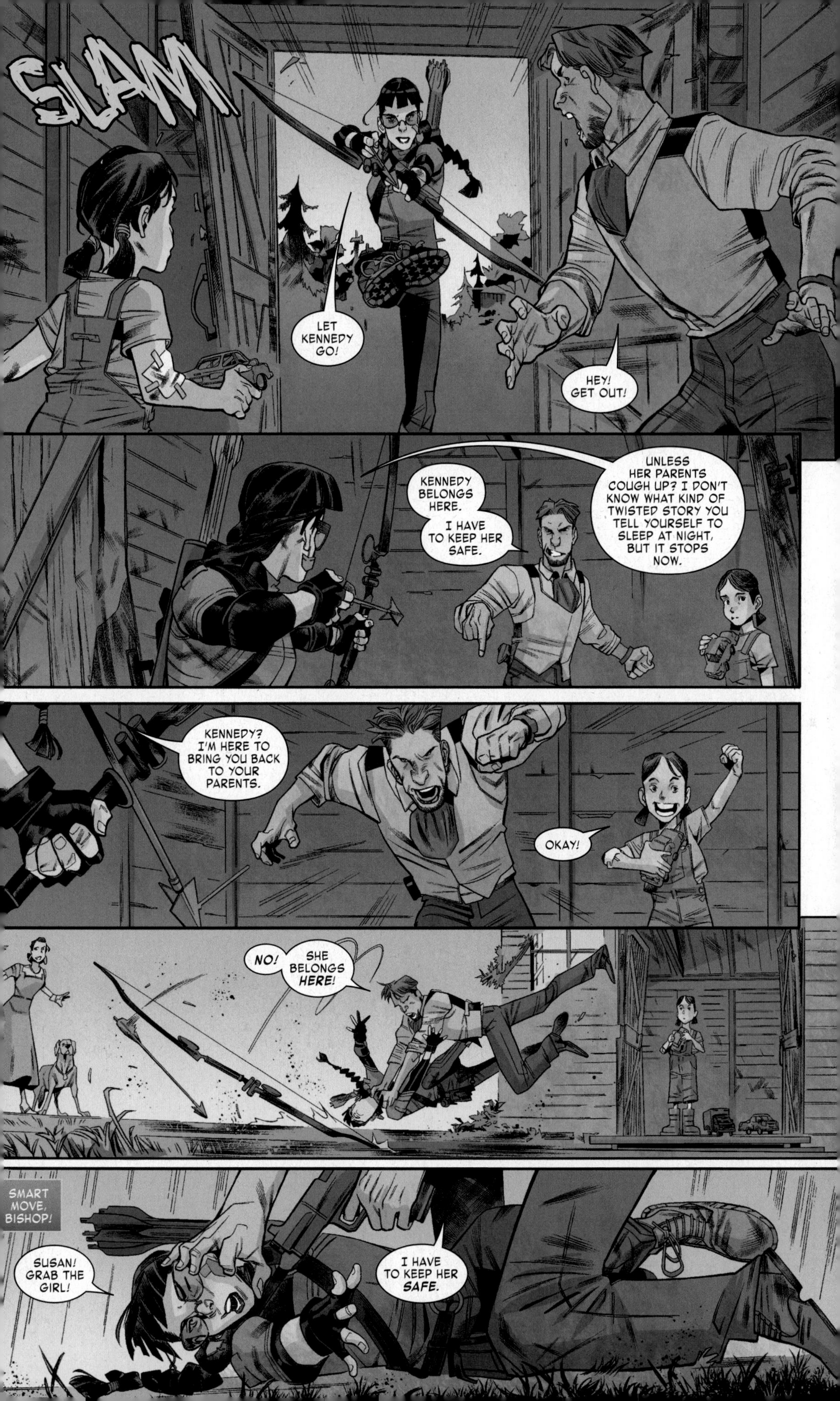
SLAM
LET KENNEDY GO!
HEY! GET OUT!
KENNEDY BELONGS HERE.
I HAVE TO KEEP HER SAFE.
UNLESS HER PARENTS COUGH UP? I DON'T KNOW WHAT KIND OF TWISTED STORY YOU TELL YOURSELF TO SLEEP AT NIGHT, BUT IT STOPS NOW.
KENNEDY? I'M HERE TO BRING YOU BACK TO YOUR PARENTS.
OKAY!
NO!
SHE BELONGS HERE!
SMART MOVE, BISHOP!
SUSAN! GRAB THE GIRL!
I HAVE TO KEEP HER SAFE.

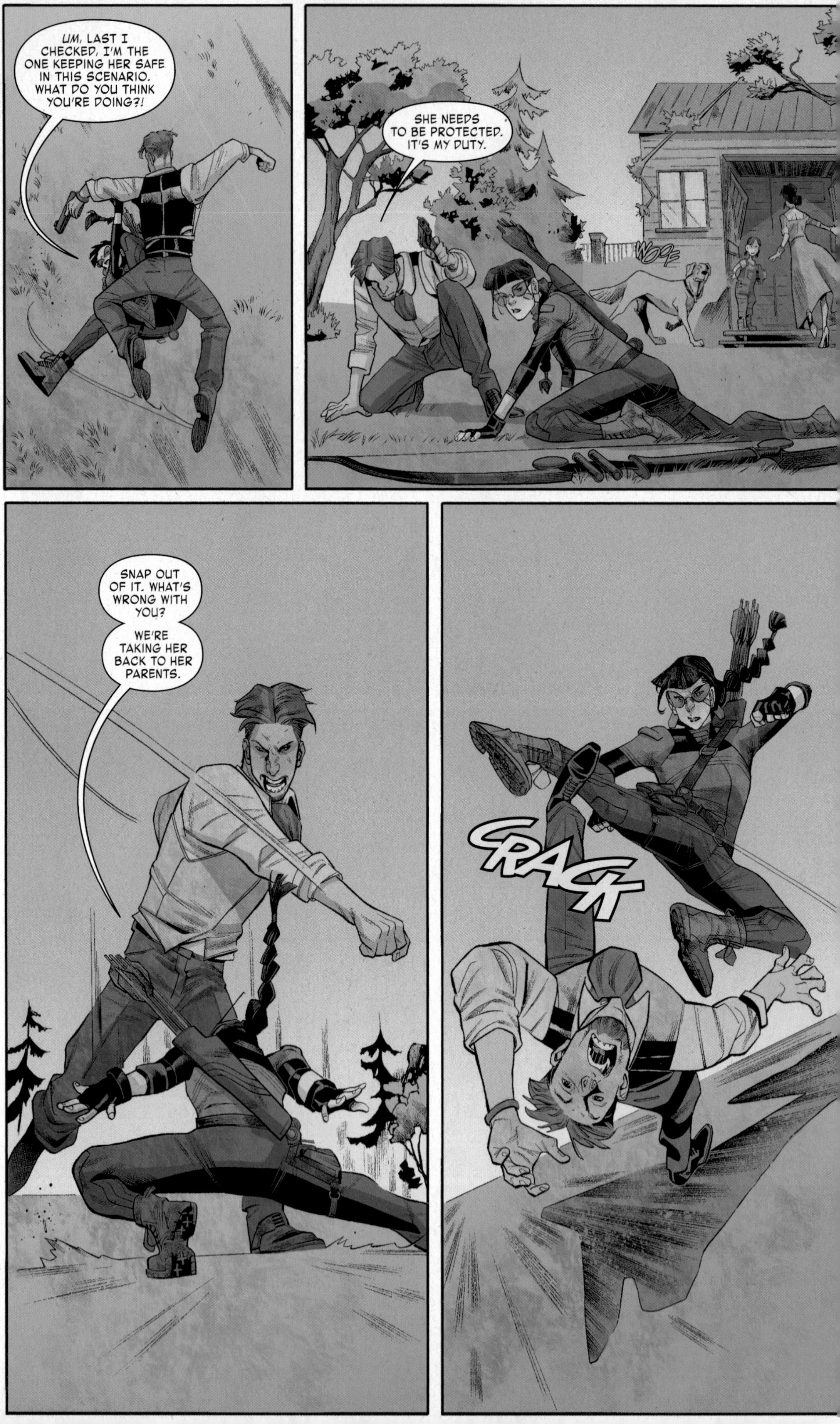
UM, LAST I CHECKED, I'M THE ONE KEEPING HER SAFE IN THIS SCENARIO. WHAT DO YOU THINK YOU'RE DOING?!
SHE NEEDS TO BE PROTECTED. IT'S MY DUTY.
WOOF
SNAP OUT OF IT. WHAT'S WRONG WITH YOU?
WE'RE TAKING HER BACK TO HER PARENTS.
CRACK

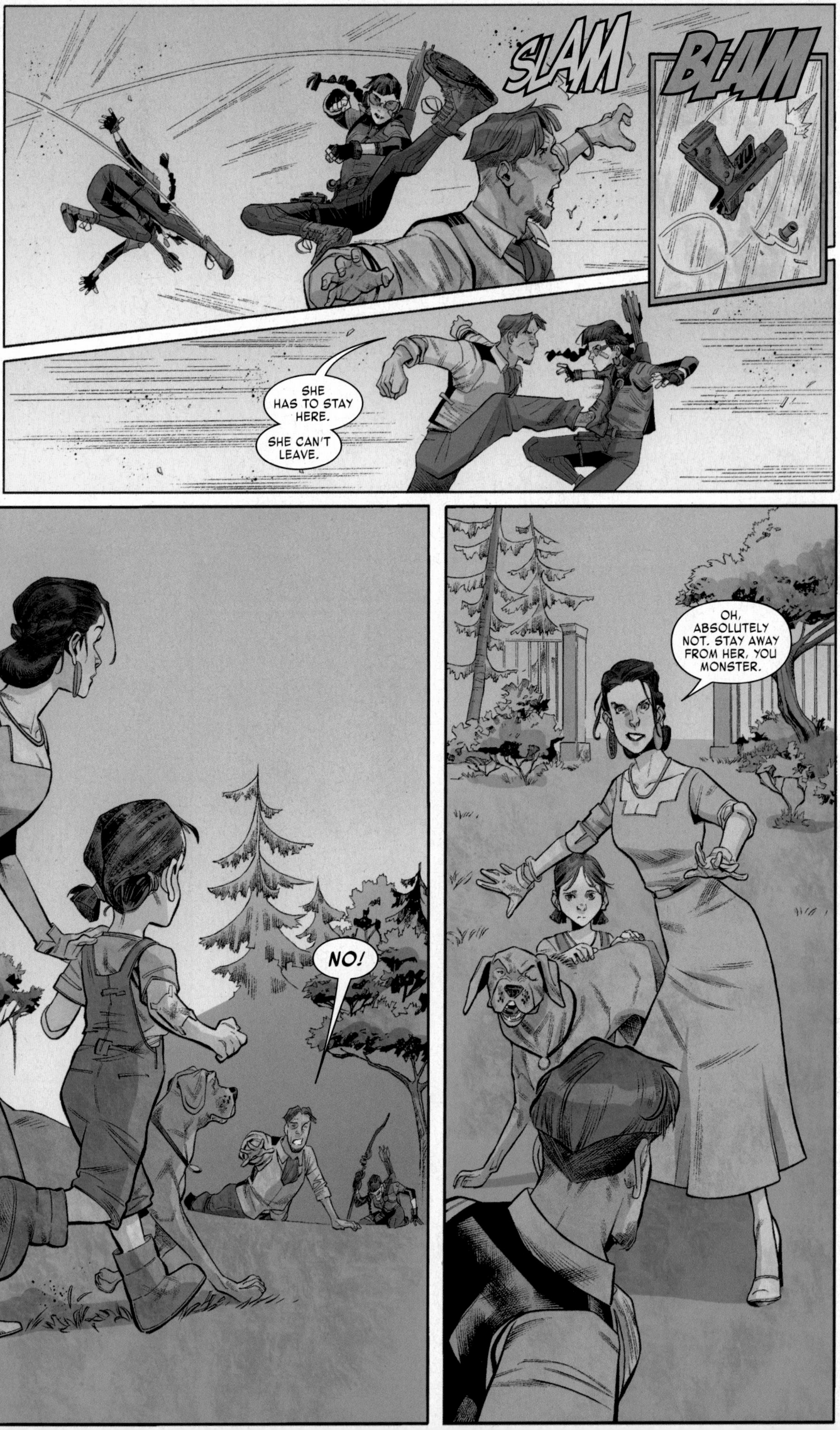
SLAM
BLAM
SHE HAS TO STAY HERE.
SHE CAN'T LEAVE.
NO!
OH, ABSOLUTELY NOT. STAY AWAY FROM HER, YOU MONSTER.

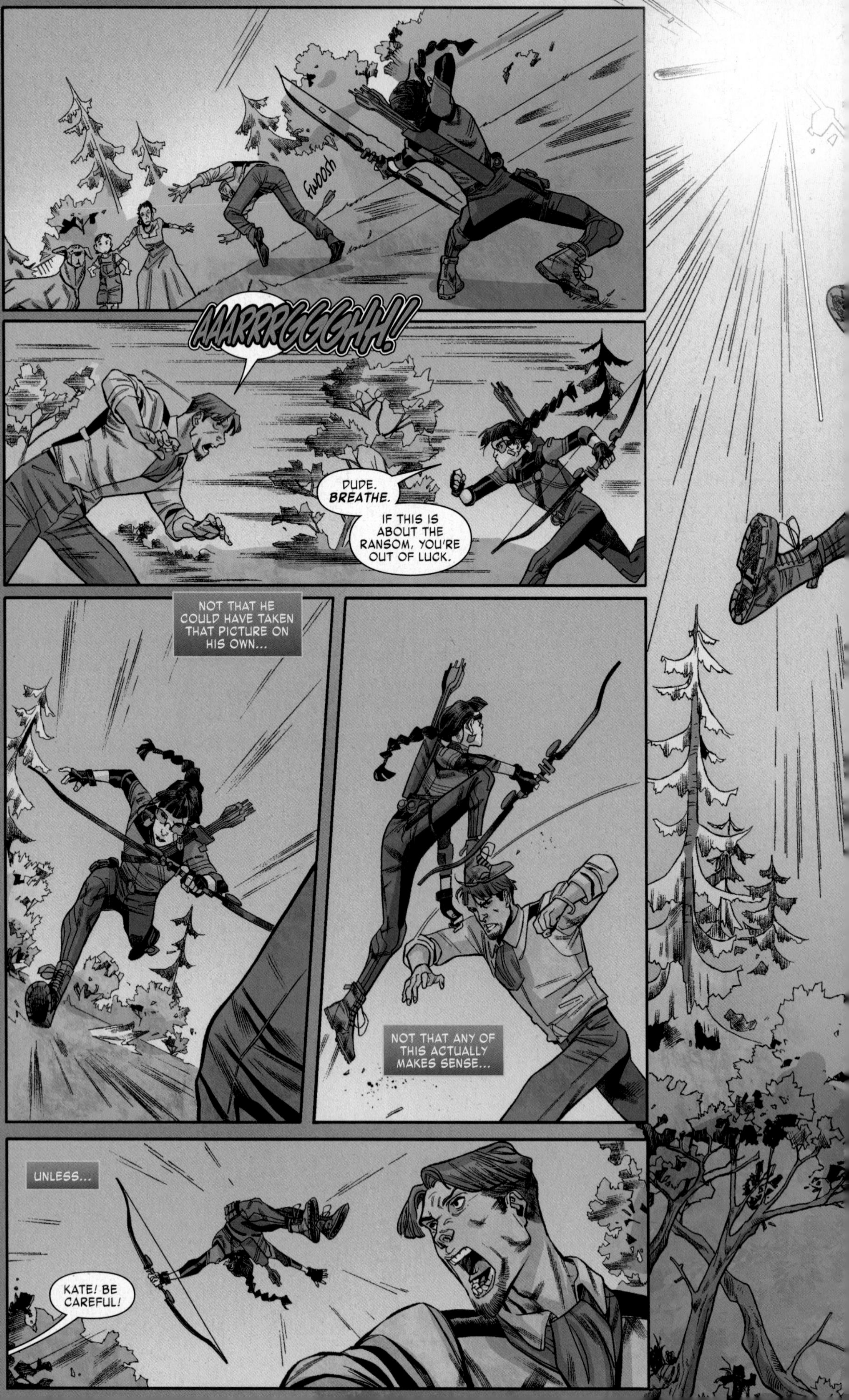
FWOOSH
AAARRRGGGHH!
DUDE. BREATHE.
IF THIS IS ABOUT THE RANSOM, YOU'RE OUT OF LUCK.
NOT THAT HE COULD HAVE TAKEN THAT PICTURE ON HIS OWN...
NOT THAT ANY OF THIS ACTUALLY MAKES SENSE...
UNLESS...
KATE! BE CAREFUL!

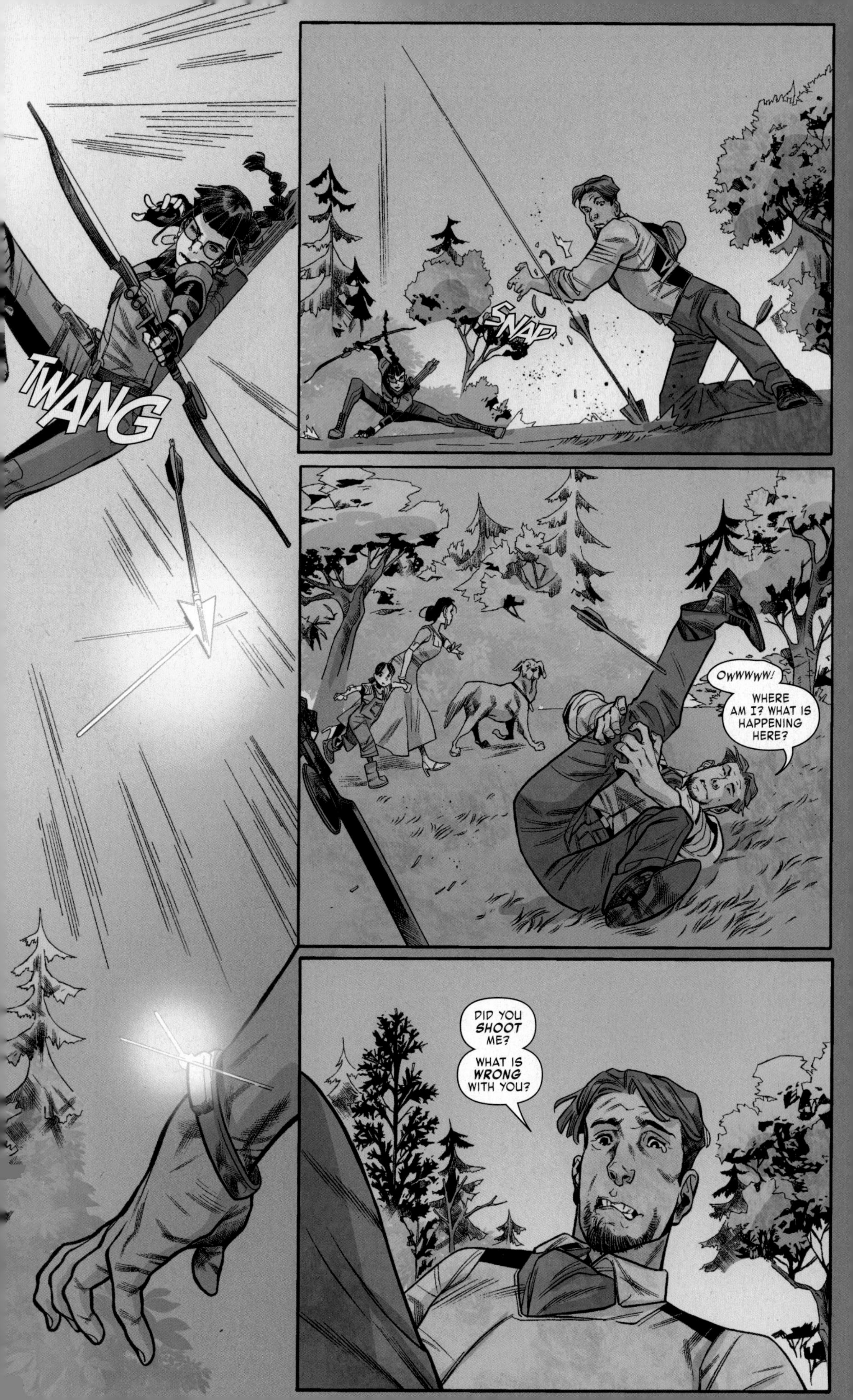
TWANG
SNAP
OWWWWW!
WHERE AM I? WHAT IS HAPPENING HERE?
DID YOU SHOOT ME?
WHAT IS WRONG WITH YOU?

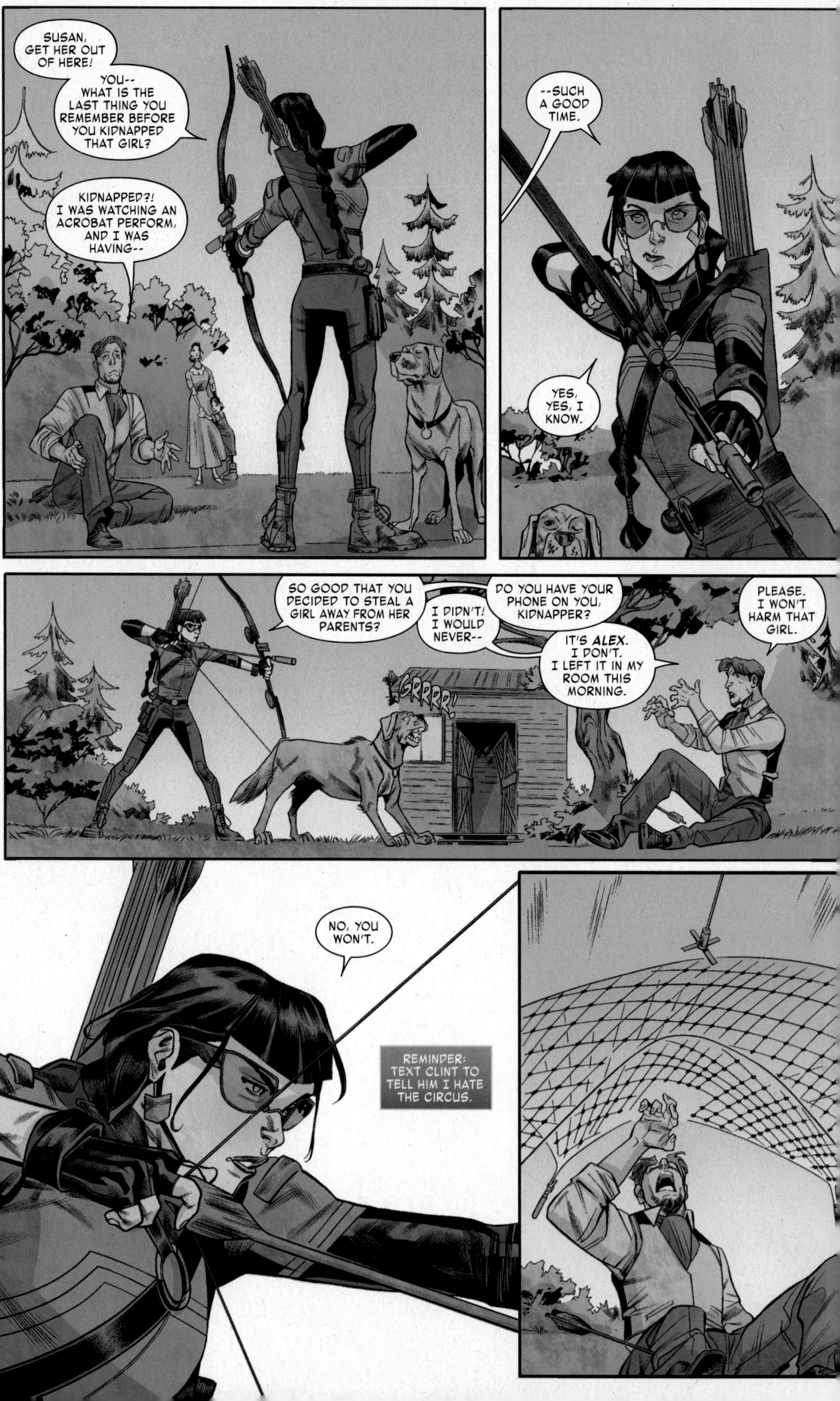
SUSAN, GET HER OUT OF HERE!
YOU-- WHAT IS THE LAST THING YOU REMEMBER BEFORE YOU KIDNAPPED THAT GIRL?
KIDNAPPED?! I WAS WATCHING AN ACROBAT PERFORM, AND I WAS HAVING--
--SUCH A GOOD TIME.
YES, YES, I KNOW.
SO GOOD THAT YOU DECIDED TO STEAL A GIRL AWAY FROM HER PARENTS?
I DIDN'T! I WOULD NEVER--
DO YOU HAVE YOUR PHONE ON YOU, KIDNAPPER?
IT'S ALEX. I DON'T. I LEFT IT IN MY ROOM THIS MORNING.
GRRRR!
PLEASE. I WON'T HARM THAT GIRL.
NO, YOU WON'T.
REMINDER: TEXT CLINT TO TELL HIM I HATE THE CIRCUS.

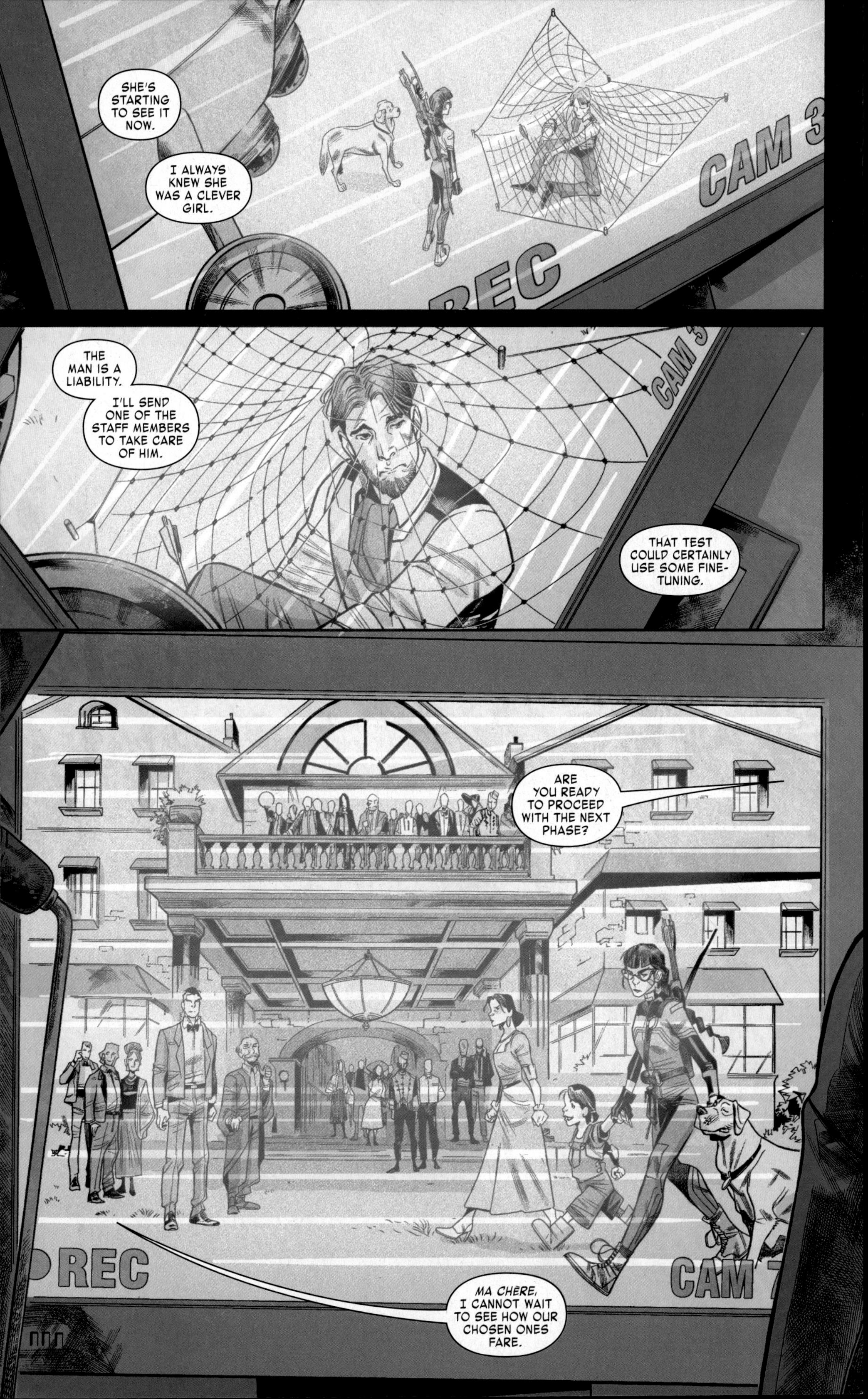
SHE'S STARTING TO SEE IT NOW.
I ALWAYS KNEW SHE WAS A CLEVER GIRL.
CAM 3
REC
THE MAN IS A LIABILITY.
I'LL SEND ONE OF THE STAFF MEMBERS TO TAKE CARE OF HIM.
CAM 3
THAT TEST COULD CERTAINLY USE SOME FINE-TUNING.
ARE YOU READY TO PROCEED WITH THE NEXT PHASE?
REC
CAM 7
MA CHÈRE, I CANNOT WAIT TO SEE HOW OUR CHOSEN ONES FARE.

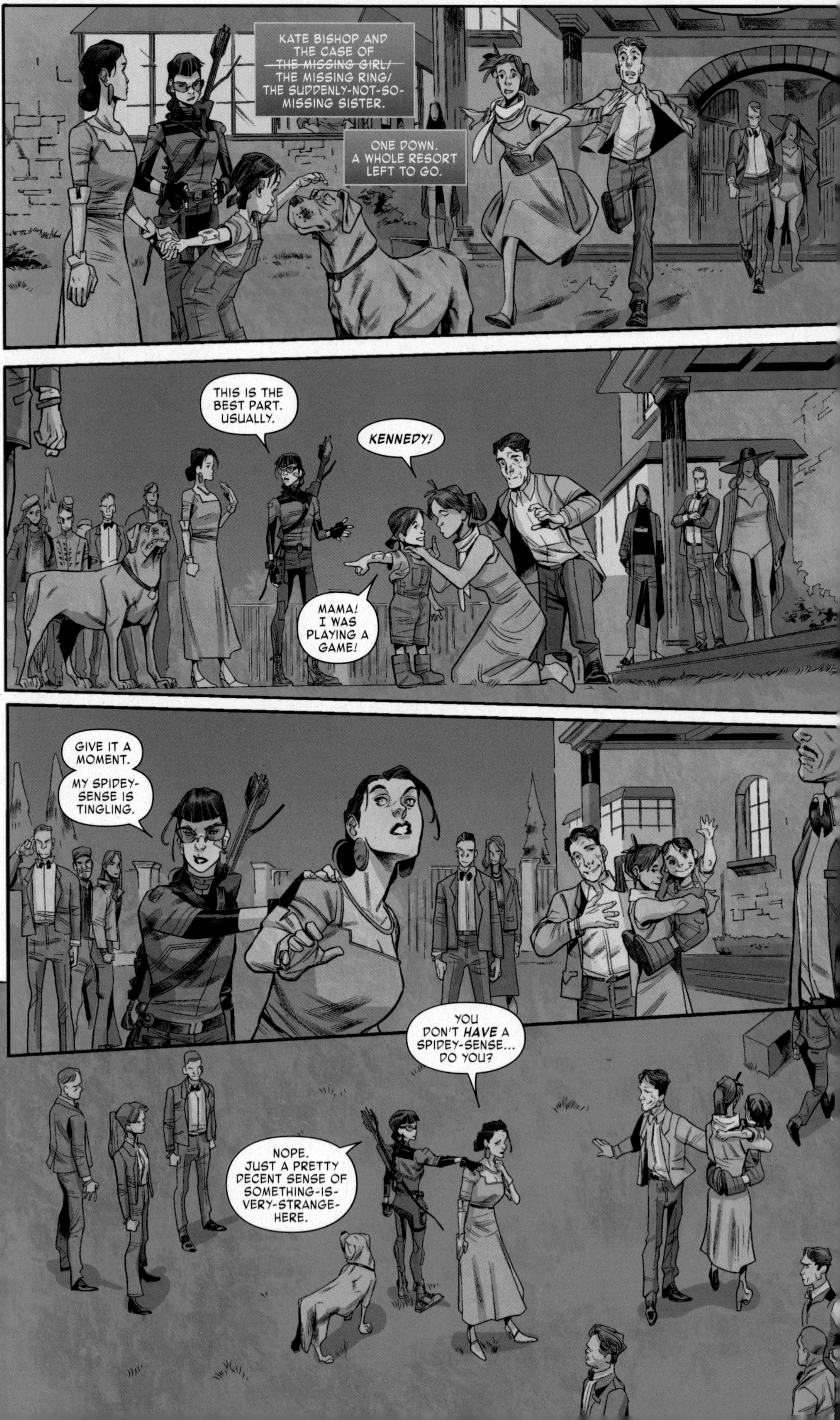

KATE BISHOP AND THE CASE OF ~~THE MISSING GIRL/~~ THE MISSING RING/ THE SUDDENLY-NOT-SO-MISSING SISTER.
ONE DOWN. A WHOLE RESORT LEFT TO GO.
THIS IS THE BEST PART. USUALLY.
KENNEDY!
MAMA! I WAS PLAYING A GAME!
GIVE IT A MOMENT.
MY SPIDEY-SENSE IS TINGLING.
YOU DON'T *HAVE* A SPIDEY-SENSE... DO YOU?
NOPE. JUST A PRETTY DECENT SENSE OF SOMETHING-IS-VERY-STRANGE-HERE.

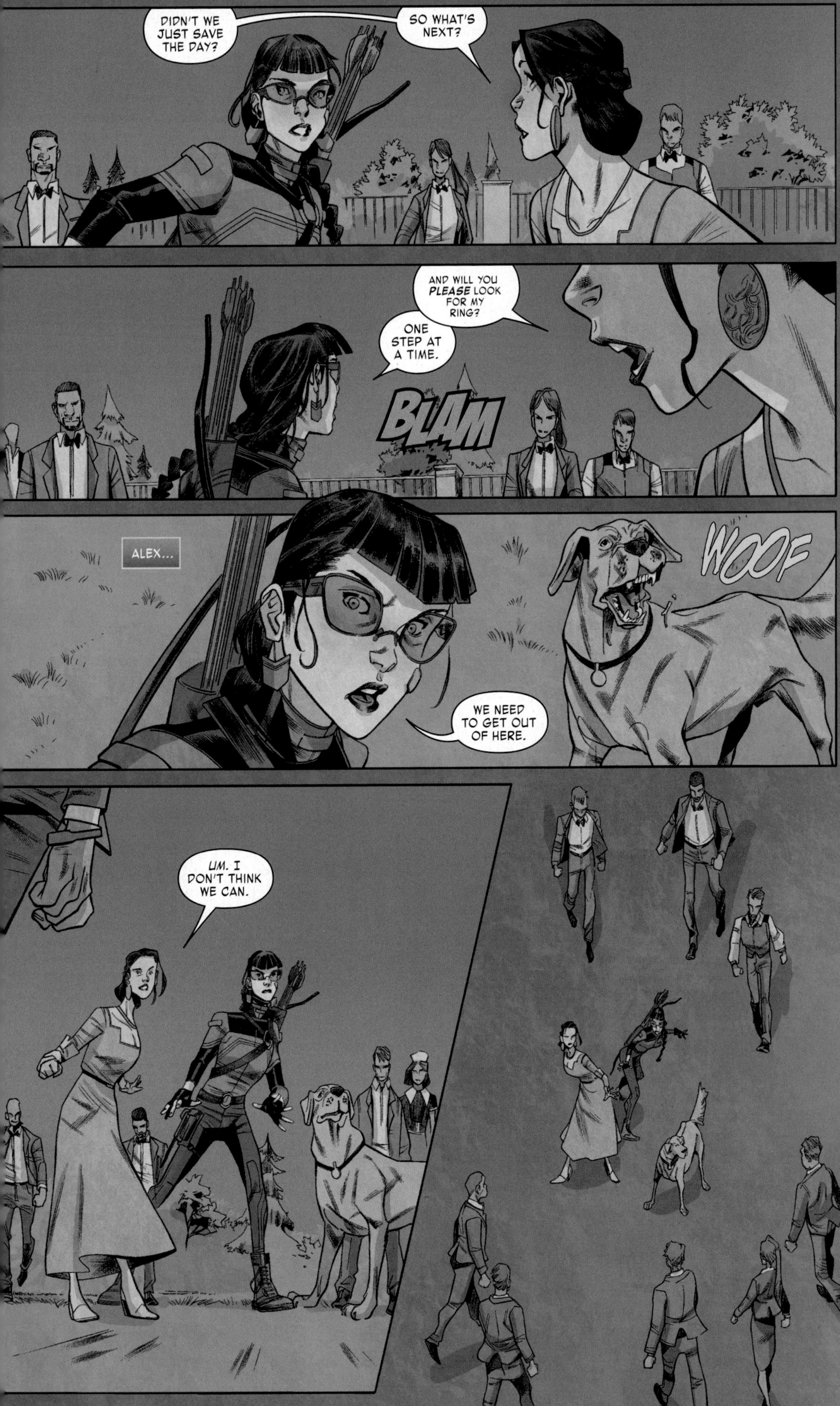

DIDN'T WE JUST SAVE THE DAY?
SO WHAT'S NEXT?
AND WILL YOU *PLEASE* LOOK FOR MY RING?
ONE STEP AT A TIME.
BLAM
ALEX...
WOOF
WE NEED TO GET OUT OF HERE.
UM. I DON'T THINK WE CAN.

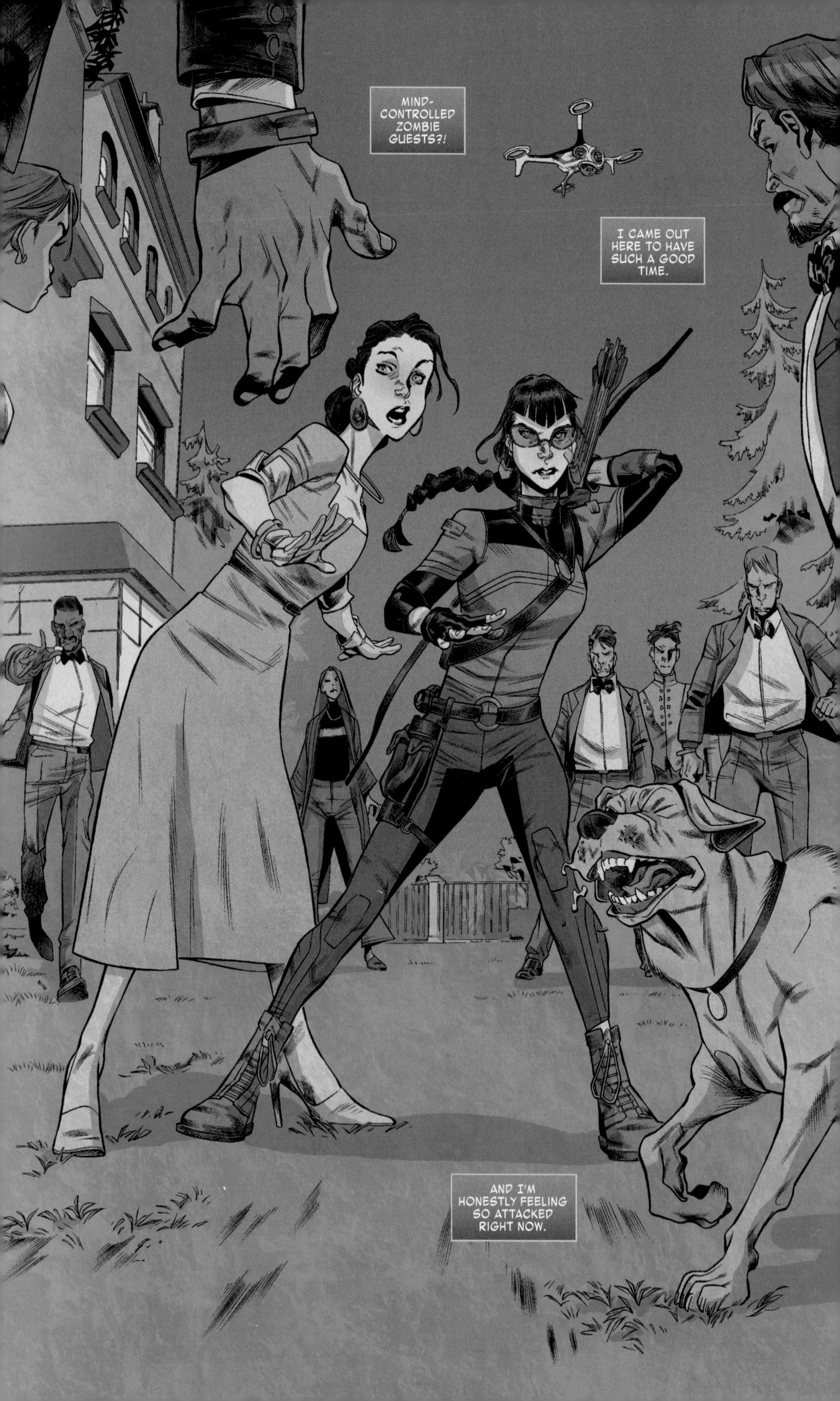
MIND-CONTROLLED ZOMBIE GUESTS?!
I CAME OUT HERE TO HAVE SUCH A GOOD TIME.
AND I'M HONESTLY FEELING SO ATTACKED RIGHT NOW.

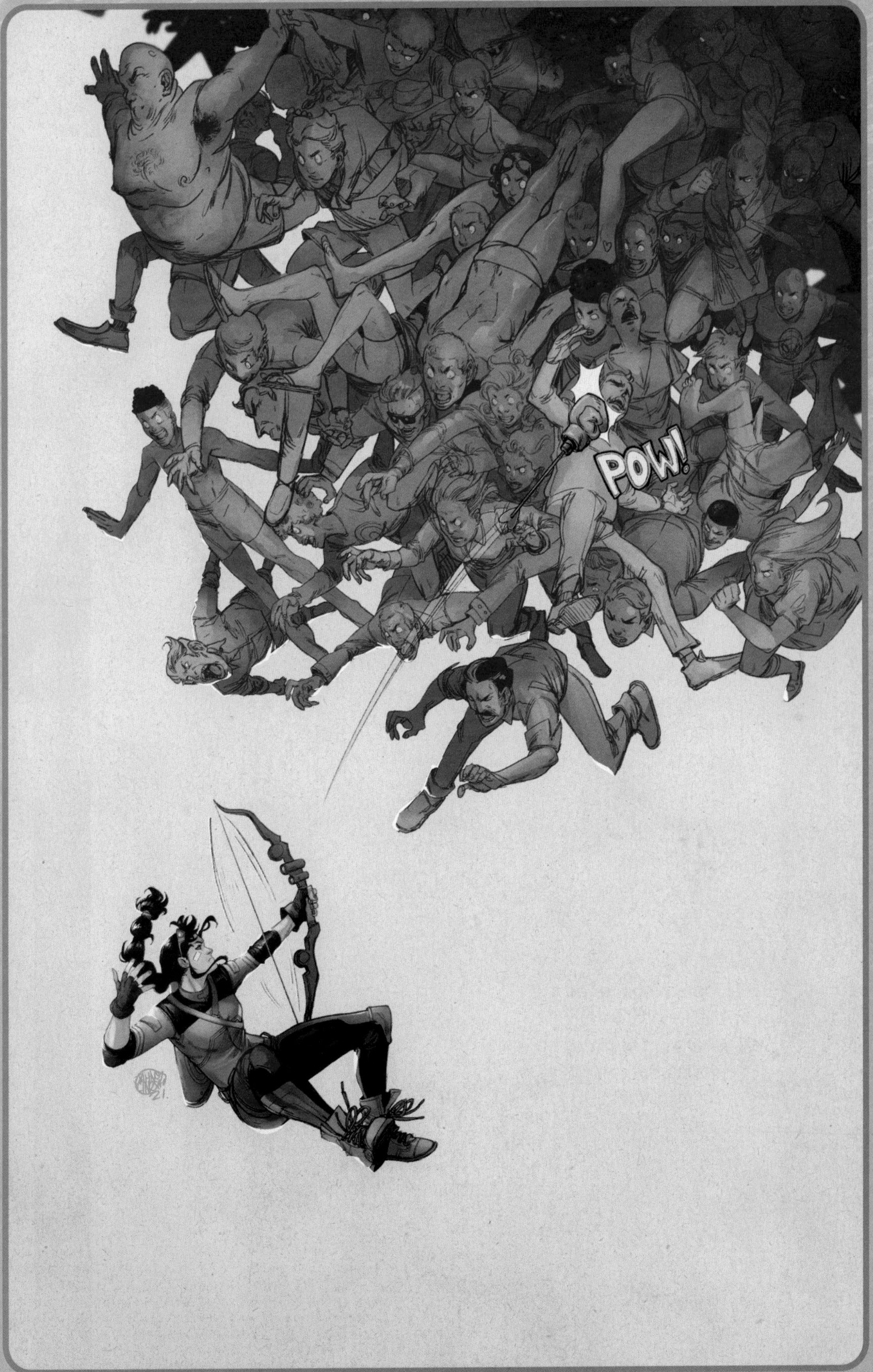
POW!

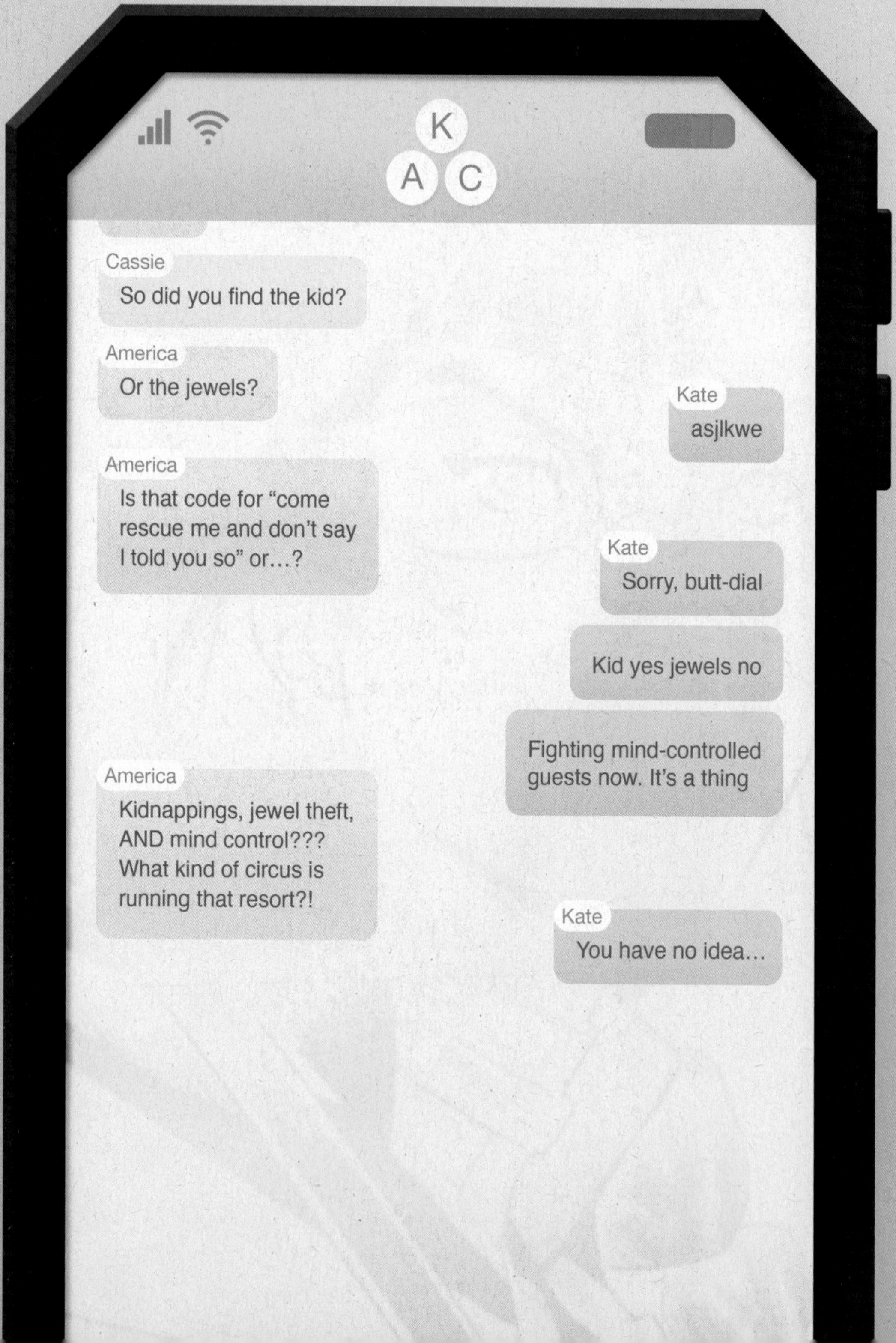
K
A
C
Cassie
So did you find the kid?
America
Or the jewels?
Kate
asjlkwe
America
Is that code for "come rescue me and don't say I told you so" or…?
Kate
Sorry, butt-dial
Kid yes jewels no
Fighting mind-controlled guests now. It's a thing
America
Kidnappings, jewel theft, AND mind control??? What kind of circus is running that resort?!
Kate
You have no idea…

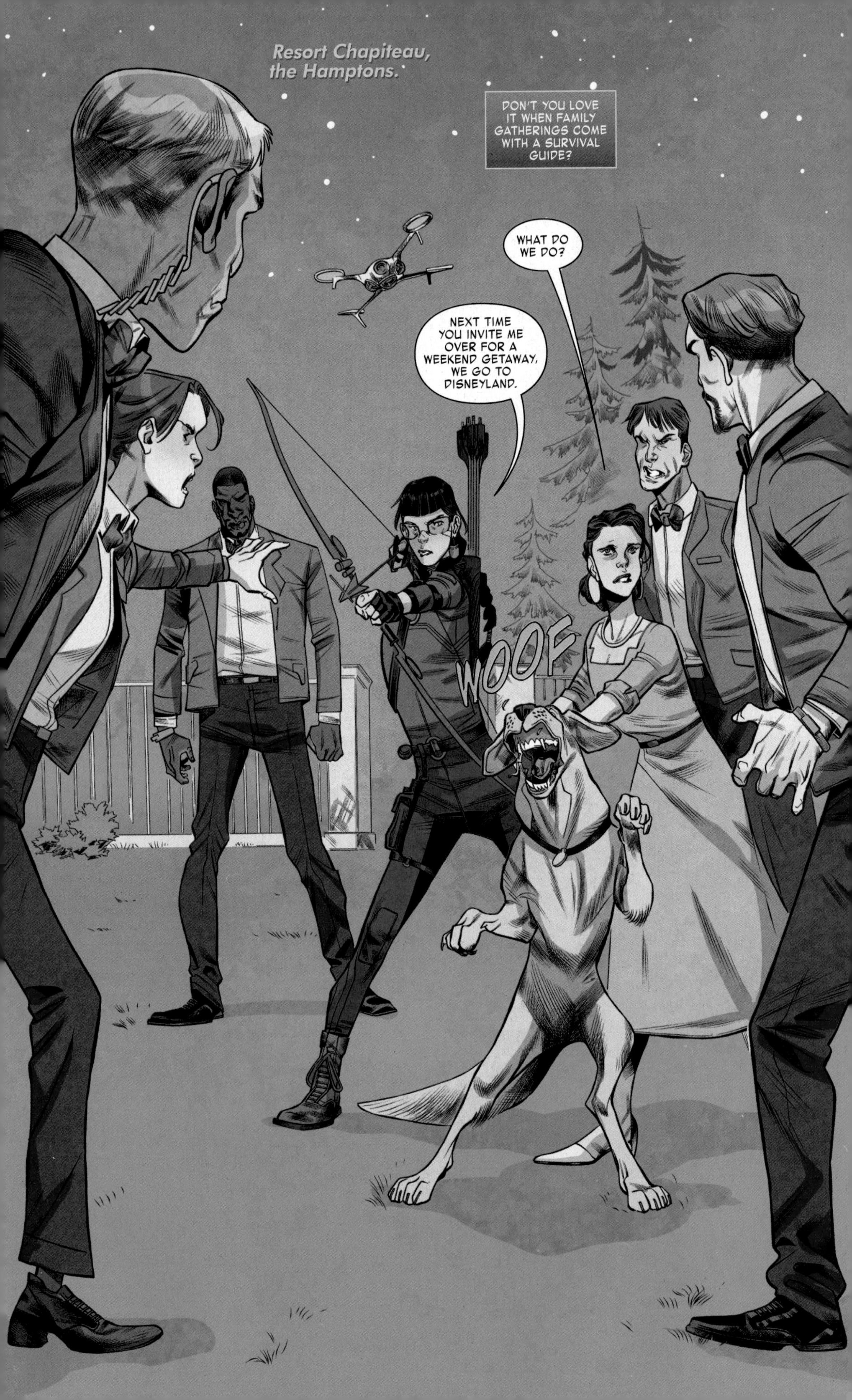
Resort Chapiteau, the Hamptons.
DON'T YOU LOVE IT WHEN FAMILY GATHERINGS COME WITH A SURVIVAL GUIDE?
WHAT DO WE DO?
NEXT TIME YOU INVITE ME OVER FOR A WEEKEND GETAWAY, WE GO TO DISNEYLAND.
WOOF

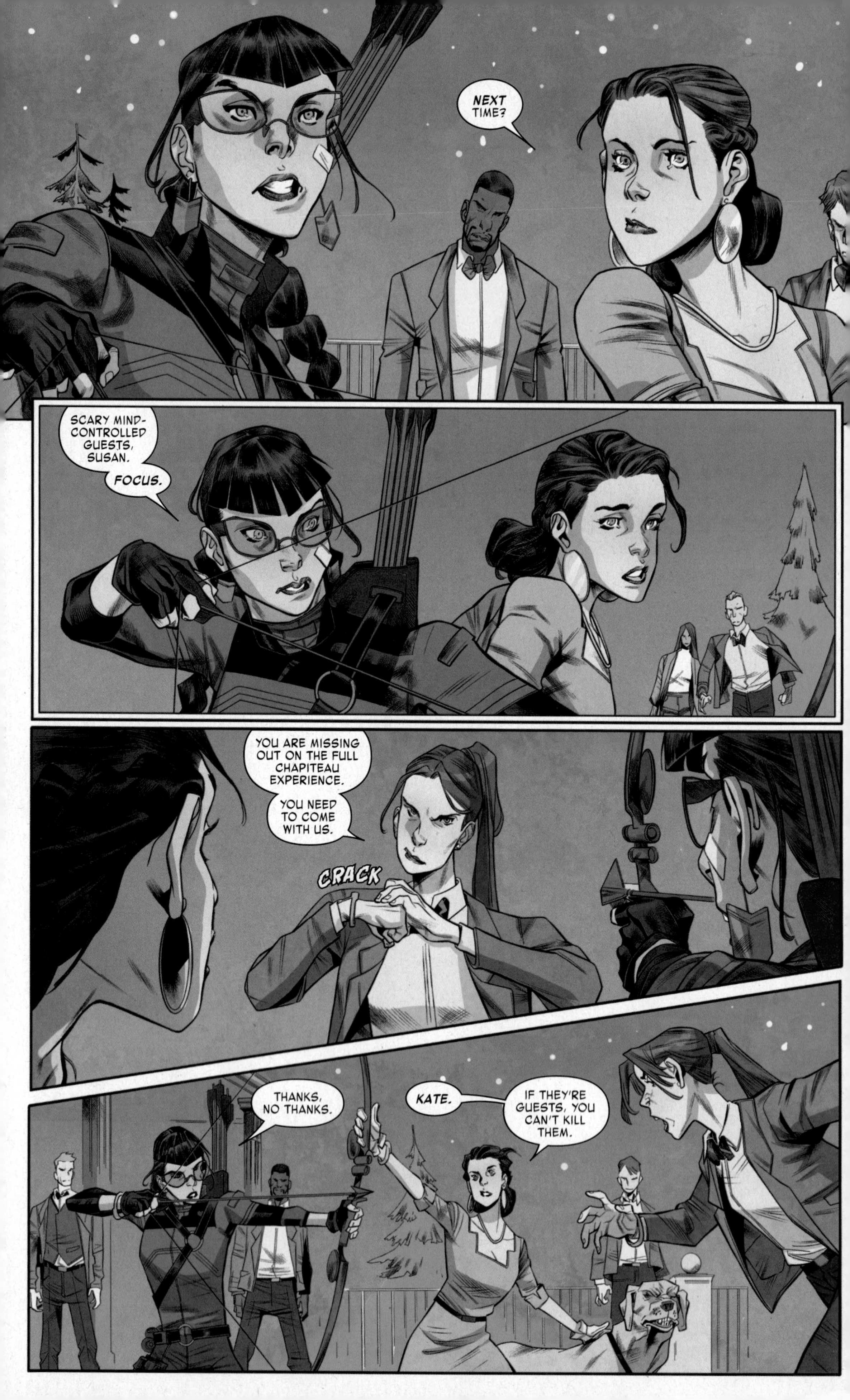
NEXT TIME?
SCARY MIND-CONTROLLED GUESTS, SUSAN.
FOCUS.
YOU ARE MISSING OUT ON THE FULL CHAPITEAU EXPERIENCE.
YOU NEED TO COME WITH US.
CRACK
THANKS, NO THANKS.
KATE.
IF THEY'RE GUESTS, YOU CAN'T KILL THEM.

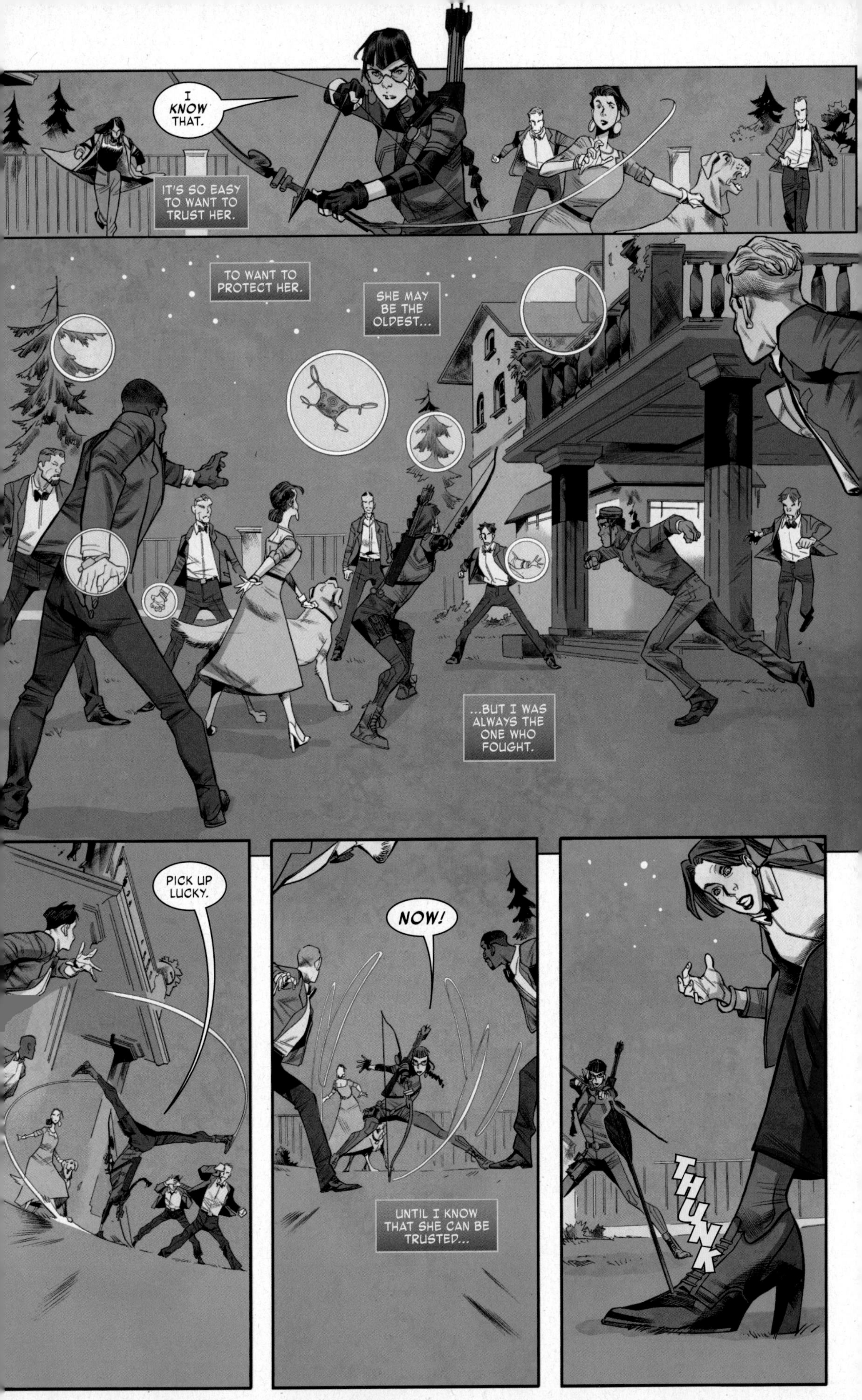
I KNOW THAT.
IT'S SO EASY TO WANT TO TRUST HER.
TO WANT TO PROTECT HER.
SHE MAY BE THE OLDEST...
...BUT I WAS ALWAYS THE ONE WHO FOUGHT.
PICK UP LUCKY.
NOW!
UNTIL I KNOW THAT SHE CAN BE TRUSTED...
THUNK

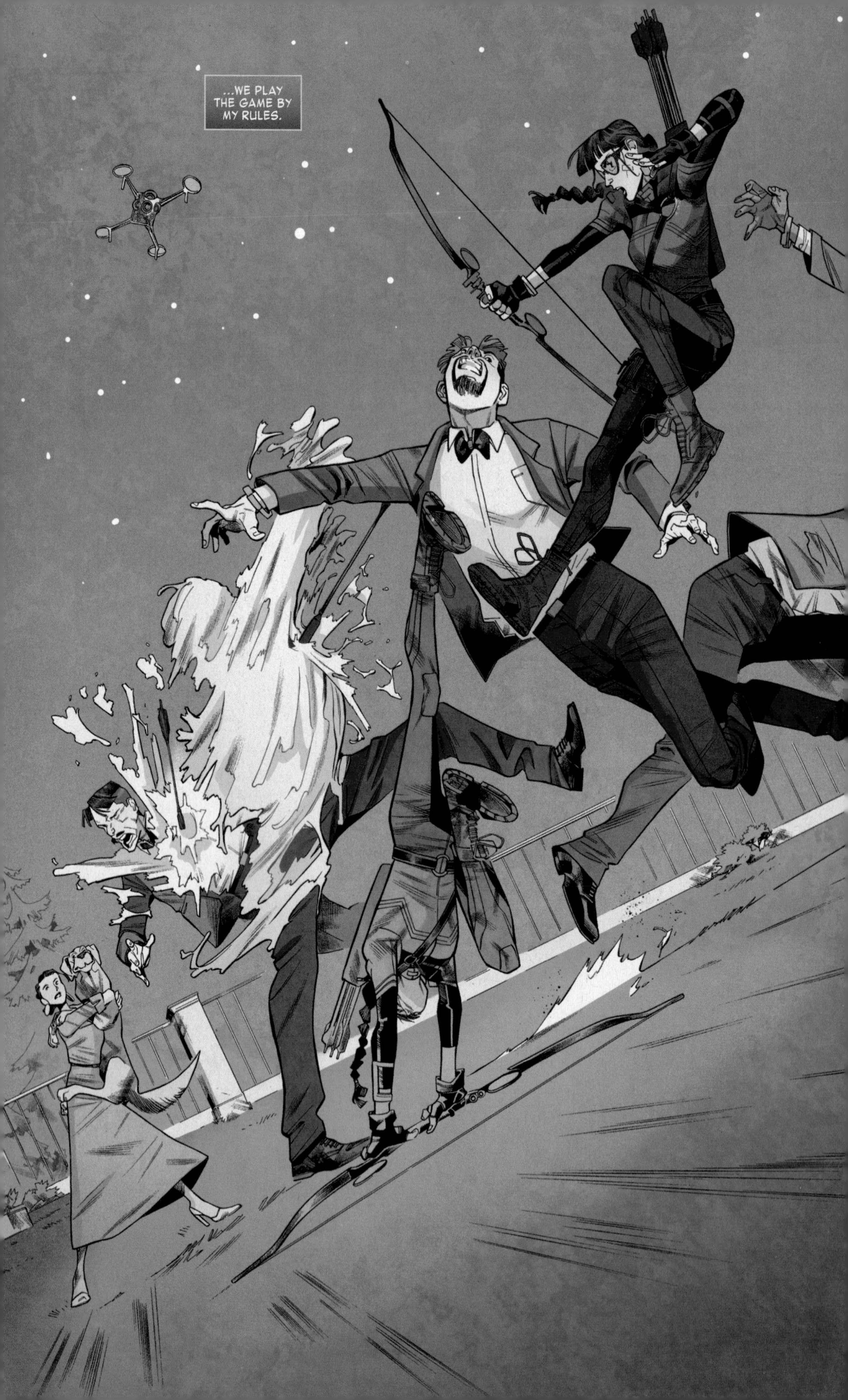
...WE PLAY THE GAME BY MY RULES.

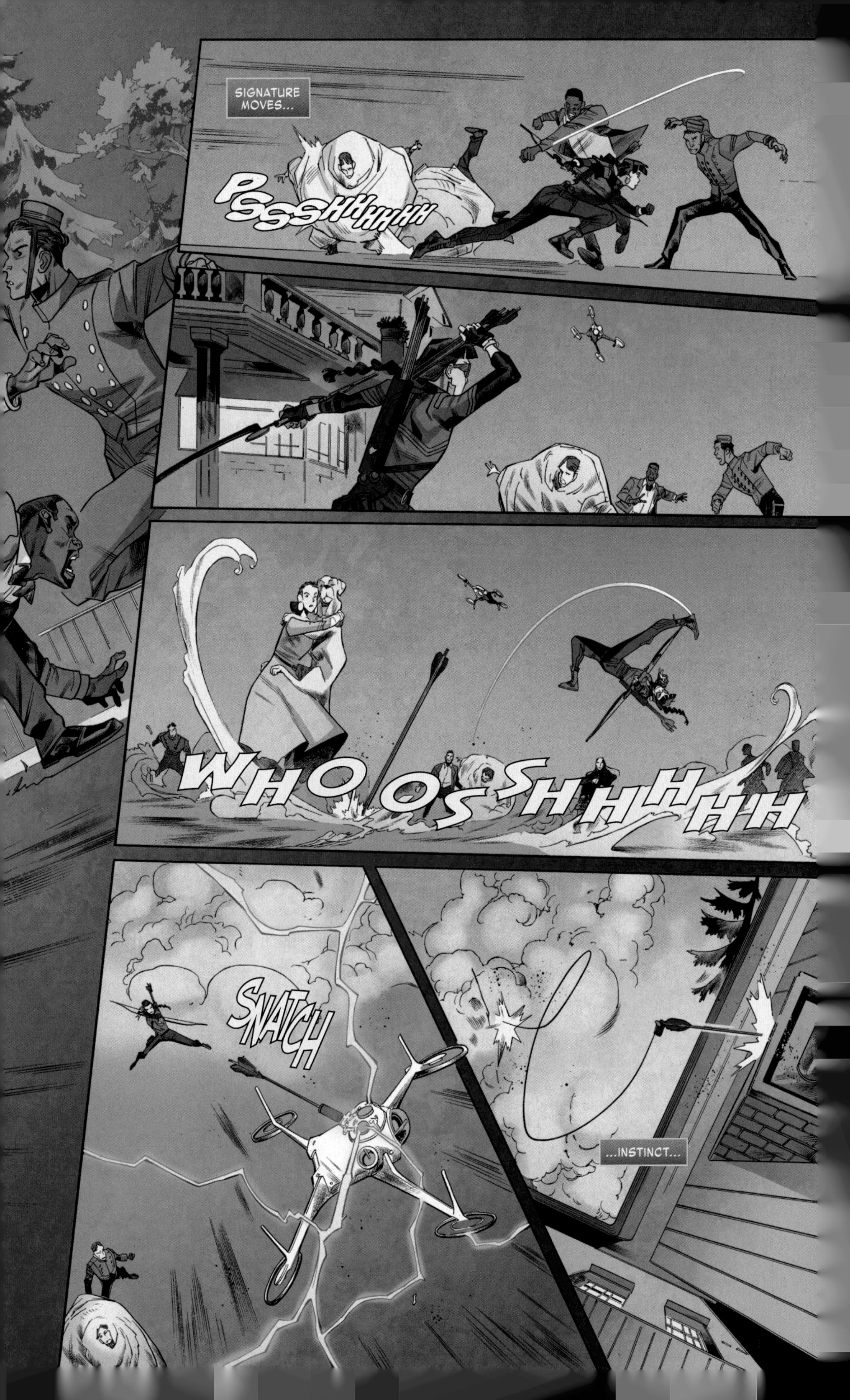
SIGNATURE MOVES...
PSSSHHHHHH
WHOOSHHHHHH
SNATCH
...INSTINCT...

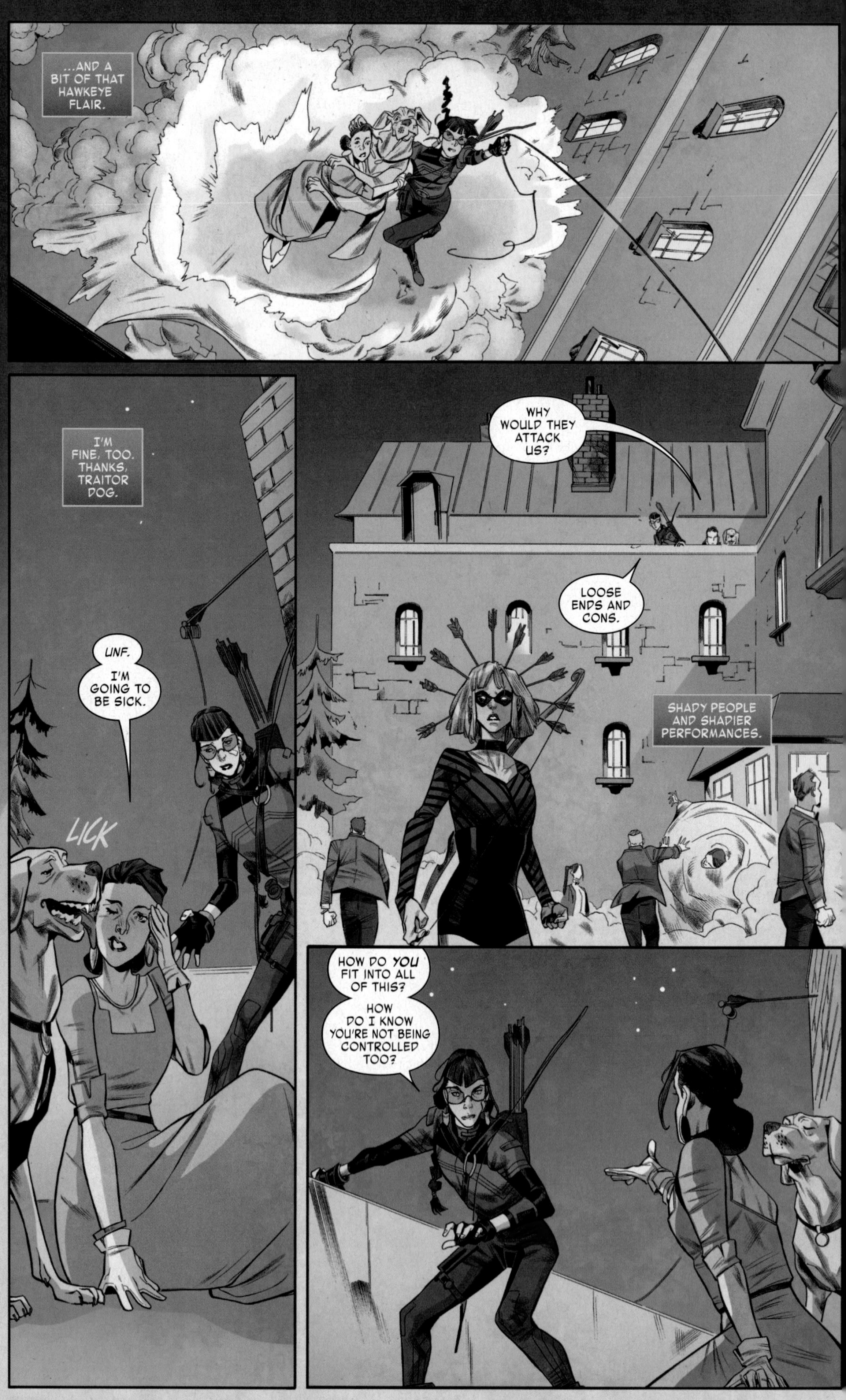
...AND A BIT OF THAT HAWKEYE FLAIR.
I'M FINE, TOO. THANKS, TRAITOR DOG.
UNF.
I'M GOING TO BE SICK.
LICK
WHY WOULD THEY ATTACK US?
LOOSE ENDS AND CONS.
SHADY PEOPLE AND SHADIER PERFORMANCES.
HOW DO YOU FIT INTO ALL OF THIS?
HOW DO I KNOW YOU'RE NOT BEING CONTROLLED TOO?

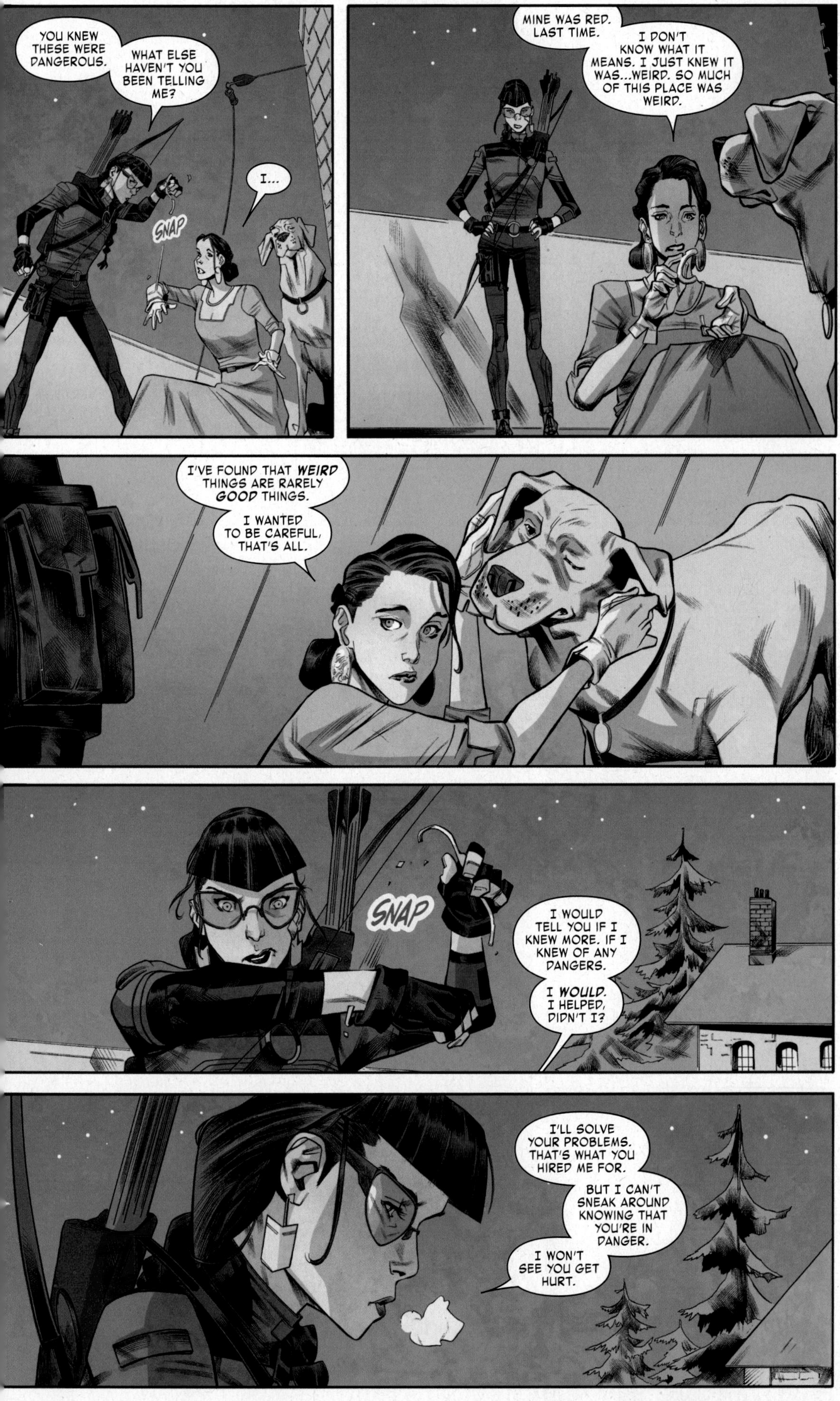

YOU KNEW THESE WERE DANGEROUS.
WHAT ELSE HAVEN'T YOU BEEN TELLING ME?
SNAP
I...
MINE WAS RED. LAST TIME.
I DON'T KNOW WHAT IT MEANS. I JUST KNEW IT WAS...WEIRD. SO MUCH OF THIS PLACE WAS WEIRD.
I'VE FOUND THAT WEIRD THINGS ARE RARELY GOOD THINGS.
I WANTED TO BE CAREFUL, THAT'S ALL.
SNAP
I WOULD TELL YOU IF I KNEW MORE. IF I KNEW OF ANY DANGERS.
I WOULD. I HELPED, DIDN'T I?
I'LL SOLVE YOUR PROBLEMS. THAT'S WHAT YOU HIRED ME FOR.
BUT I CAN'T SNEAK AROUND KNOWING THAT YOU'RE IN DANGER.
I WON'T SEE YOU GET HURT.

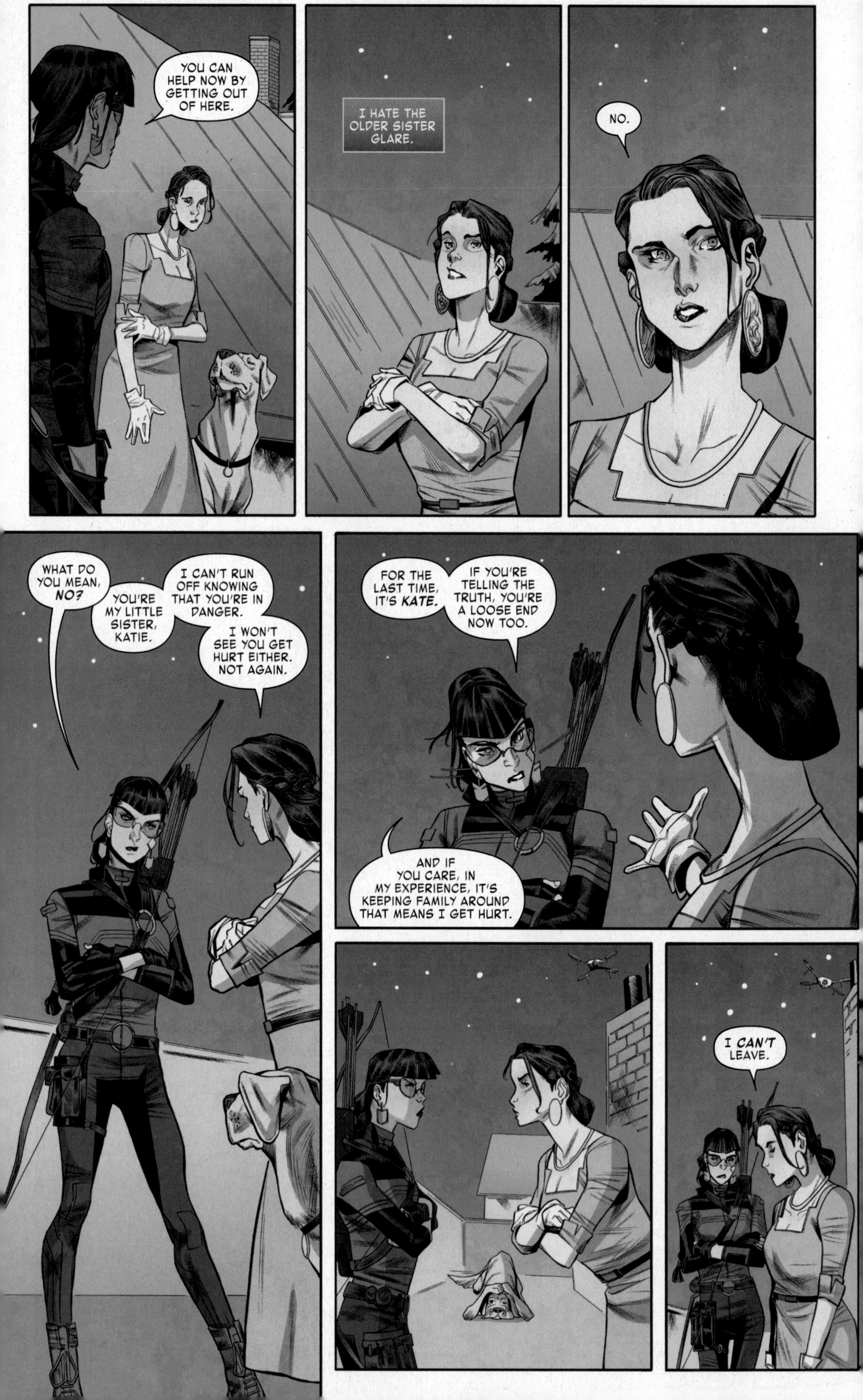

YOU CAN HELP NOW BY GETTING OUT OF HERE.
I HATE THE OLDER SISTER GLARE.
NO.
WHAT DO YOU MEAN, NO?
YOU'RE MY LITTLE SISTER, KATIE.
I CAN'T RUN OFF KNOWING THAT YOU'RE IN DANGER.
I WON'T SEE YOU GET HURT EITHER. NOT AGAIN.
FOR THE LAST TIME, IT'S KATE.
IF YOU'RE TELLING THE TRUTH, YOU'RE A LOOSE END NOW TOO.
AND IF YOU CARE, IN MY EXPERIENCE, IT'S KEEPING FAMILY AROUND THAT MEANS I GET HURT.
I CAN'T LEAVE.

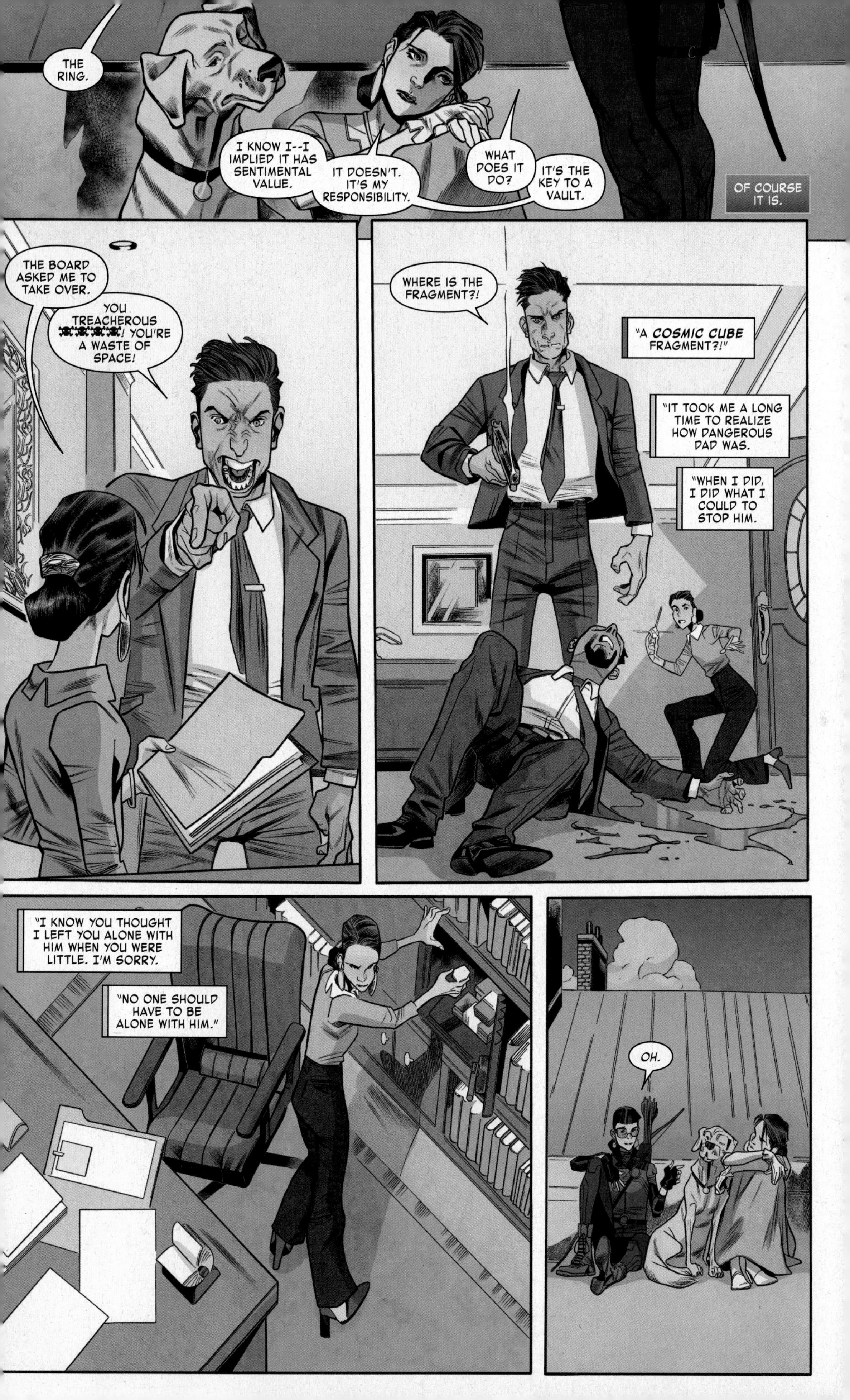
THE RING.
I KNOW I--I IMPLIED IT HAS SENTIMENTAL VALUE.
IT DOESN'T. IT'S MY RESPONSIBILITY.
WHAT DOES IT DO?
IT'S THE KEY TO A VAULT.
OF COURSE IT IS.
THE BOARD ASKED ME TO TAKE OVER.
YOU TREACHEROUS ☠☠☠☠! YOU'RE A WASTE OF SPACE!
WHERE IS THE FRAGMENT?!
"A COSMIC CUBE FRAGMENT?!"
"IT TOOK ME A LONG TIME TO REALIZE HOW DANGEROUS DAD WAS.
"WHEN I DID, I DID WHAT I COULD TO STOP HIM.
"I KNOW YOU THOUGHT I LEFT YOU ALONE WITH HIM WHEN YOU WERE LITTLE. I'M SORRY.
"NO ONE SHOULD HAVE TO BE ALONE WITH HIM."
OH.

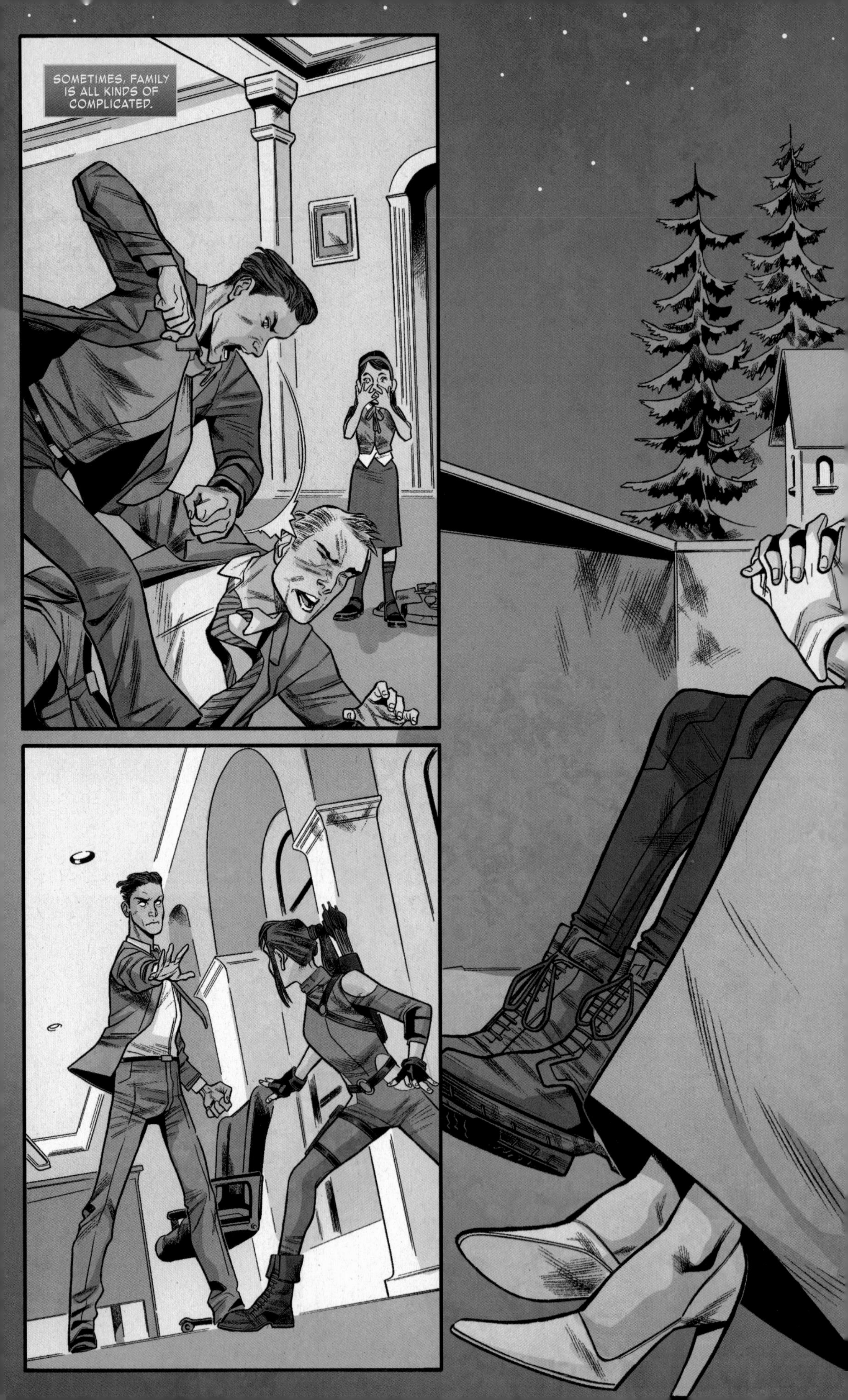
SOMETIMES, FAMILY IS ALL KINDS OF COMPLICATED.

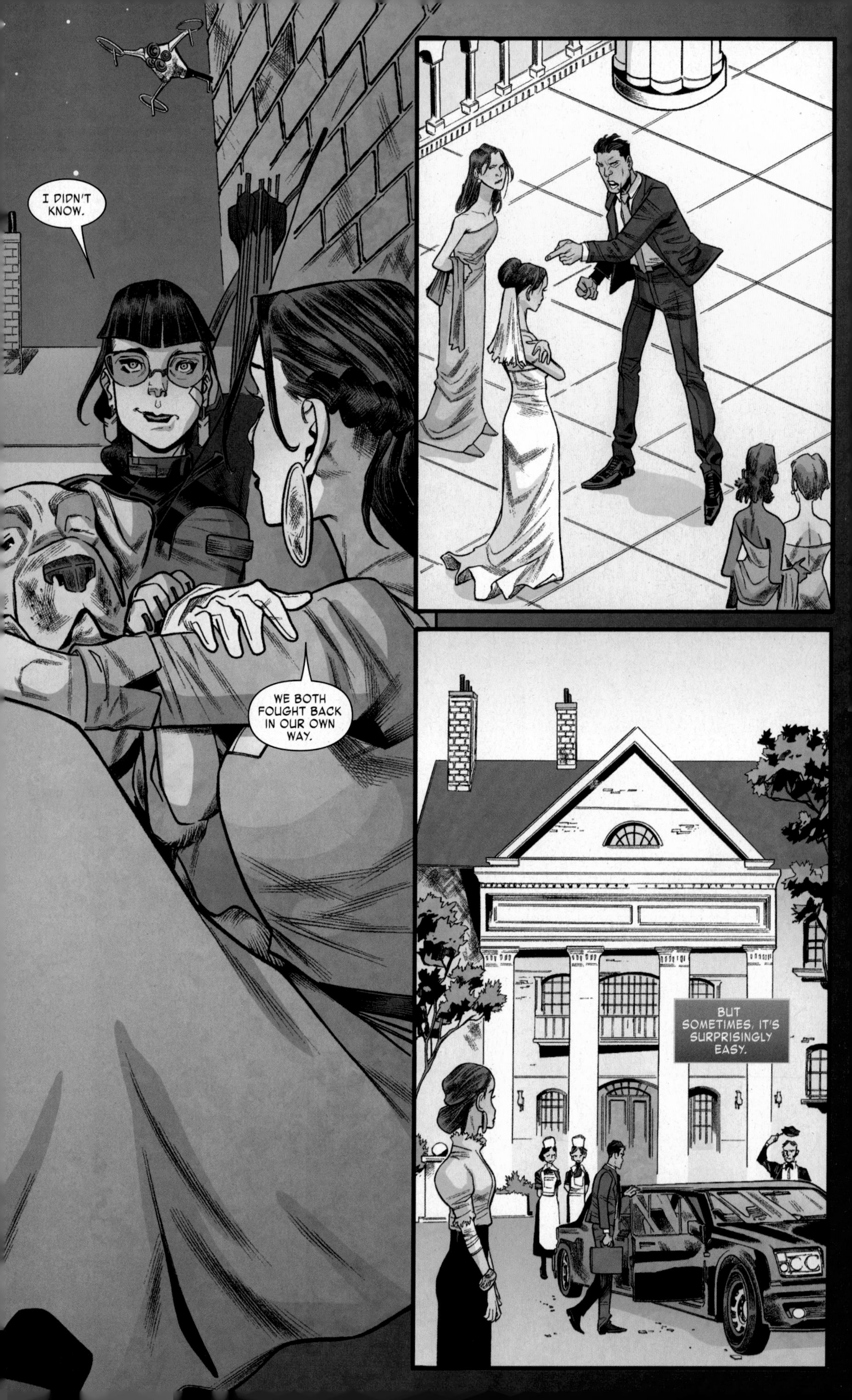
I DIDN'T KNOW.
WE BOTH FOUGHT BACK IN OUR OWN WAY.
BUT SOMETIMES, IT'S SURPRISINGLY EASY.

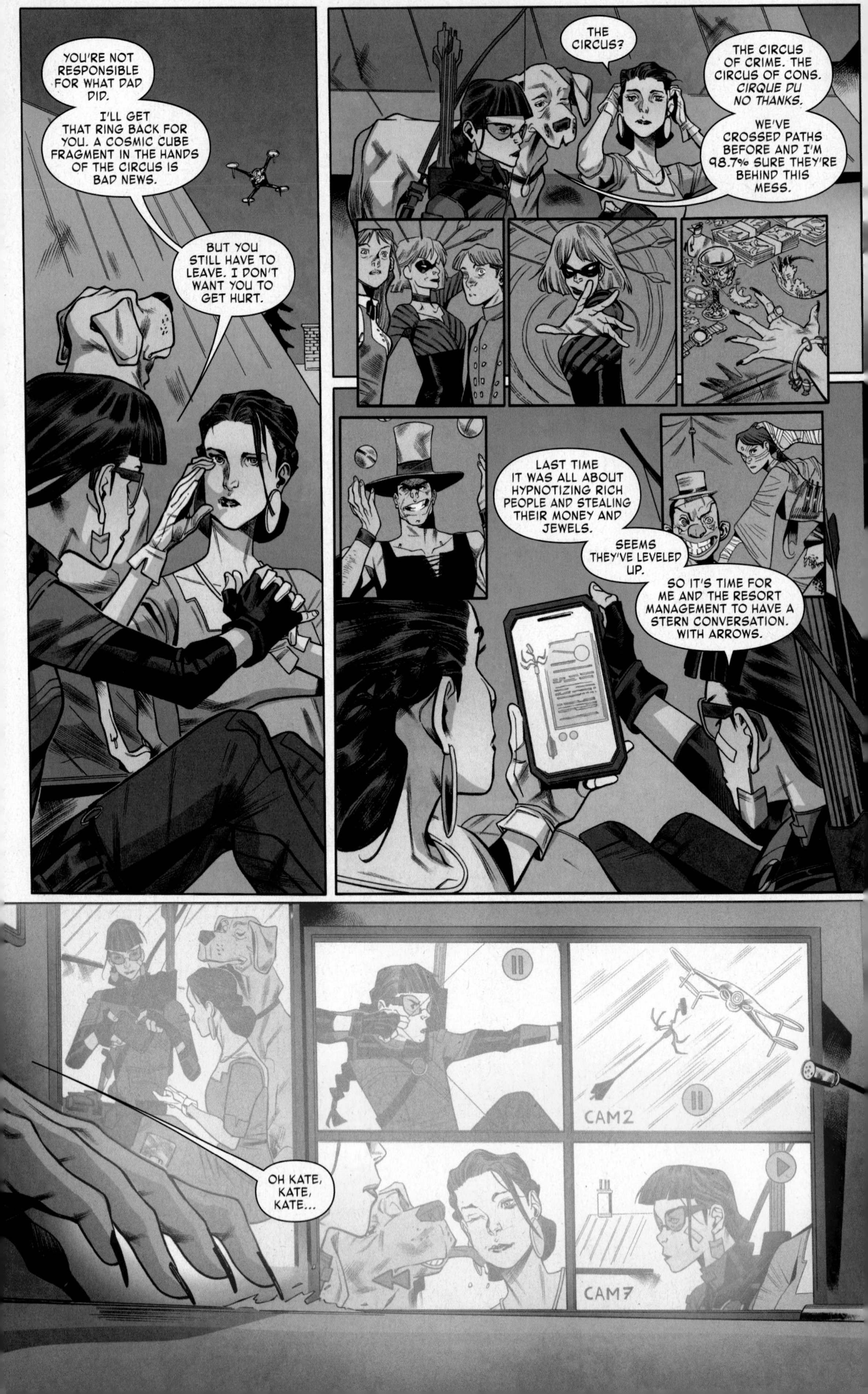
YOU'RE NOT RESPONSIBLE FOR WHAT DAD DID.
I'LL GET THAT RING BACK FOR YOU. A COSMIC CUBE FRAGMENT IN THE HANDS OF THE CIRCUS IS BAD NEWS.
BUT YOU STILL HAVE TO LEAVE. I DON'T WANT YOU TO GET HURT.
THE CIRCUS?
THE CIRCUS OF CRIME. THE CIRCUS OF CONS. CIRQUE DU NO THANKS.
WE'VE CROSSED PATHS BEFORE AND I'M 98.7% SURE THEY'RE BEHIND THIS MESS.
LAST TIME IT WAS ALL ABOUT HYPNOTIZING RICH PEOPLE AND STEALING THEIR MONEY AND JEWELS.
SEEMS THEY'VE LEVELED UP.
SO IT'S TIME FOR ME AND THE RESORT MANAGEMENT TO HAVE A STERN CONVERSATION. WITH ARROWS.
CAM2
OH KATE, KATE, KATE...
CAM7

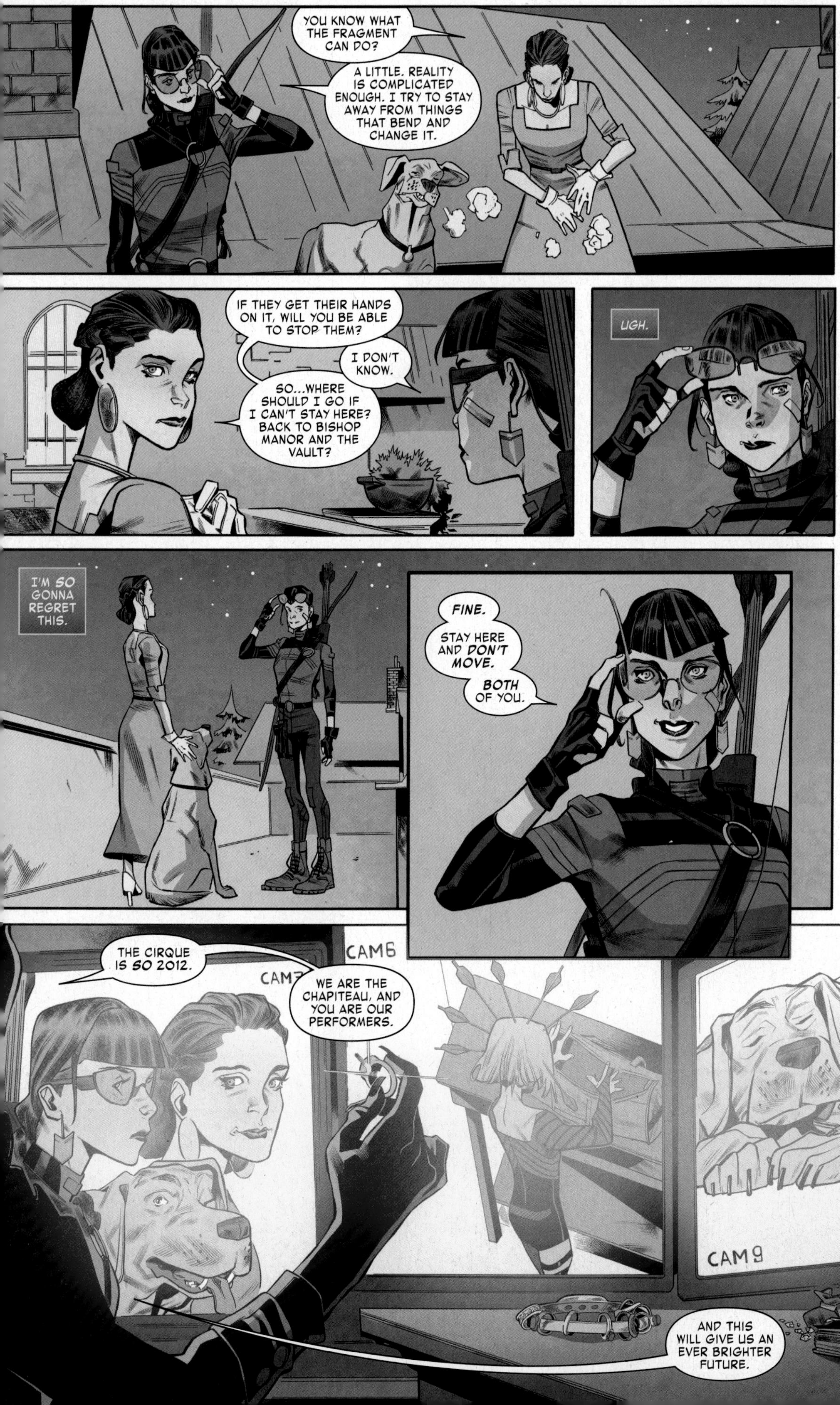

YOU KNOW WHAT THE FRAGMENT CAN DO?
A LITTLE. REALITY IS COMPLICATED ENOUGH. I TRY TO STAY AWAY FROM THINGS THAT BEND AND CHANGE IT.
IF THEY GET THEIR HANDS ON IT, WILL YOU BE ABLE TO STOP THEM?
I DON'T KNOW.
SO...WHERE SHOULD I GO IF I CAN'T STAY HERE? BACK TO BISHOP MANOR AND THE VAULT?
UGH.
I'M SO GONNA REGRET THIS.
FINE.
STAY HERE AND DON'T MOVE.
BOTH OF YOU.
CAM6
CAM7
THE CIRQUE IS SO 2012.
WE ARE THE CHAPITEAU, AND YOU ARE OUR PERFORMERS.
CAM9
AND THIS WILL GIVE US AN EVER BRIGHTER FUTURE.

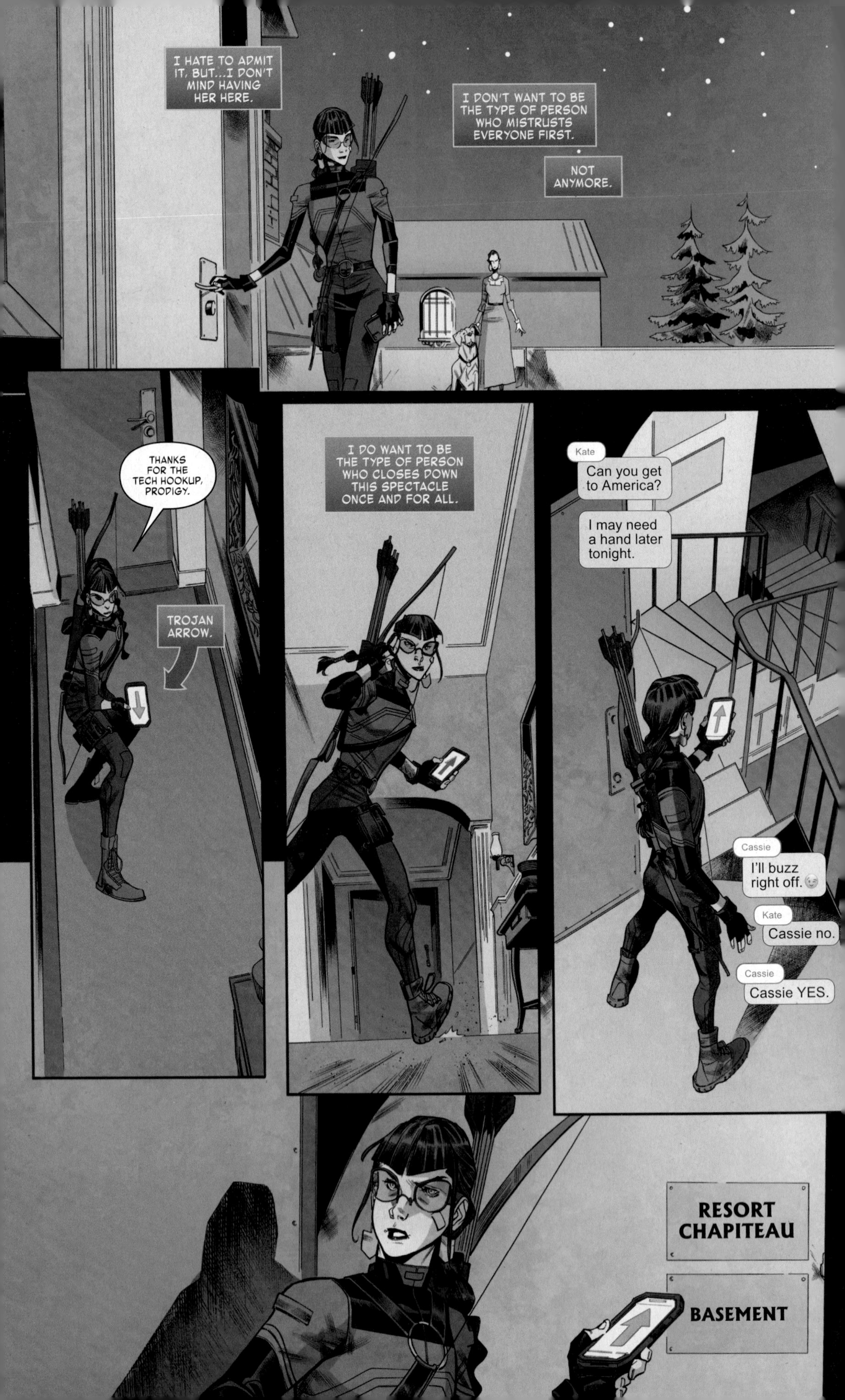
I HATE TO ADMIT IT, BUT...I DON'T MIND HAVING HER HERE.
I DON'T WANT TO BE THE TYPE OF PERSON WHO MISTRUSTS EVERYONE FIRST.
NOT ANYMORE.
THANKS FOR THE TECH HOOKUP, PRODIGY.
TROJAN ARROW.
I DO WANT TO BE THE TYPE OF PERSON WHO CLOSES DOWN THIS SPECTACLE ONCE AND FOR ALL.
Kate
Can you get to America?
I may need a hand later tonight.
Cassie
I'll buzz right off.
Kate
Cassie no.
Cassie
Cassie YES.
RESORT CHAPITEAU
BASEMENT

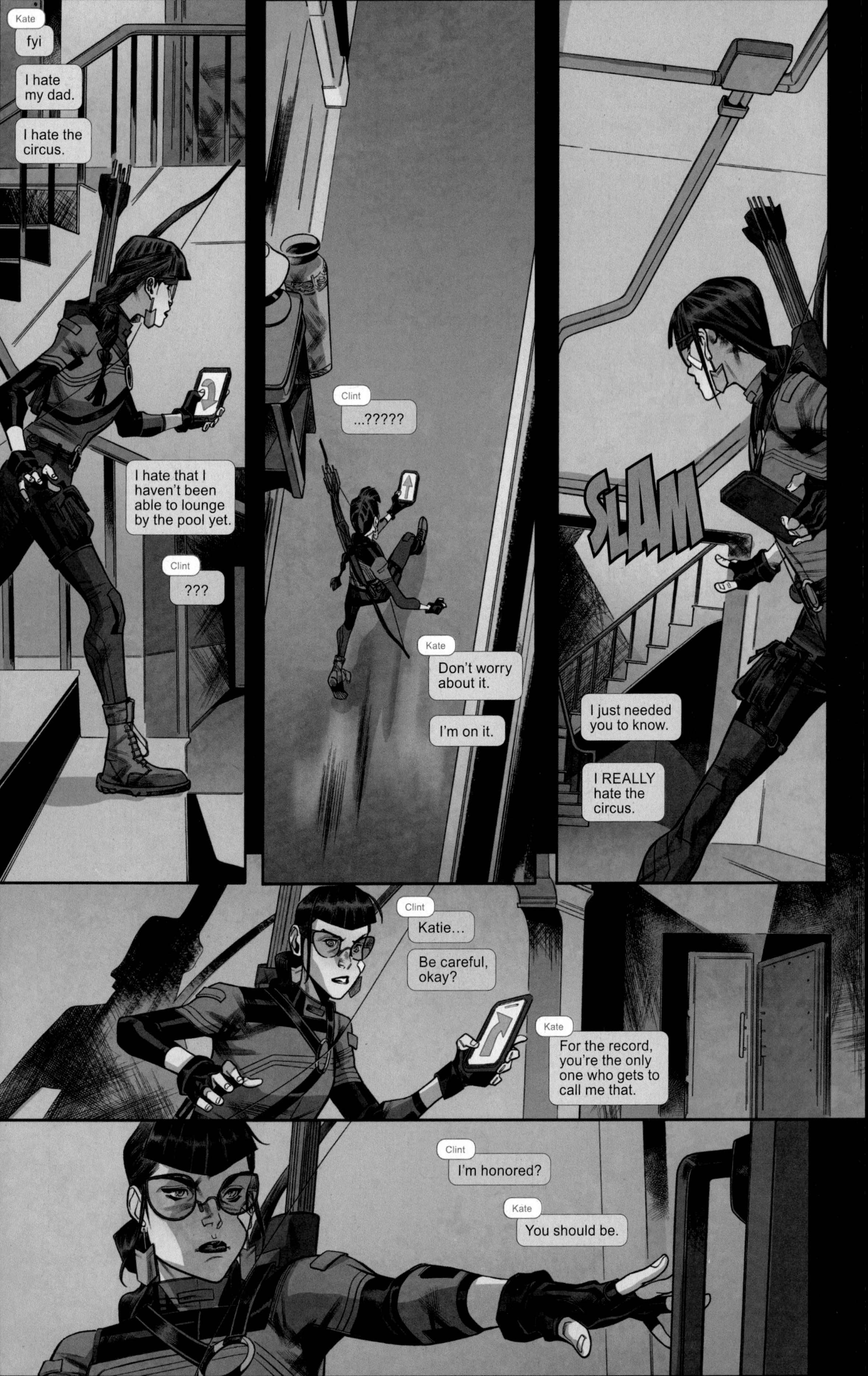
Kate
fyi
I hate my dad.
I hate the circus.
I hate that I haven't been able to lounge by the pool yet.
Clint
???
Clint
...?????
Kate
Don't worry about it.
I'm on it.
SLAM
I just needed you to know.
I REALLY hate the circus.
Clint
Katie...
Be careful, okay?
Kate
For the record, you're the only one who gets to call me that.
Clint
I'm honored?
Kate
You should be.

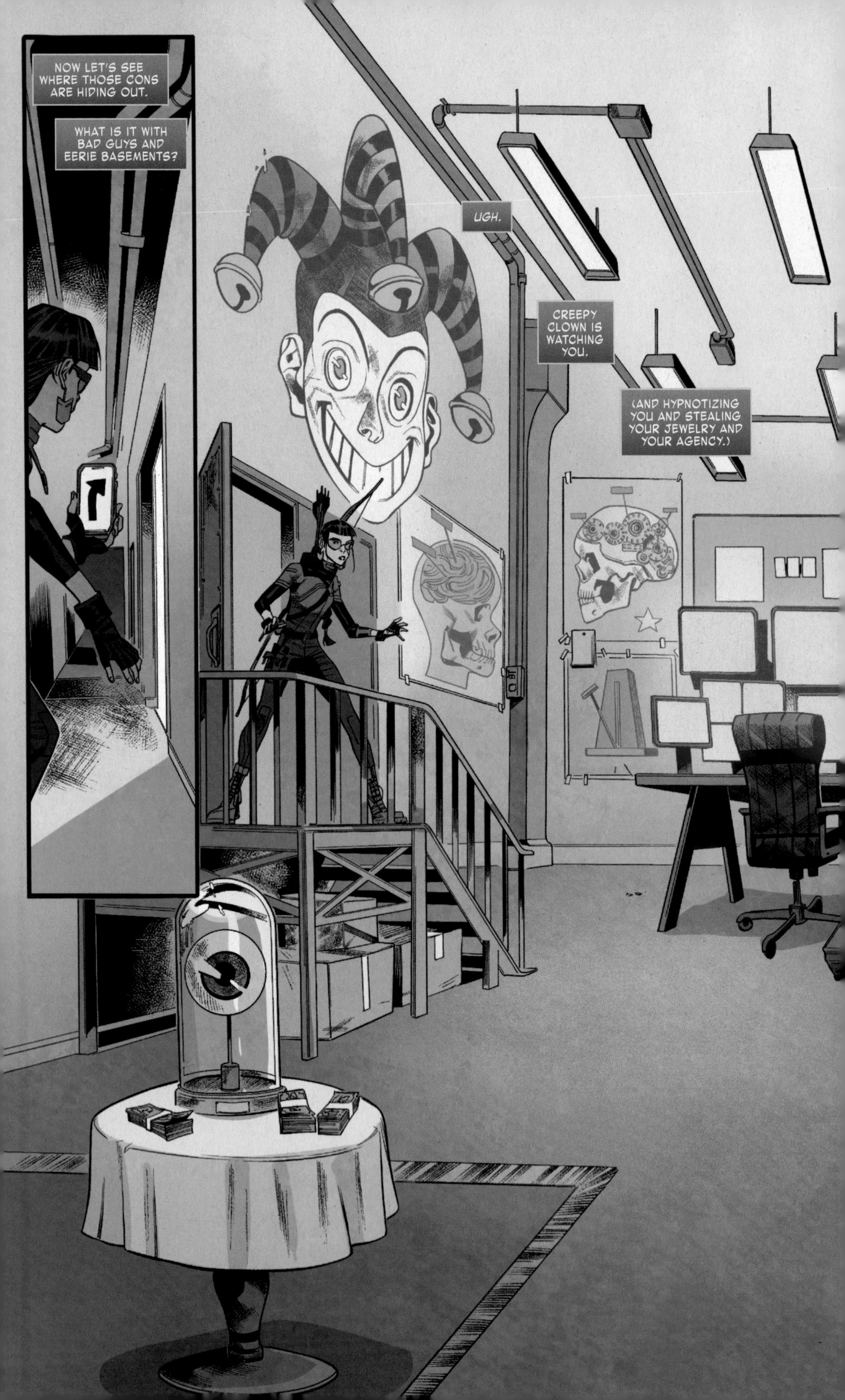
NOW LET'S SEE WHERE THOSE CONS ARE HIDING OUT.
WHAT IS IT WITH BAD GUYS AND EERIE BASEMENTS?
UGH.
CREEPY CLOWN IS WATCHING YOU.
(AND HYPNOTIZING YOU AND STEALING YOUR JEWELRY AND YOUR AGENCY.)

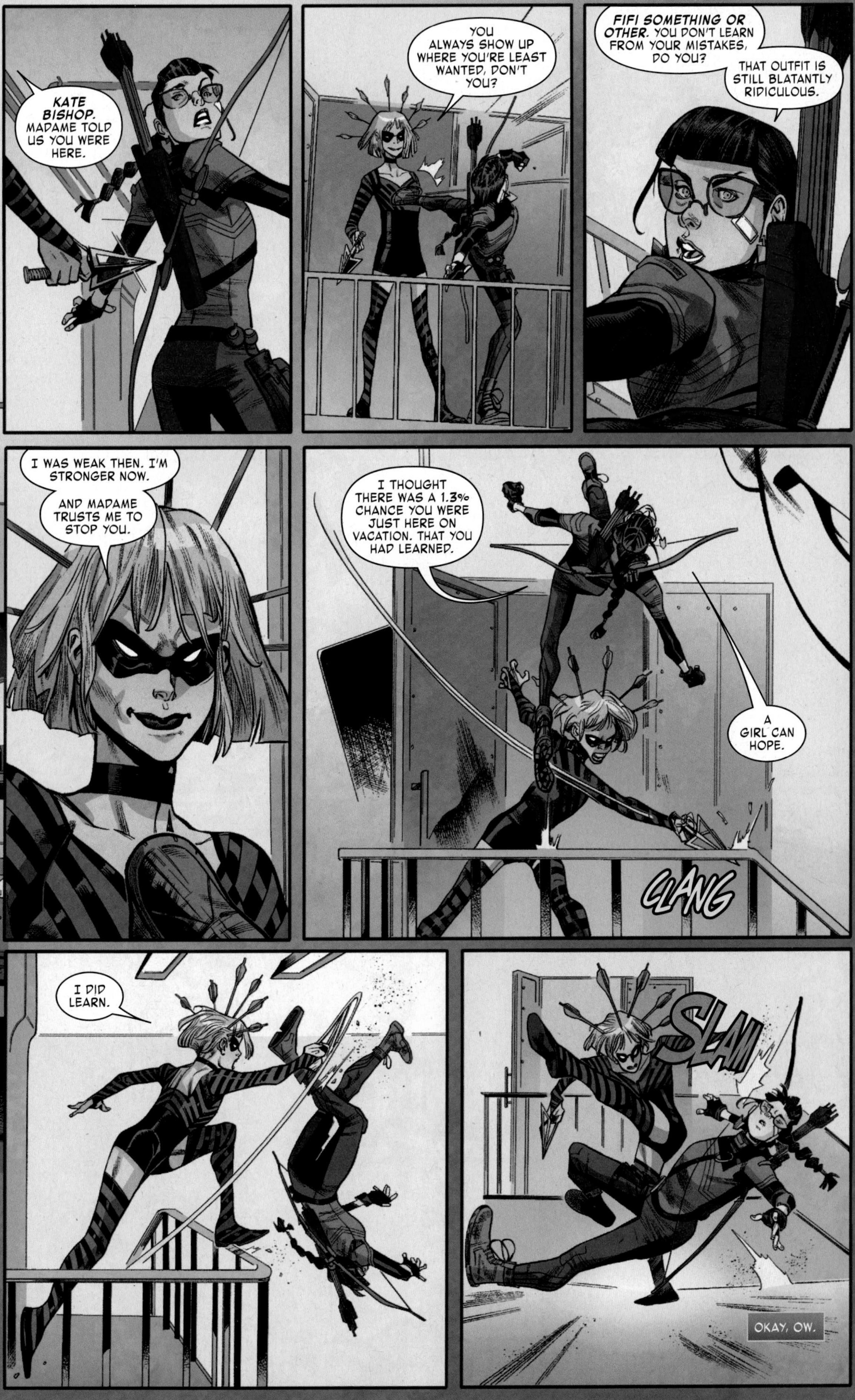
KATE BISHOP. MADAME TOLD US YOU WERE HERE.
YOU ALWAYS SHOW UP WHERE YOU'RE LEAST WANTED, DON'T YOU?
FIFI SOMETHING OR OTHER. YOU DON'T LEARN FROM YOUR MISTAKES, DO YOU?
THAT OUTFIT IS STILL BLATANTLY RIDICULOUS.
I WAS WEAK THEN. I'M STRONGER NOW.
AND MADAME TRUSTS ME TO STOP YOU.
I THOUGHT THERE WAS A 1.3% CHANCE YOU WERE JUST HERE ON VACATION. THAT YOU HAD LEARNED.
A GIRL CAN HOPE.
CLANG
I DID LEARN.
SLAM
OKAY, OW.

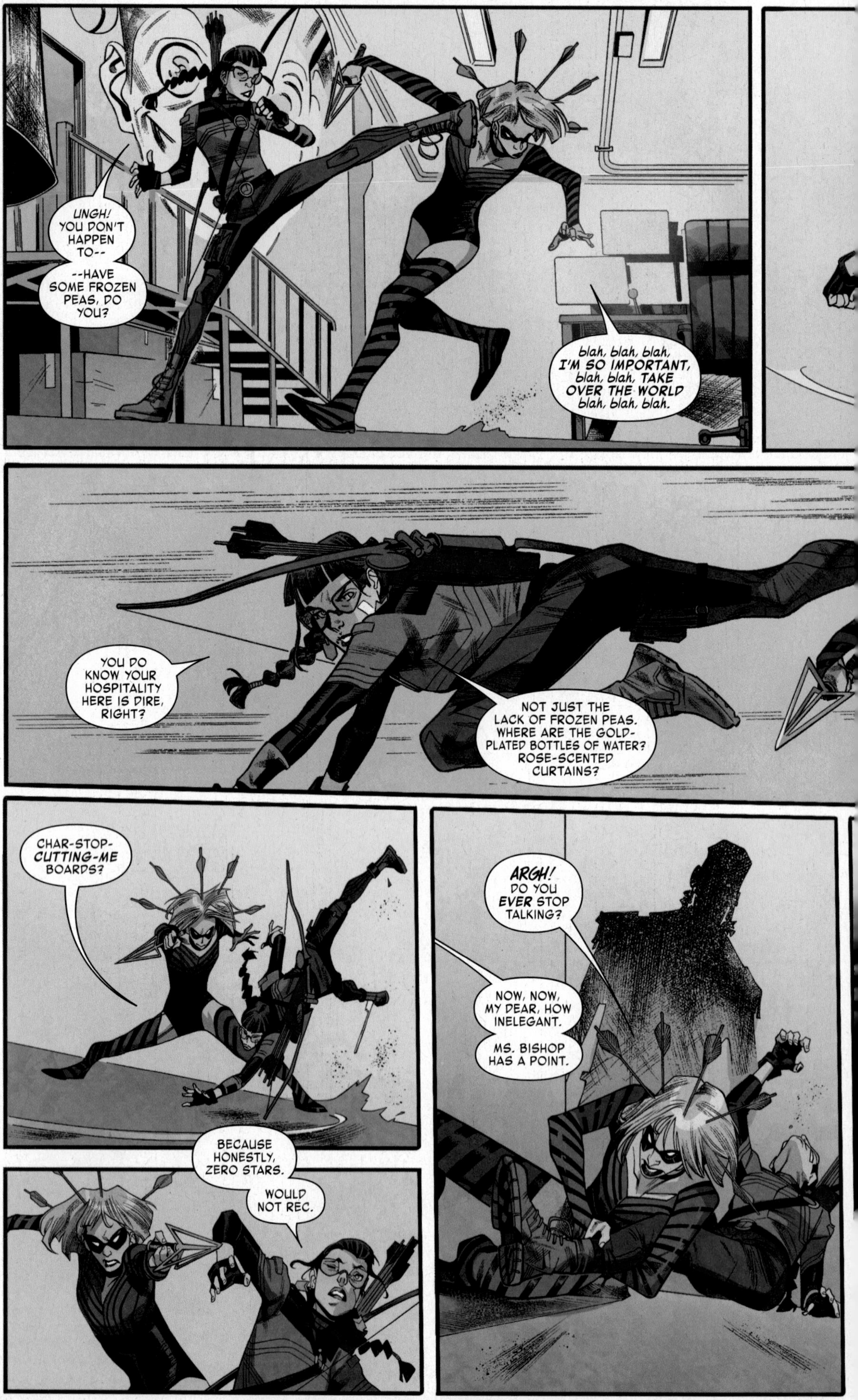
UNGH! YOU DON'T HAPPEN TO--
--HAVE SOME FROZEN PEAS, DO YOU?
blah, blah, blah, I'M SO IMPORTANT, blah, blah, TAKE OVER THE WORLD blah, blah, blah.
YOU DO KNOW YOUR HOSPITALITY HERE IS DIRE, RIGHT?
NOT JUST THE LACK OF FROZEN PEAS. WHERE ARE THE GOLD-PLATED BOTTLES OF WATER? ROSE-SCENTED CURTAINS?
CHAR-STOP-CUTTING-ME BOARDS?
BECAUSE HONESTLY, ZERO STARS.
WOULD NOT REC.
ARGH! DO YOU EVER STOP TALKING?
NOW, NOW, MY DEAR, HOW INELEGANT.
MS. BISHOP HAS A POINT.

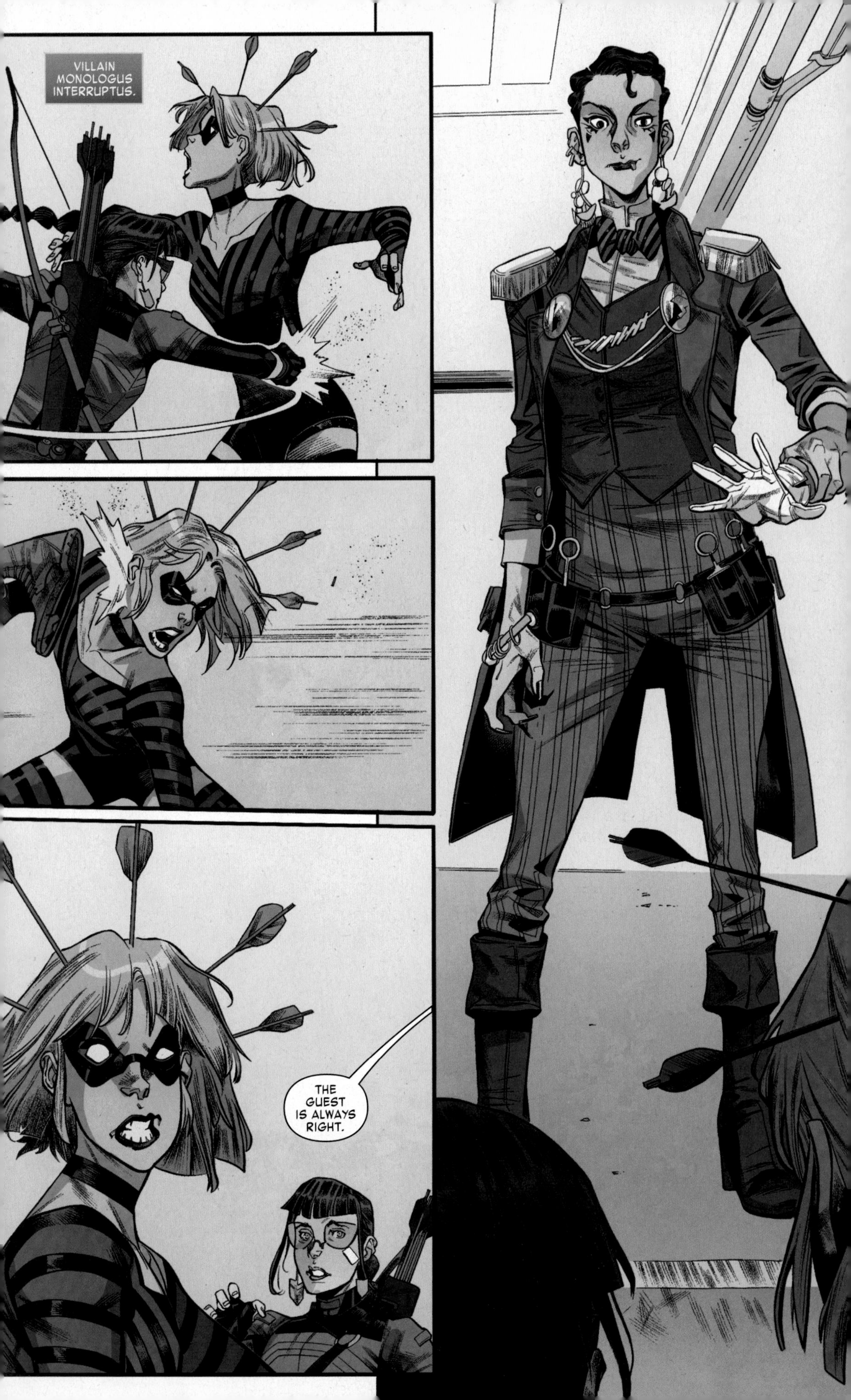
VILLAIN MONOLOGUS INTERRUPTUS.
THE GUEST IS ALWAYS RIGHT.

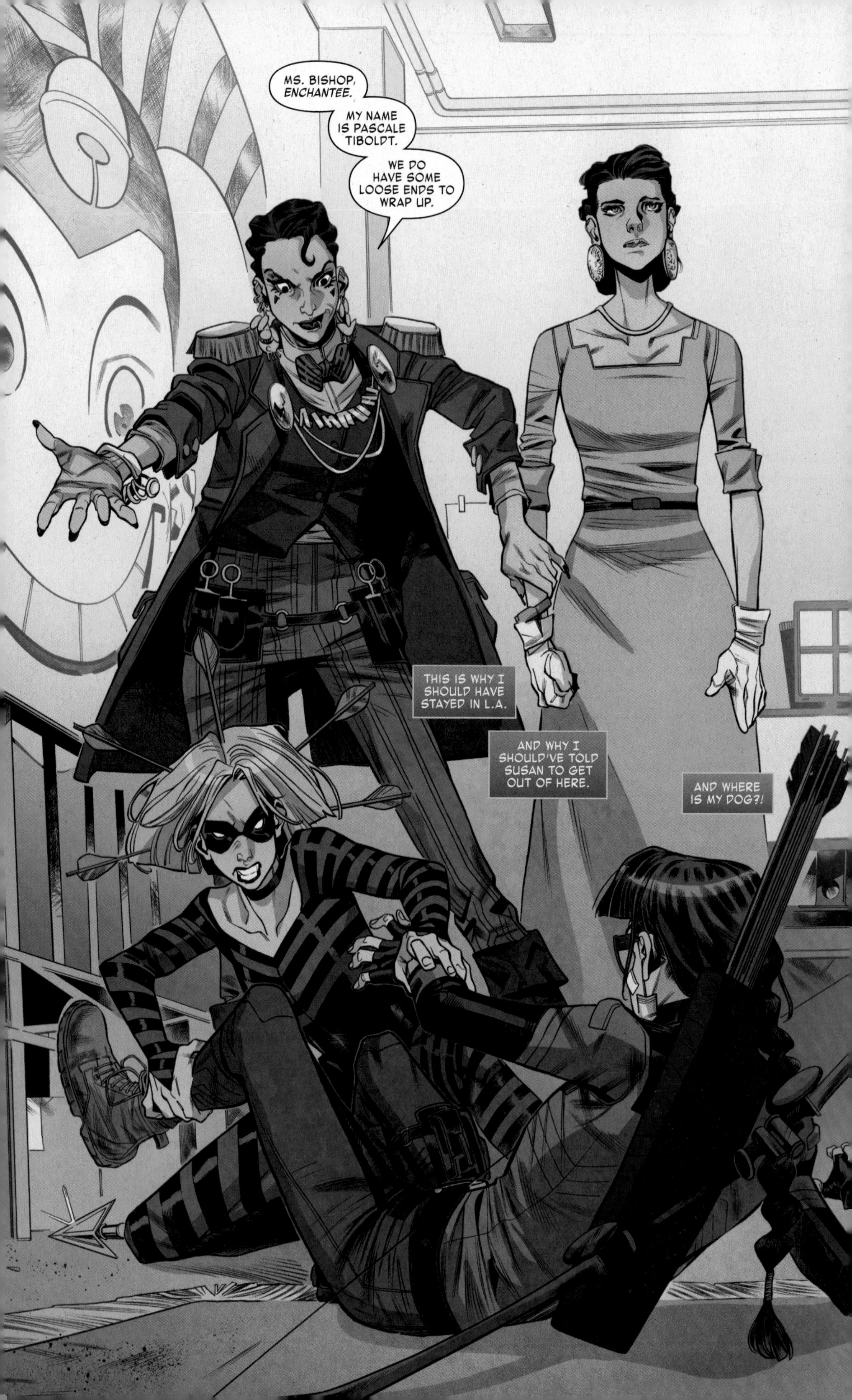
MS. BISHOP, ENCHANTÉE.
MY NAME IS PASCALE TIBOLDT.
WE DO HAVE SOME LOOSE ENDS TO WRAP UP.
THIS IS WHY I SHOULD HAVE STAYED IN L.A.
AND WHY I SHOULD'VE TOLD SUSAN TO GET OUT OF HERE.
AND WHERE IS MY DOG?!

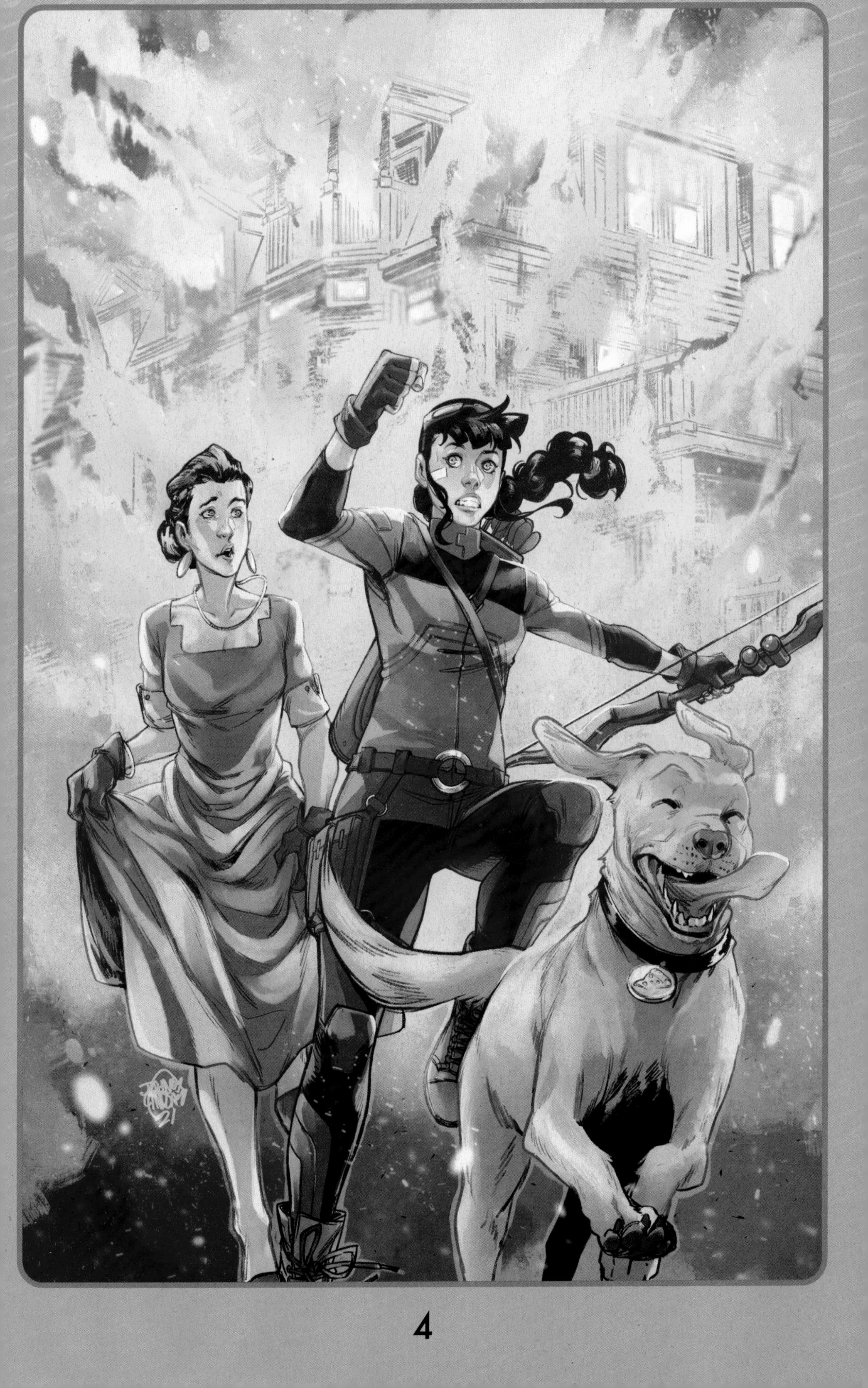

4

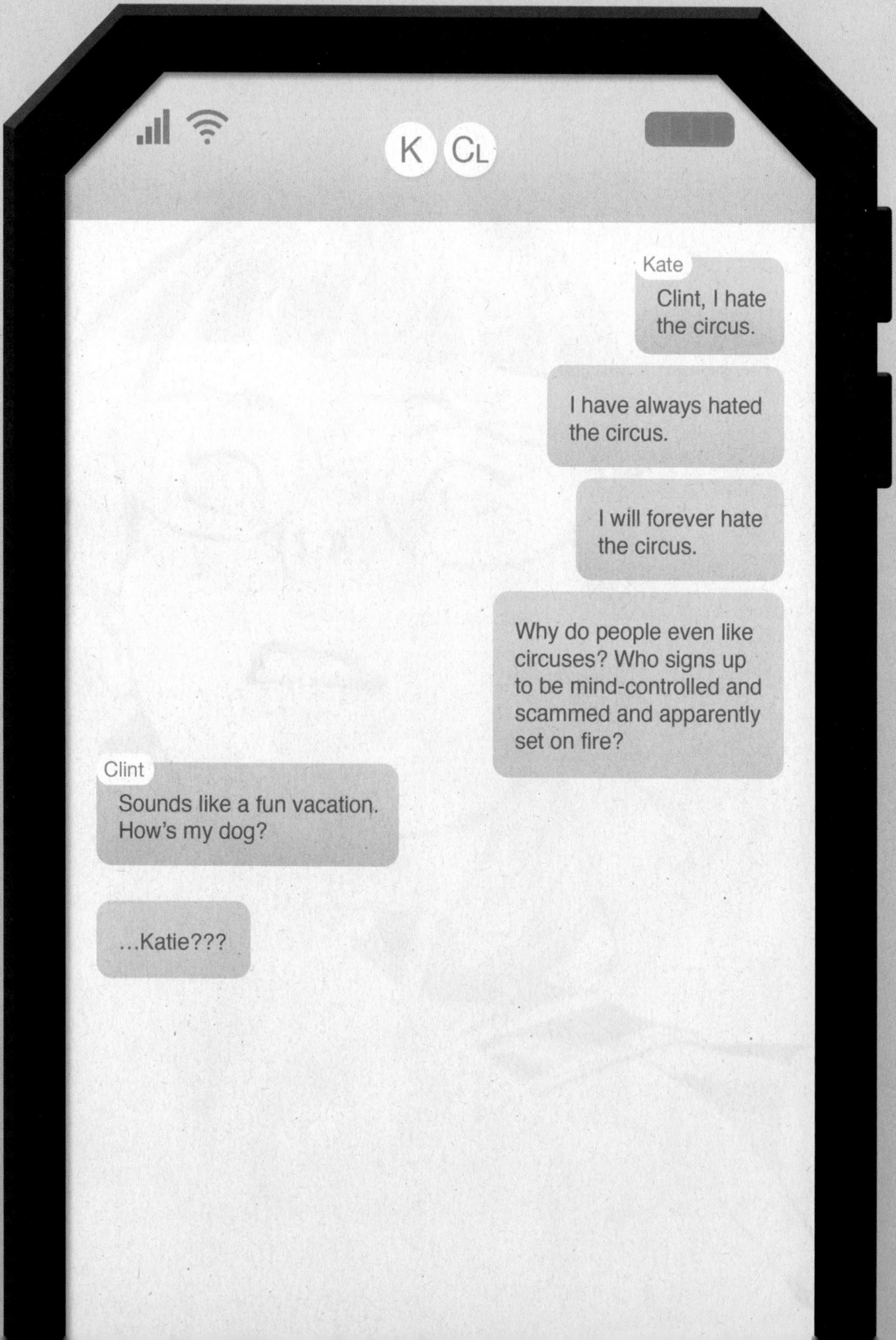

K
CL
Kate
Clint, I hate the circus.
I have always hated the circus.
I will forever hate the circus.
Why do people even like circuses? Who signs up to be mind-controlled and scammed and apparently set on fire?
Clint
Sounds like a fun vacation. How's my dog?
...Katie???

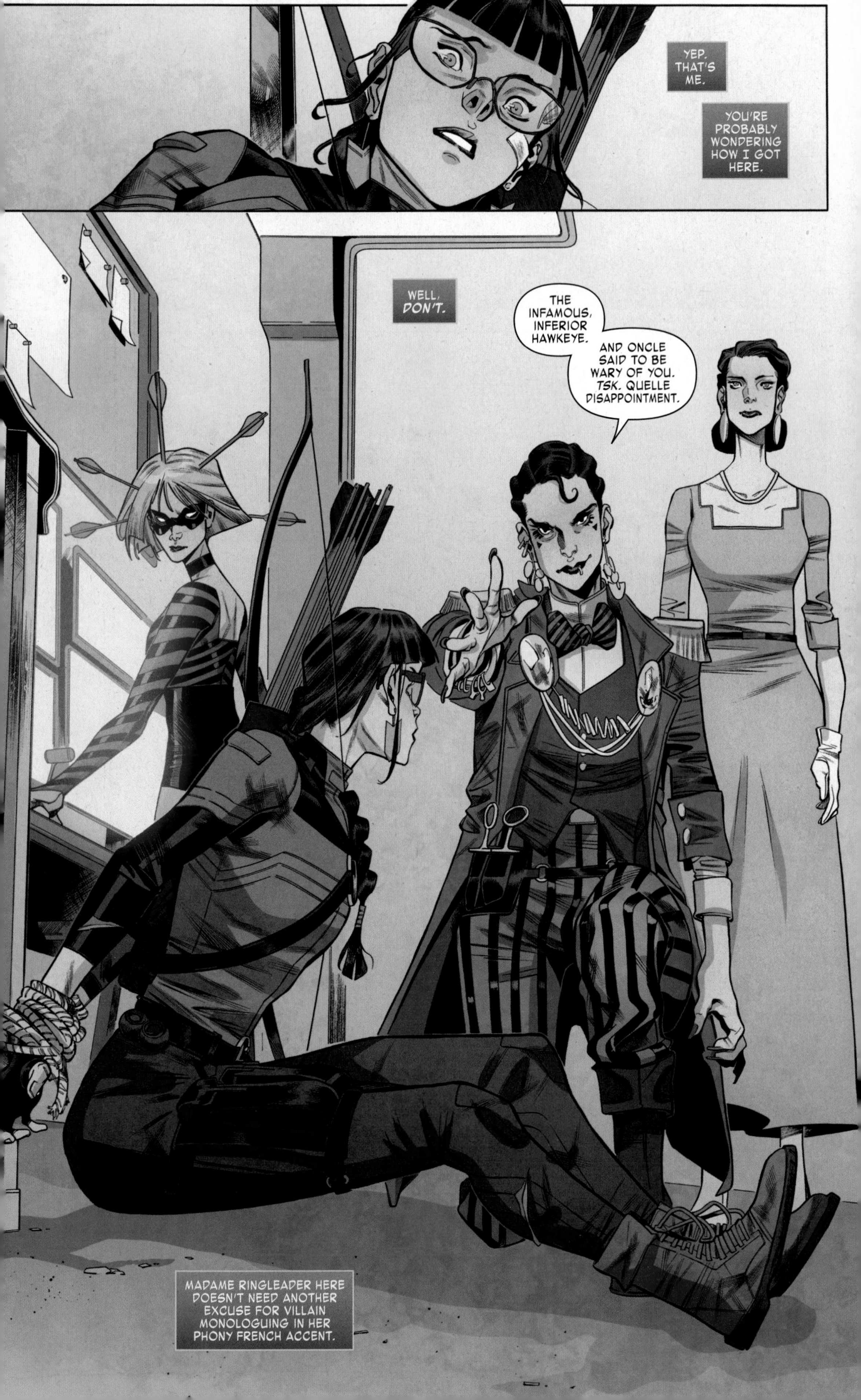
YEP. THAT'S ME.
YOU'RE PROBABLY WONDERING HOW I GOT HERE.
WELL, *DON'T.*
THE INFAMOUS, INFERIOR HAWKEYE.
AND ONCLE SAID TO BE WARY OF YOU. *TSK.* QUELLE DISAPPOINTMENT.
MADAME RINGLEADER HERE DOESN'T NEED ANOTHER EXCUSE FOR VILLAIN MONOLOGUING IN HER PHONY FRENCH ACCENT.

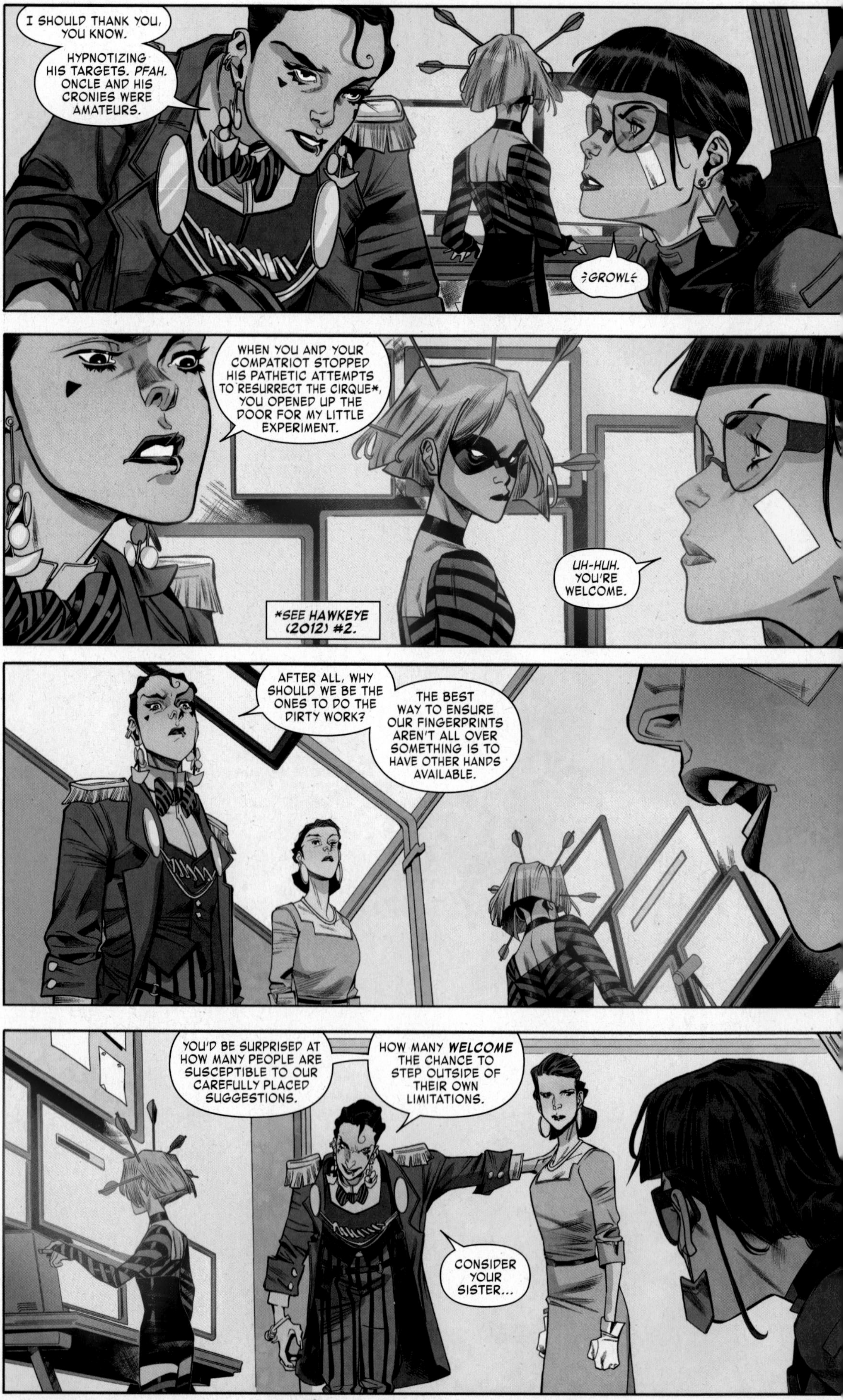

I SHOULD THANK YOU, YOU KNOW.
HYPNOTIZING HIS TARGETS. PFAH. ONCLE AND HIS CRONIES WERE AMATEURS.
GROWL
WHEN YOU AND YOUR COMPATRIOT STOPPED HIS PATHETIC ATTEMPTS TO RESURRECT THE CIRQUE*, YOU OPENED UP THE DOOR FOR MY LITTLE EXPERIMENT.
*SEE HAWKEYE (2012) #2.
UH-HUH. YOU'RE WELCOME.
AFTER ALL, WHY SHOULD WE BE THE ONES TO DO THE DIRTY WORK?
THE BEST WAY TO ENSURE OUR FINGERPRINTS AREN'T ALL OVER SOMETHING IS TO HAVE OTHER HANDS AVAILABLE.
YOU'D BE SURPRISED AT HOW MANY PEOPLE ARE SUSCEPTIBLE TO OUR CAREFULLY PLACED SUGGESTIONS.
HOW MANY WELCOME THE CHANCE TO STEP OUTSIDE OF THEIR OWN LIMITATIONS.
CONSIDER YOUR SISTER...

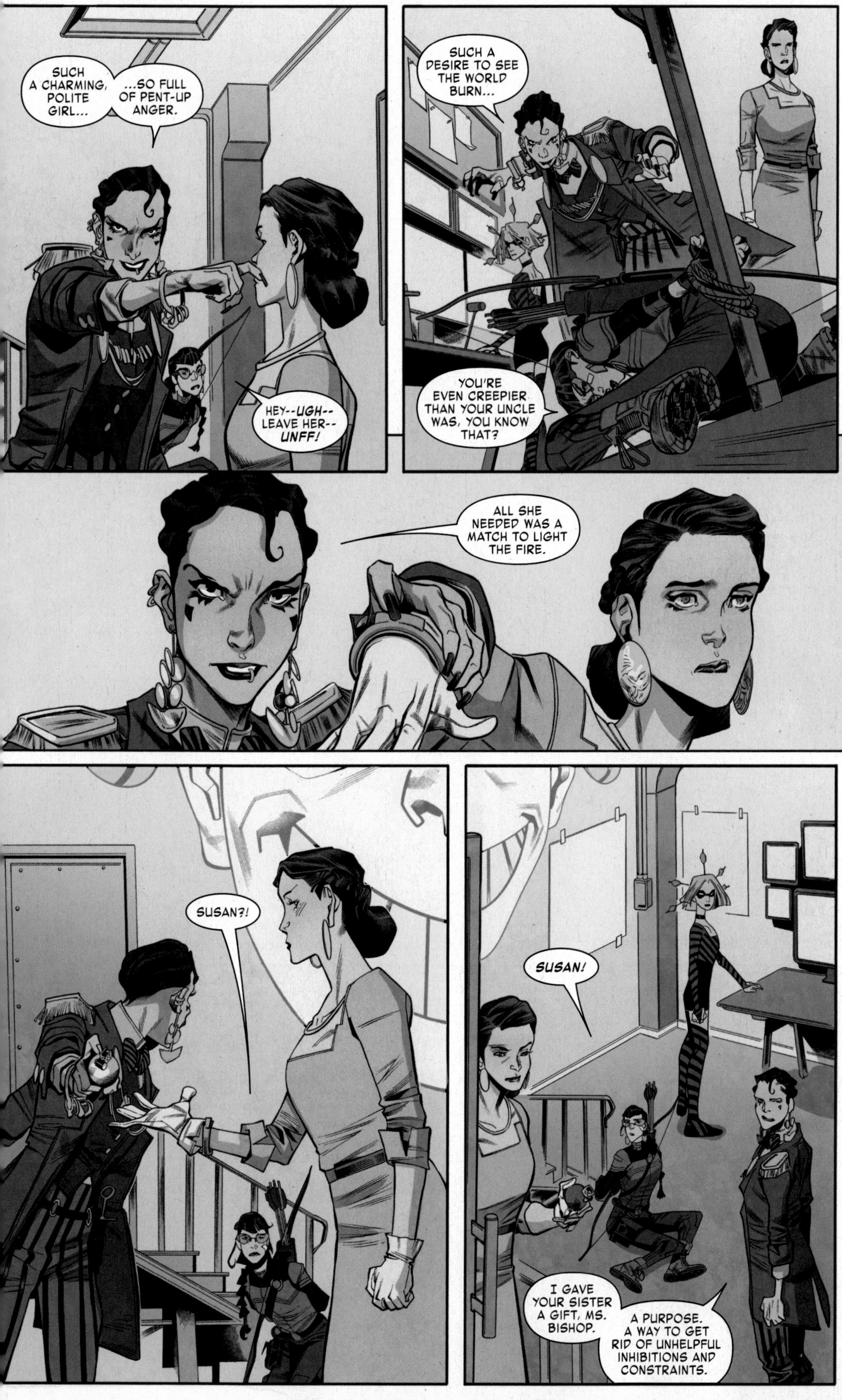
SUCH A CHARMING, POLITE GIRL...
...SO FULL OF PENT-UP ANGER.
HEY--UGH--LEAVE HER--UNFF!
SUCH A DESIRE TO SEE THE WORLD BURN...
YOU'RE EVEN CREEPIER THAN YOUR UNCLE WAS, YOU KNOW THAT?
ALL SHE NEEDED WAS A MATCH TO LIGHT THE FIRE.
SUSAN?!
SUSAN!
I GAVE YOUR SISTER A GIFT, MS. BISHOP.
A PURPOSE. A WAY TO GET RID OF UNHELPFUL INHIBITIONS AND CONSTRAINTS.

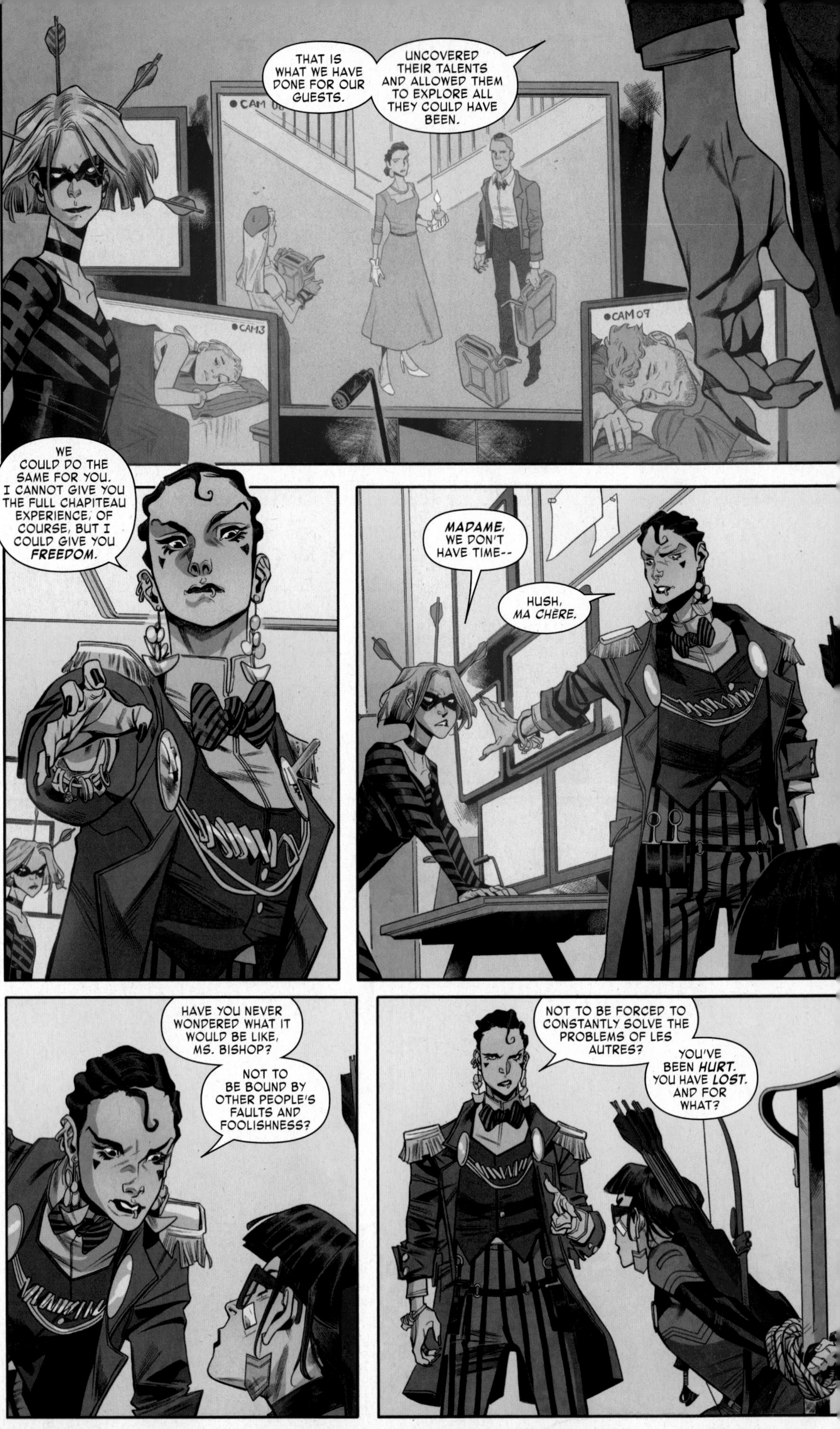
THAT IS WHAT WE HAVE DONE FOR OUR GUESTS.
UNCOVERED THEIR TALENTS AND ALLOWED THEM TO EXPLORE ALL THEY COULD HAVE BEEN.
CAM 3
CAM 07
WE COULD DO THE SAME FOR YOU. I CANNOT GIVE YOU THE FULL CHAPITEAU EXPERIENCE, OF COURSE, BUT I COULD GIVE YOU *FREEDOM.*
MADAME, WE DON'T HAVE TIME--
HUSH, *MA CHÈRE.*
HAVE YOU NEVER WONDERED WHAT IT WOULD BE LIKE, MS. BISHOP?
NOT TO BE BOUND BY OTHER PEOPLE'S FAULTS AND FOOLISHNESS?
NOT TO BE FORCED TO CONSTANTLY SOLVE THE PROBLEMS OF LES AUTRES?
YOU'VE BEEN *HURT.* YOU HAVE *LOST.* AND FOR WHAT?

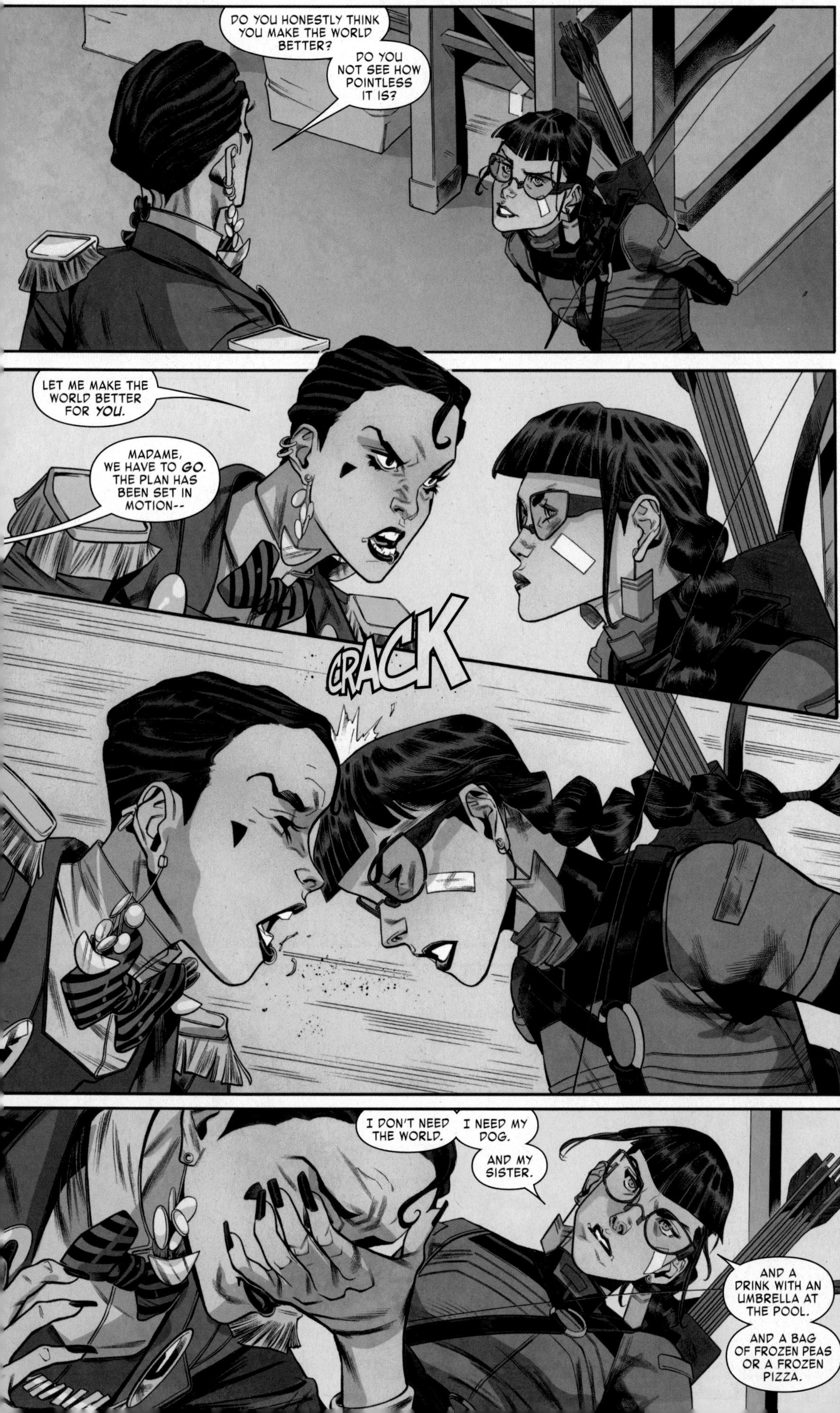
DO YOU HONESTLY THINK YOU MAKE THE WORLD BETTER?
DO YOU NOT SEE HOW POINTLESS IT IS?
LET ME MAKE THE WORLD BETTER FOR YOU.
MADAME, WE HAVE TO GO. THE PLAN HAS BEEN SET IN MOTION--
CRACK
I DON'T NEED THE WORLD.
I NEED MY DOG.
AND MY SISTER.
AND A DRINK WITH AN UMBRELLA AT THE POOL.
AND A BAG OF FROZEN PEAS OR A FROZEN PIZZA.

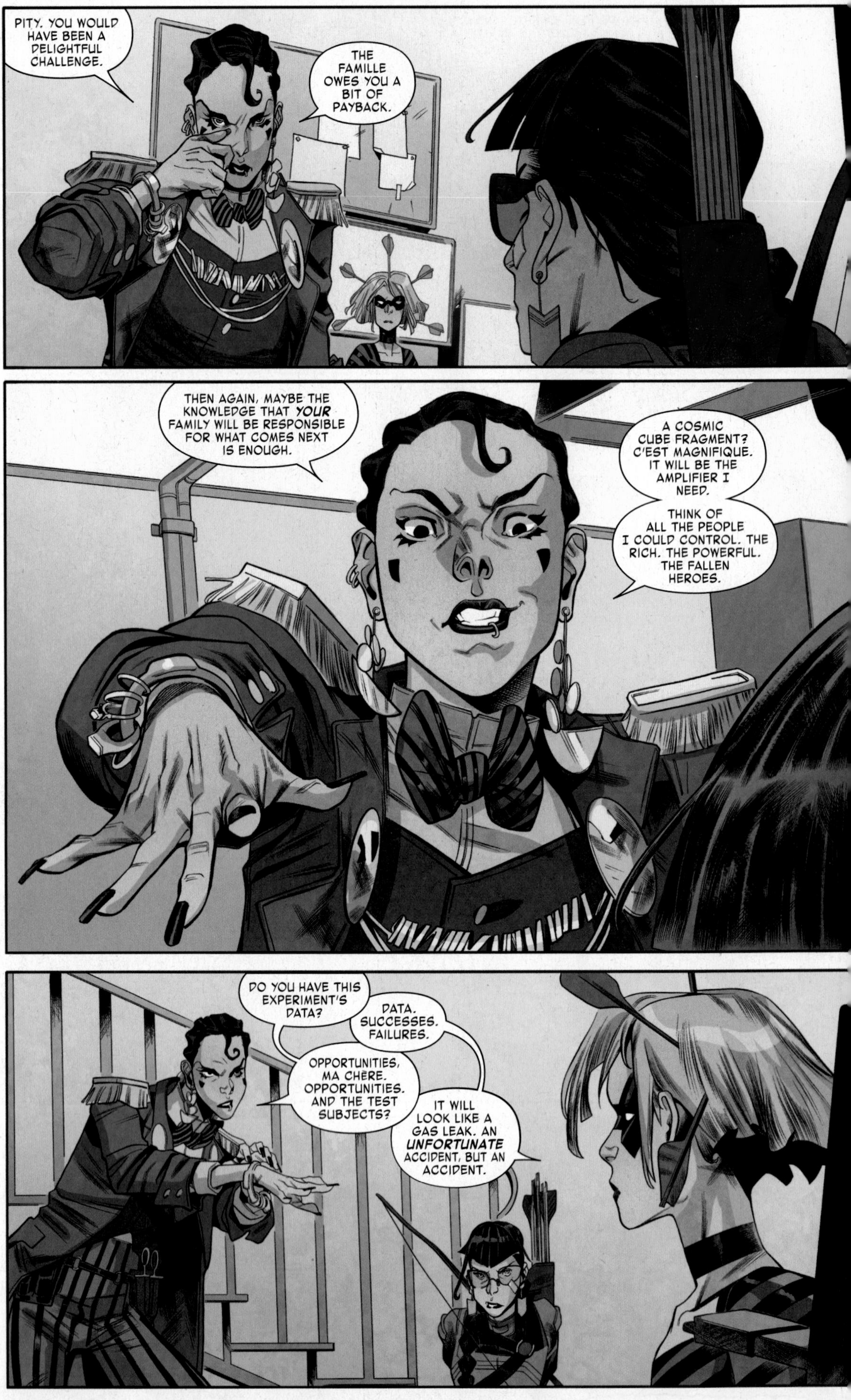
PITY. YOU WOULD HAVE BEEN A DELIGHTFUL CHALLENGE.
THE FAMILLE OWES YOU A BIT OF PAYBACK.
THEN AGAIN, MAYBE THE KNOWLEDGE THAT *YOUR* FAMILY WILL BE RESPONSIBLE FOR WHAT COMES NEXT IS ENOUGH.
A COSMIC CUBE FRAGMENT? C'EST MAGNIFIQUE. IT WILL BE THE AMPLIFIER I NEED.
THINK OF ALL THE PEOPLE I COULD CONTROL. THE RICH. THE POWERFUL. THE FALLEN HEROES.
DO YOU HAVE THIS EXPERIMENT'S DATA?
DATA. SUCCESSES. FAILURES.
OPPORTUNITIES, MA CHÈRE. OPPORTUNITIES. AND THE TEST SUBJECTS?
IT WILL LOOK LIKE A GAS LEAK. AN *UNFORTUNATE* ACCIDENT, BUT AN ACCIDENT.

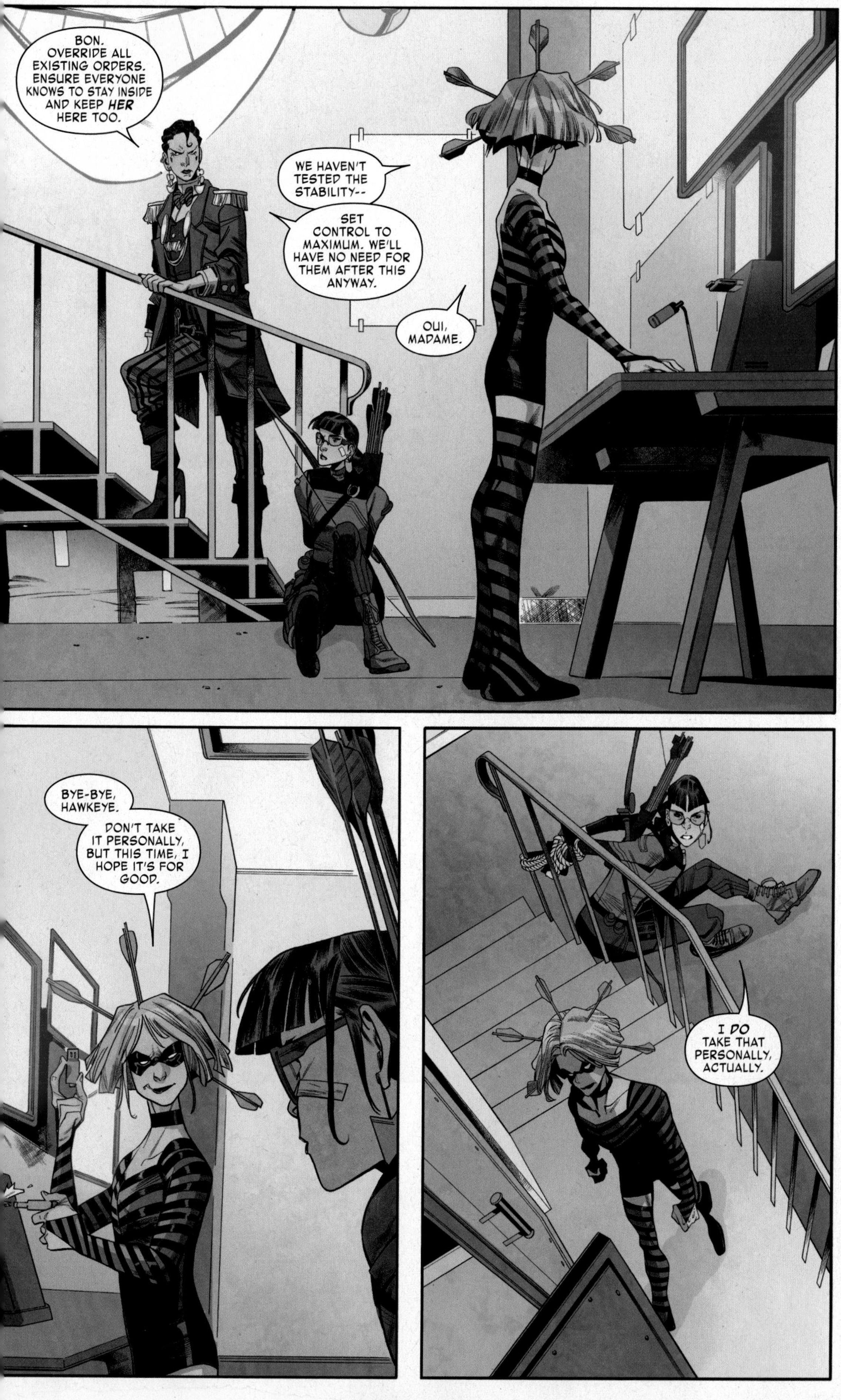
BON. OVERRIDE ALL EXISTING ORDERS. ENSURE EVERYONE KNOWS TO STAY INSIDE AND KEEP *HER* HERE TOO.
WE HAVEN'T TESTED THE STABILITY--
SET CONTROL TO MAXIMUM. WE'LL HAVE NO NEED FOR THEM AFTER THIS ANYWAY.
OUI, MADAME.
BYE-BYE, HAWKEYE.
DON'T TAKE IT PERSONALLY, BUT THIS TIME, I HOPE IT'S FOR GOOD.
I *DO* TAKE THAT PERSONALLY, ACTUALLY.

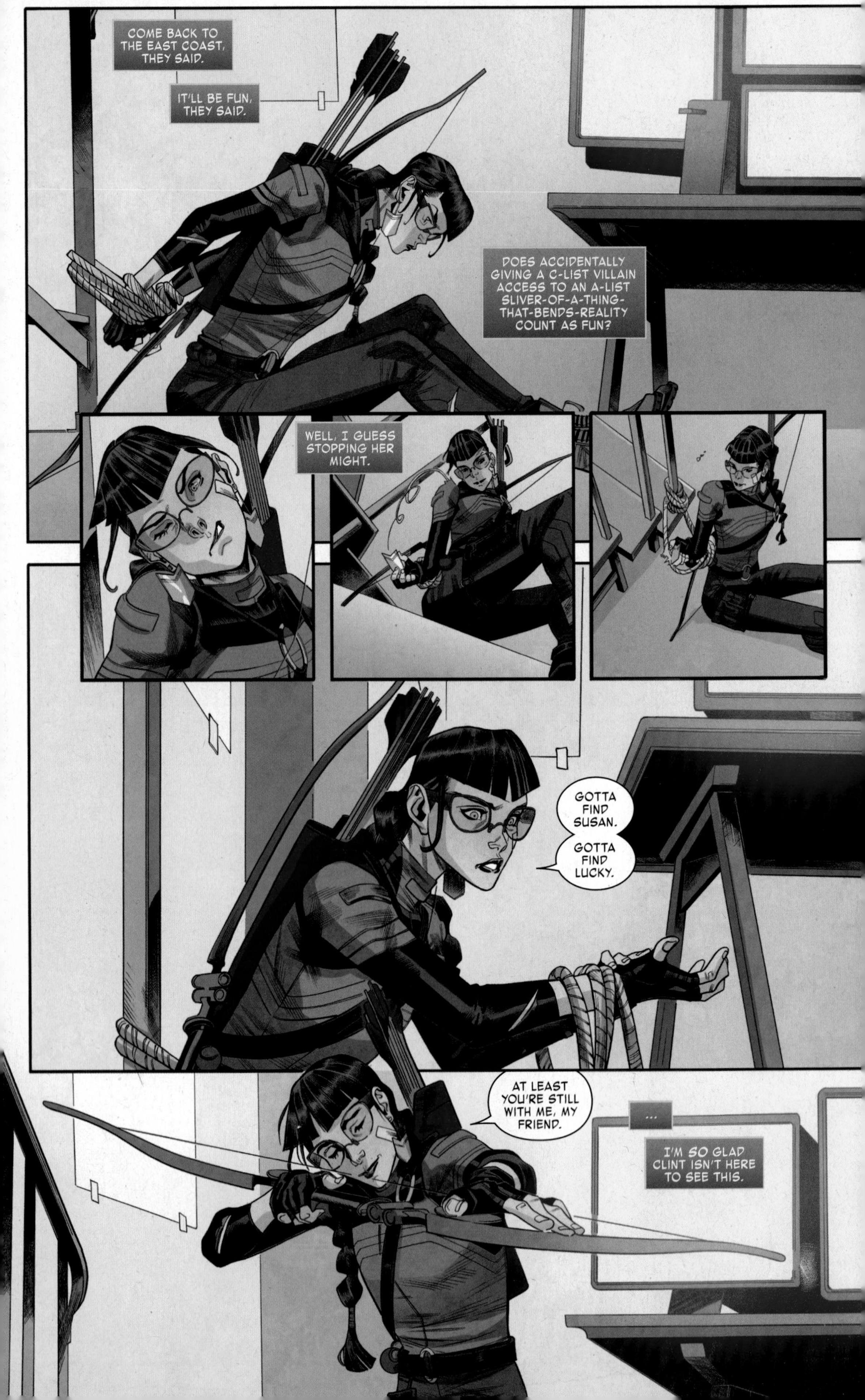
COME BACK TO THE EAST COAST, THEY SAID.
IT'LL BE FUN, THEY SAID.
DOES ACCIDENTALLY GIVING A C-LIST VILLAIN ACCESS TO AN A-LIST SLIVER-OF-A-THING-THAT-BENDS-REALITY COUNT AS FUN?
WELL, I GUESS STOPPING HER MIGHT.
GOTTA FIND SUSAN.
GOTTA FIND LUCKY.
AT LEAST YOU'RE STILL WITH ME, MY FRIEND.
...
I'M SO GLAD CLINT ISN'T HERE TO SEE THIS.

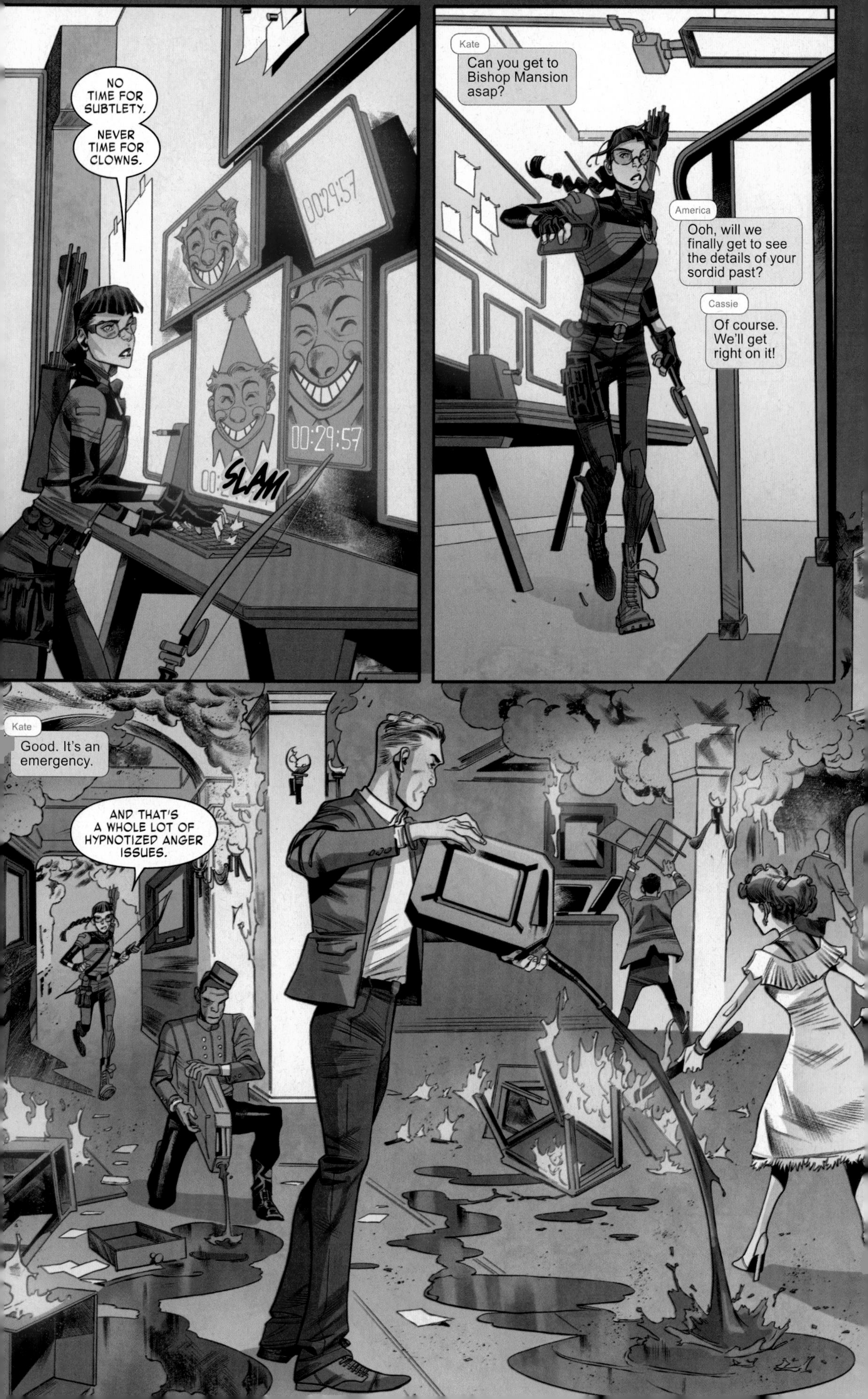
NO TIME FOR SUBTLETY.
NEVER TIME FOR CLOWNS.
00:29:57
00:29:57
SLAM
Kate
Can you get to Bishop Mansion asap?
America
Ooh, will we finally get to see the details of your sordid past?
Cassie
Of course. We'll get right on it!
Kate
Good. It's an emergency.
AND THAT'S A WHOLE LOT OF HYPNOTIZED ANGER ISSUES.

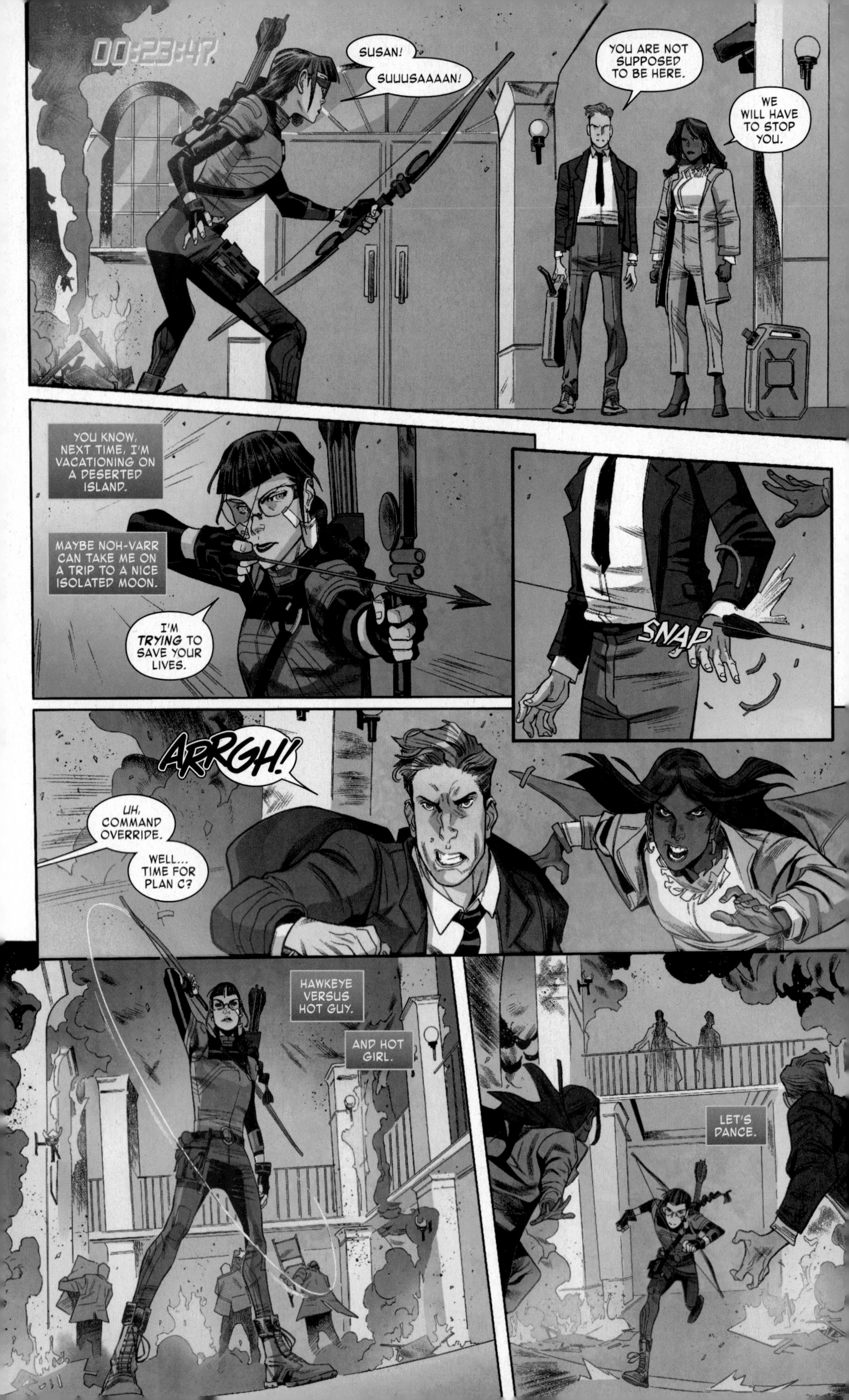
00:23:47
SUSAN!
SUUUSAAAAN!
YOU ARE NOT SUPPOSED TO BE HERE.
WE WILL HAVE TO STOP YOU.
YOU KNOW, NEXT TIME, I'M VACATIONING ON A DESERTED ISLAND.
MAYBE NOH-VARR CAN TAKE ME ON A TRIP TO A NICE ISOLATED MOON.
I'M TRYING TO SAVE YOUR LIVES.
SNAP
ARRGH!
UH, COMMAND OVERRIDE.
WELL... TIME FOR PLAN C?
HAWKEYE VERSUS HOT GUY.
AND HOT GIRL.
LET'S DANCE.

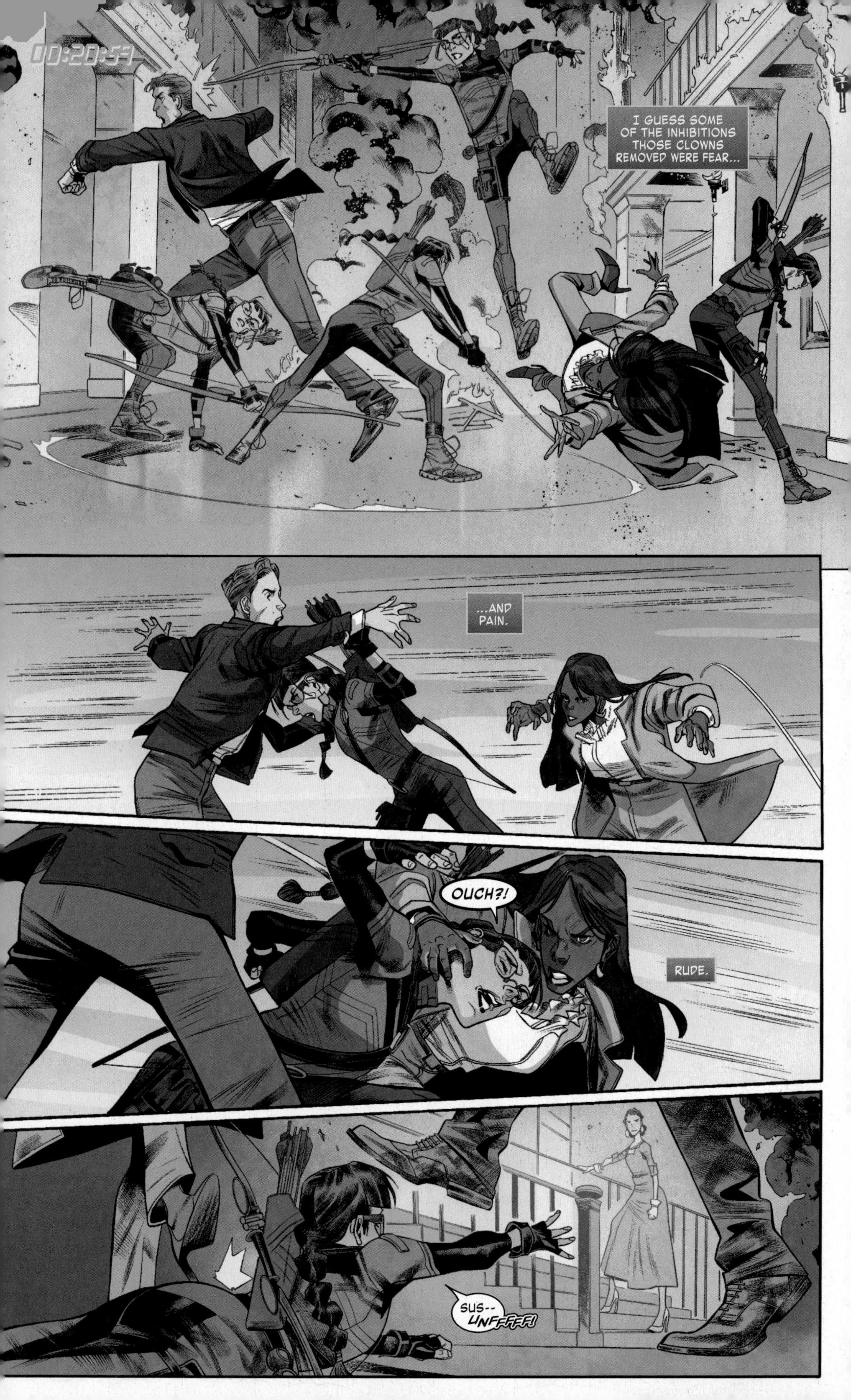
00:20:59
I GUESS SOME OF THE INHIBITIONS THOSE CLOWNS REMOVED WERE FEAR...
...AND PAIN.
OUCH?!
RUDE.
SUS-- UNFFFFF!

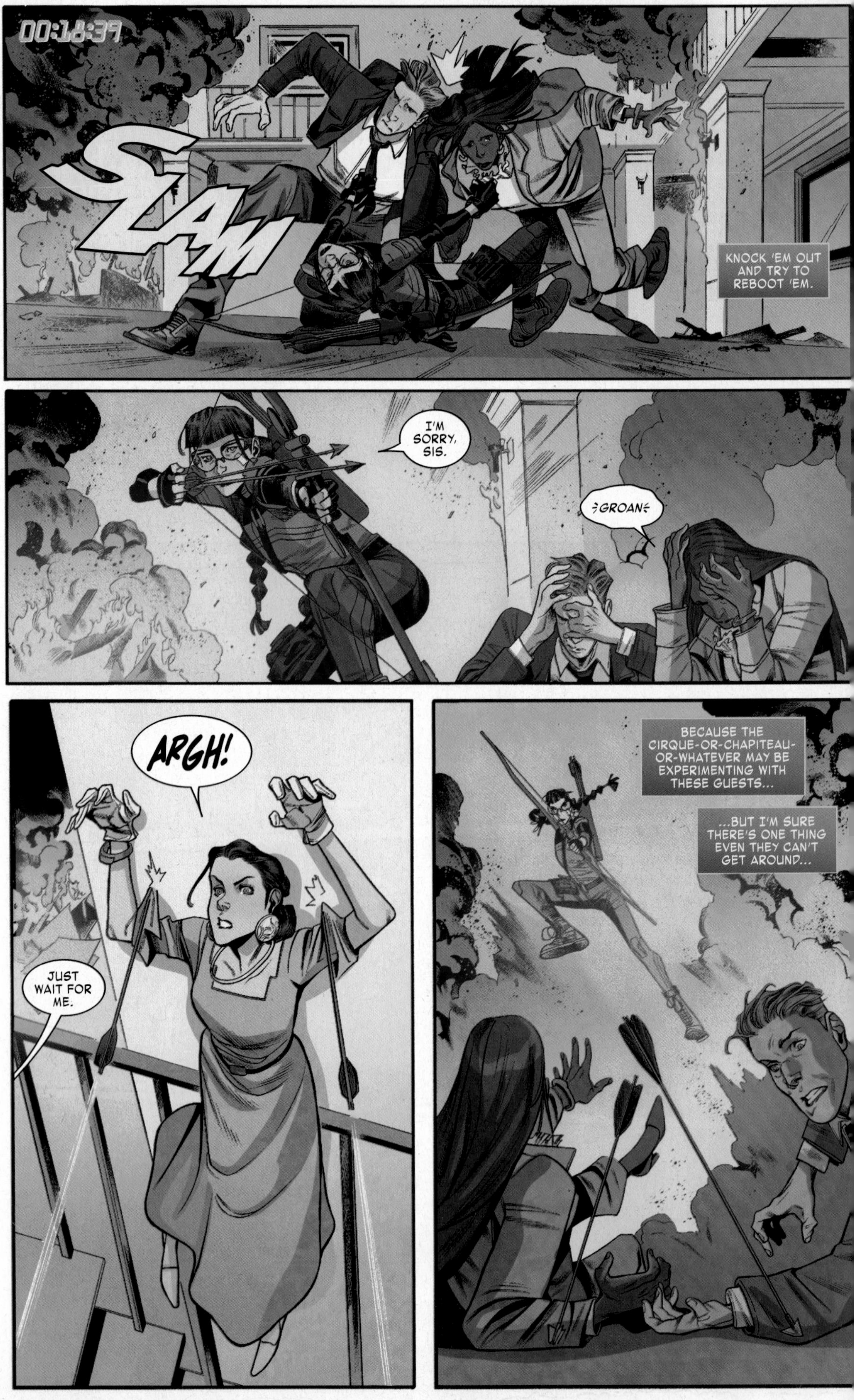

00:18:39
SLAM
KNOCK 'EM OUT AND TRY TO REBOOT 'EM.
I'M SORRY, SIS.
GROAN
ARGH!
JUST WAIT FOR ME.
BECAUSE THE CIRQUE-OR-CHAPITEAU-OR-WHATEVER MAY BE EXPERIMENTING WITH THESE GUESTS...
...BUT I'M SURE THERE'S ONE THING EVEN THEY CAN'T GET AROUND...

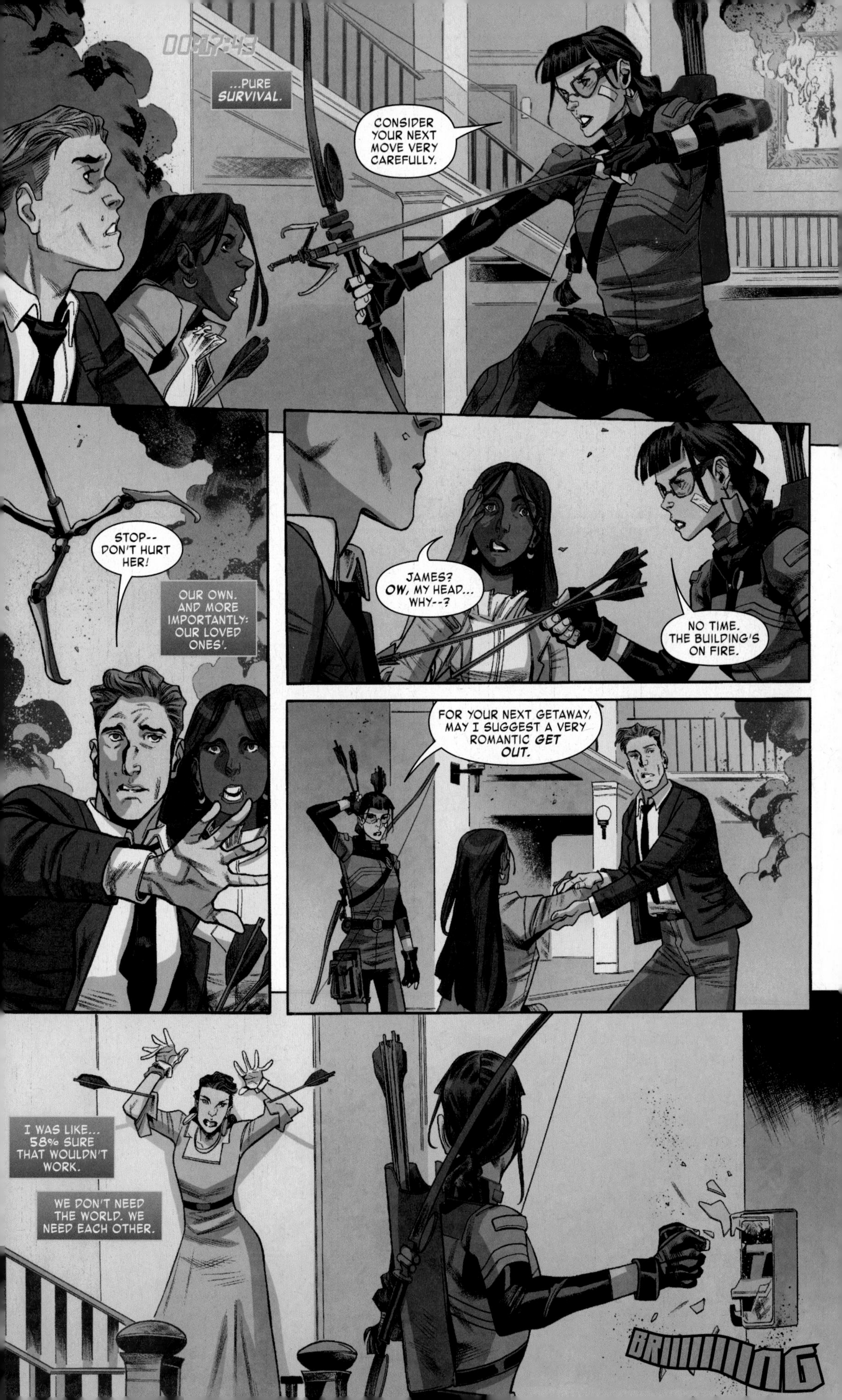

00:17:43
...PURE SURVIVAL.
CONSIDER YOUR NEXT MOVE VERY CAREFULLY.
STOP-- DON'T HURT HER!
OUR OWN. AND MORE IMPORTANTLY: OUR LOVED ONES!
JAMES? OW, MY HEAD... WHY--?
NO TIME. THE BUILDING'S ON FIRE.
FOR YOUR NEXT GETAWAY, MAY I SUGGEST A VERY ROMANTIC GET OUT.
I WAS LIKE... 58% SURE THAT WOULDN'T WORK.
WE DON'T NEED THE WORLD. WE NEED EACH OTHER.
BRIIIIIING

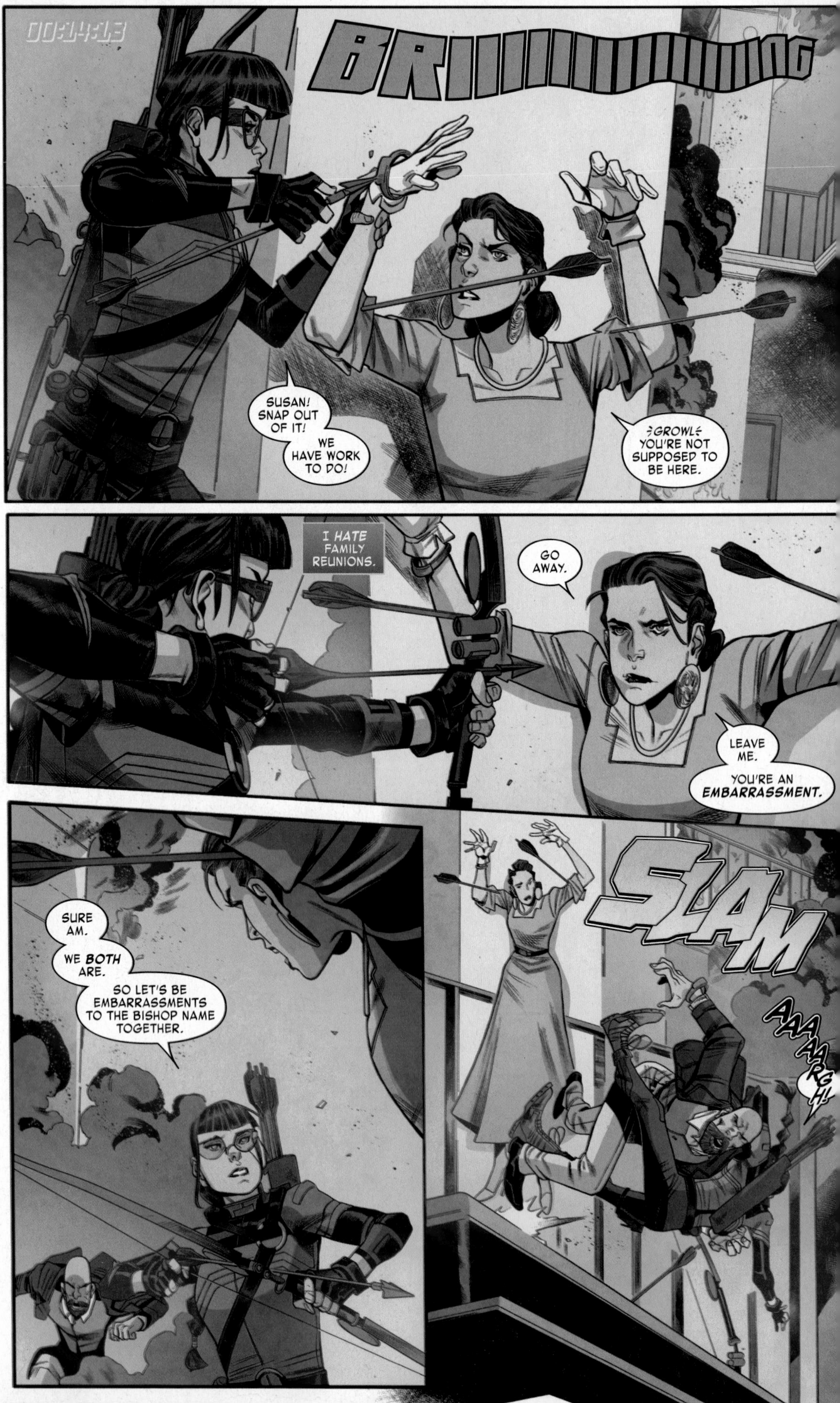

00:04:13
BRIIIIIIIIIIIIIIING
SUSAN! SNAP OUT OF IT!
WE HAVE WORK TO DO!
GROWL YOU'RE NOT SUPPOSED TO BE HERE.
I HATE FAMILY REUNIONS.
GO AWAY.
LEAVE ME.
YOU'RE AN EMBARRASSMENT.
SURE AM.
WE BOTH ARE.
SO LET'S BE EMBARRASSMENTS TO THE BISHOP NAME TOGETHER.
SLAM
AAAAARGH!

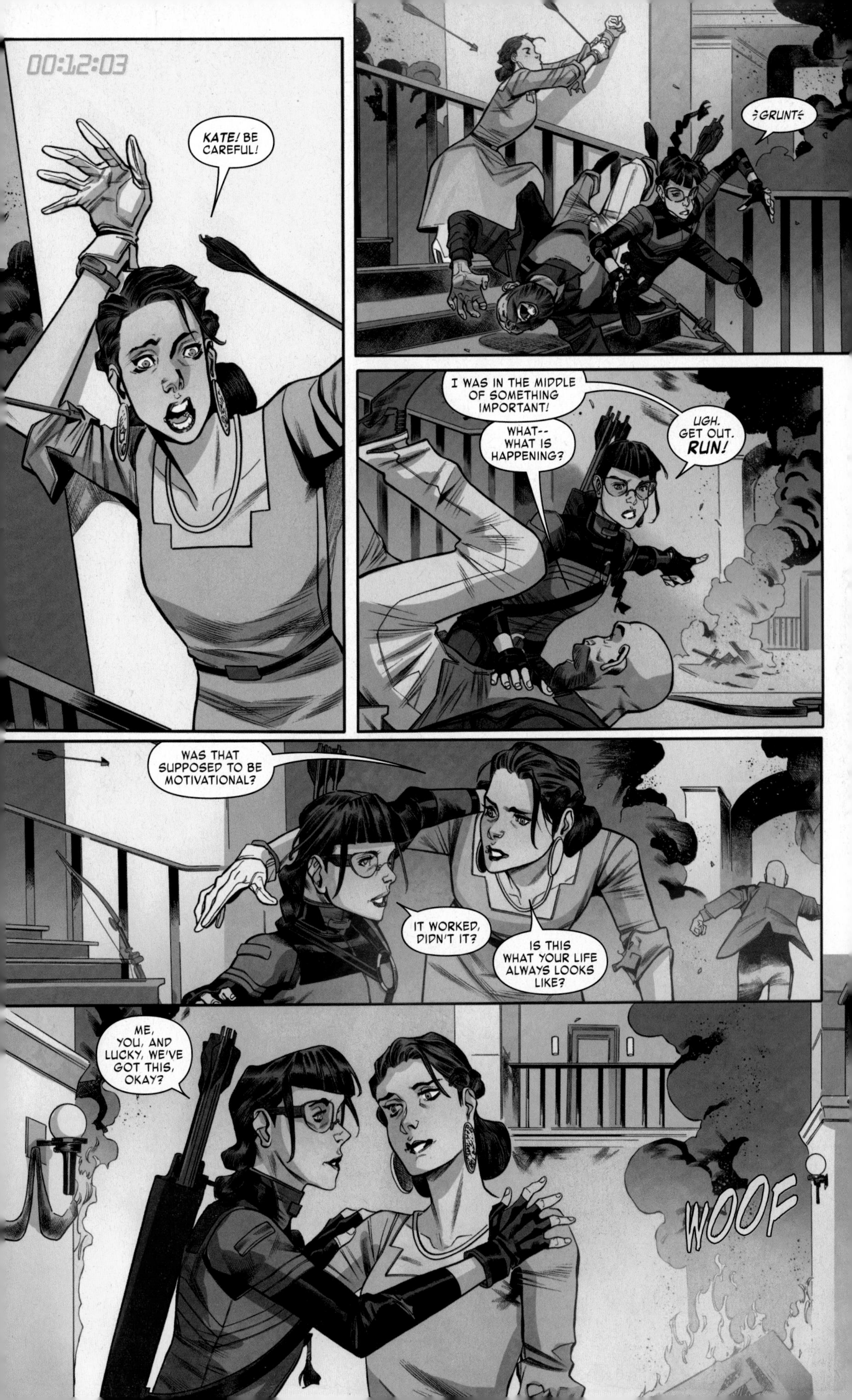
00:12:03
KATE! BE CAREFUL!
GRUNT
I WAS IN THE MIDDLE OF SOMETHING IMPORTANT!
WHAT-- WHAT IS HAPPENING?
UGH. GET OUT. RUN!
WAS THAT SUPPOSED TO BE MOTIVATIONAL?
IT WORKED, DIDN'T IT?
IS THIS WHAT YOUR LIFE ALWAYS LOOKS LIKE?
ME, YOU, AND LUCKY, WE'VE GOT THIS, OKAY?
WOOF

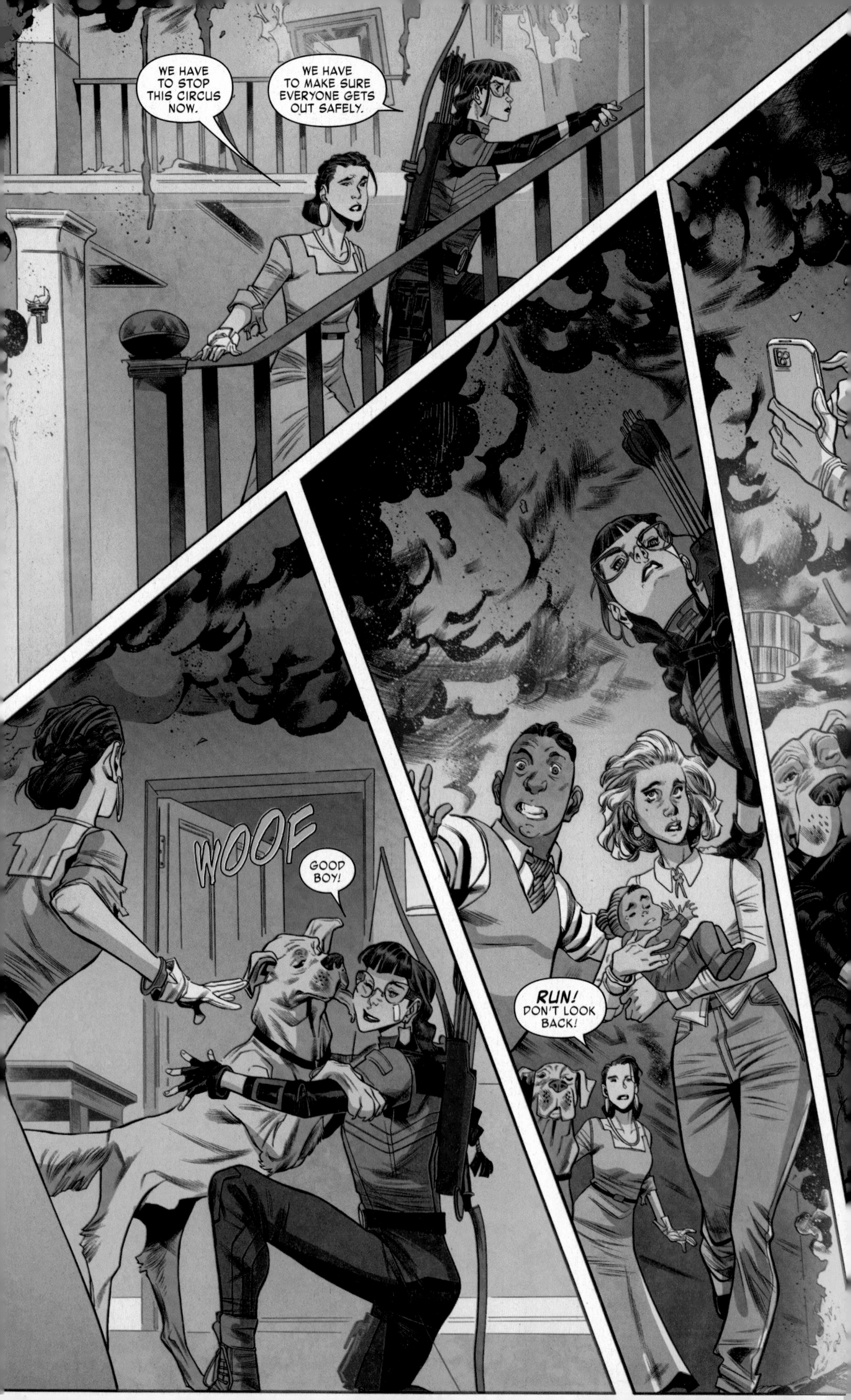
WE HAVE TO STOP THIS CIRCUS NOW.
WE HAVE TO MAKE SURE EVERYONE GETS OUT SAFELY.
WOOF
GOOD BOY!
RUN! DON'T LOOK BACK!

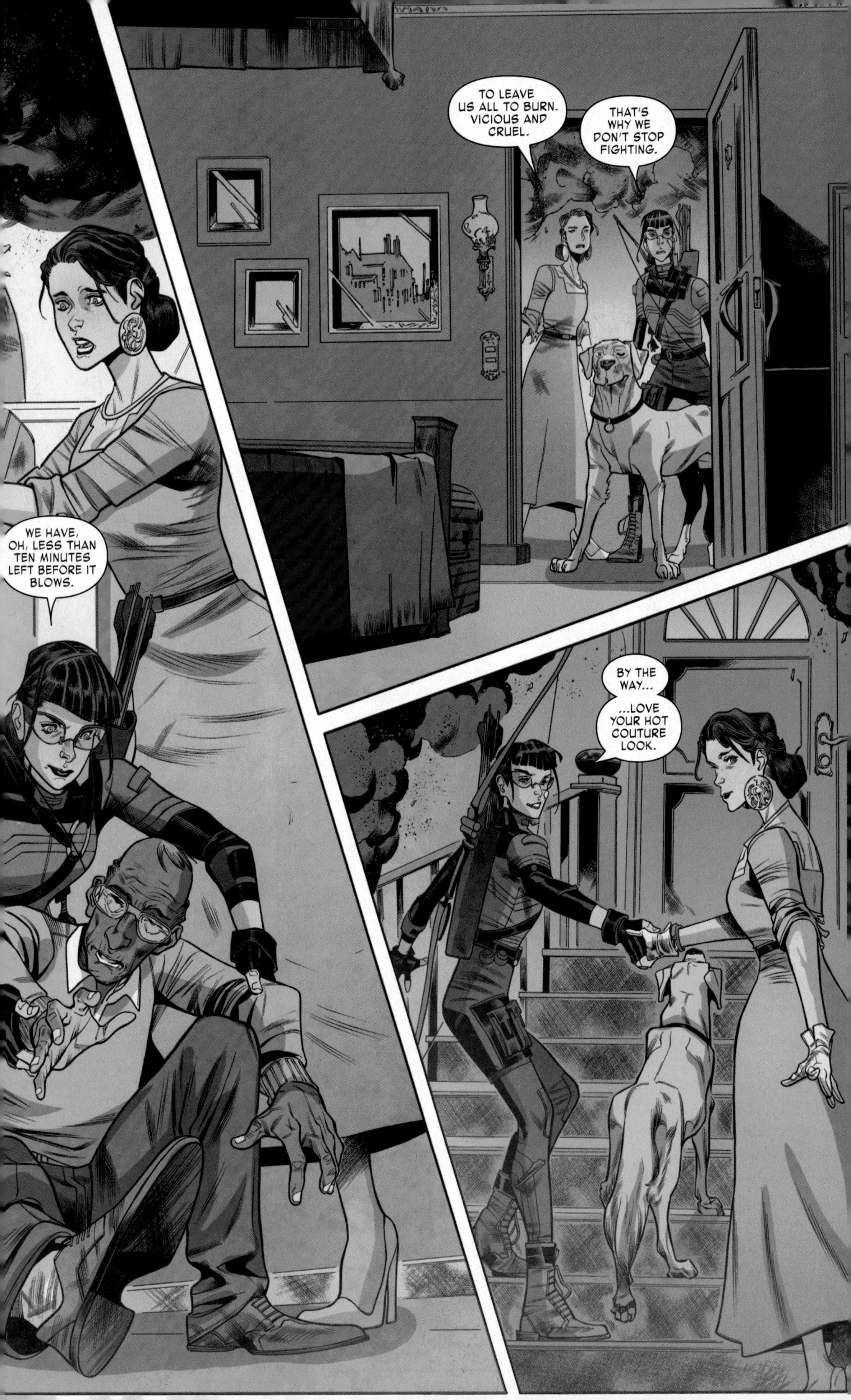
TO LEAVE US ALL TO BURN. VICIOUS AND CRUEL.
THAT'S WHY WE DON'T STOP FIGHTING.
WE HAVE, OH, LESS THAN TEN MINUTES LEFT BEFORE IT BLOWS.
BY THE WAY...
...LOVE YOUR HOT COUTURE LOOK.

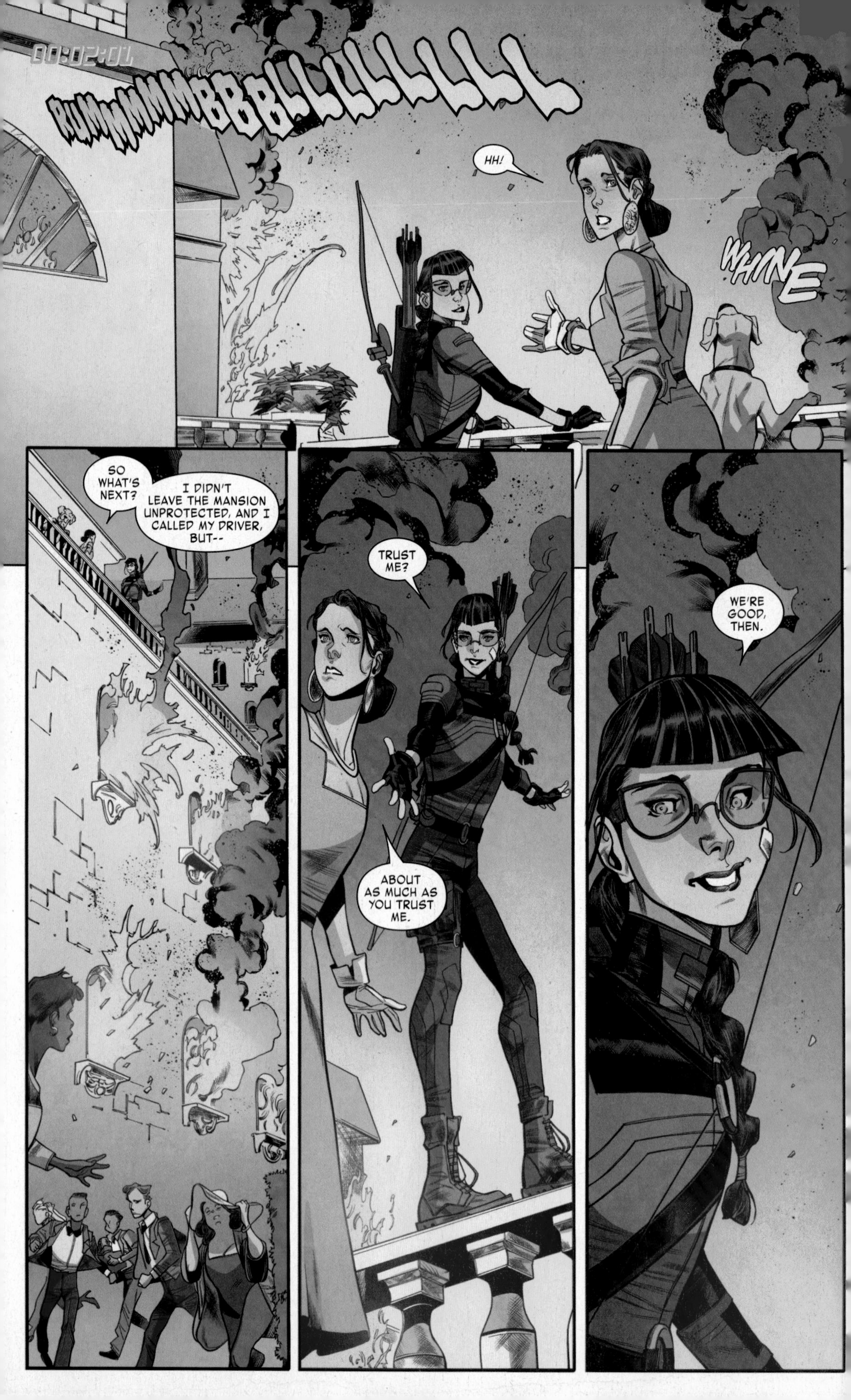
00:02:01
RUMMMMMBBBLLLLLLLL
HH!
WHINE
SO WHAT'S NEXT?
I DIDN'T LEAVE THE MANSION UNPROTECTED, AND I CALLED MY DRIVER, BUT--
TRUST ME?
ABOUT AS MUCH AS YOU TRUST ME.
WE'RE GOOD, THEN.

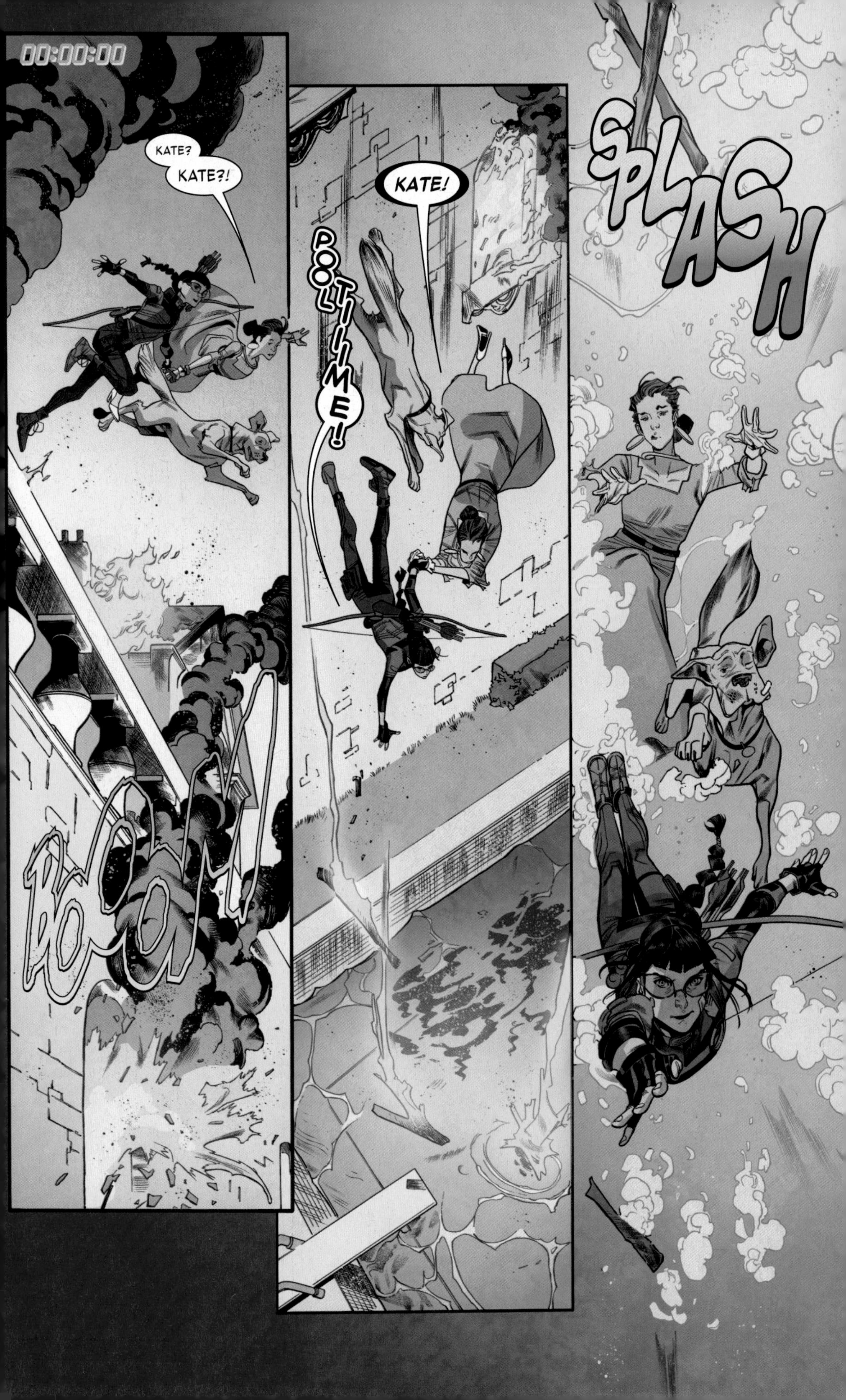
00:00:00
KATE?
KATE?!
BOOM
KATE!
POOL TIIIME!
SPLASH

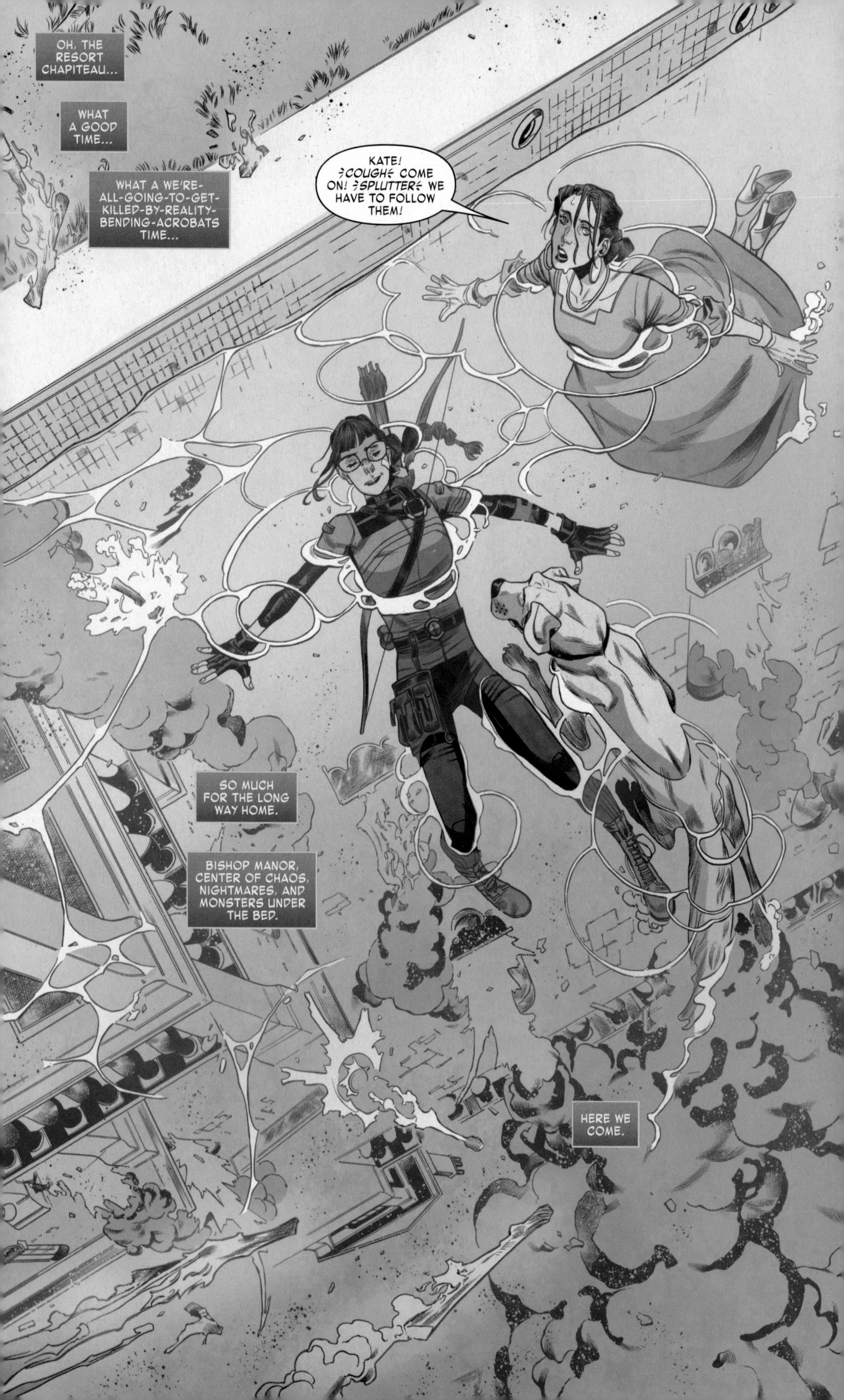
OH, THE RESORT CHAPITEAU...
WHAT A GOOD TIME...
WHAT A WE'RE-ALL-GOING-TO-GET-KILLED-BY-REALITY-BENDING-ACROBATS TIME...
KATE! ⋟COUGH⋞ COME ON! ⋟SPLUTTER⋞ WE HAVE TO FOLLOW THEM!
SO MUCH FOR THE LONG WAY HOME.
BISHOP MANOR, CENTER OF CHAOS, NIGHTMARES, AND MONSTERS UNDER THE BED.
HERE WE COME.

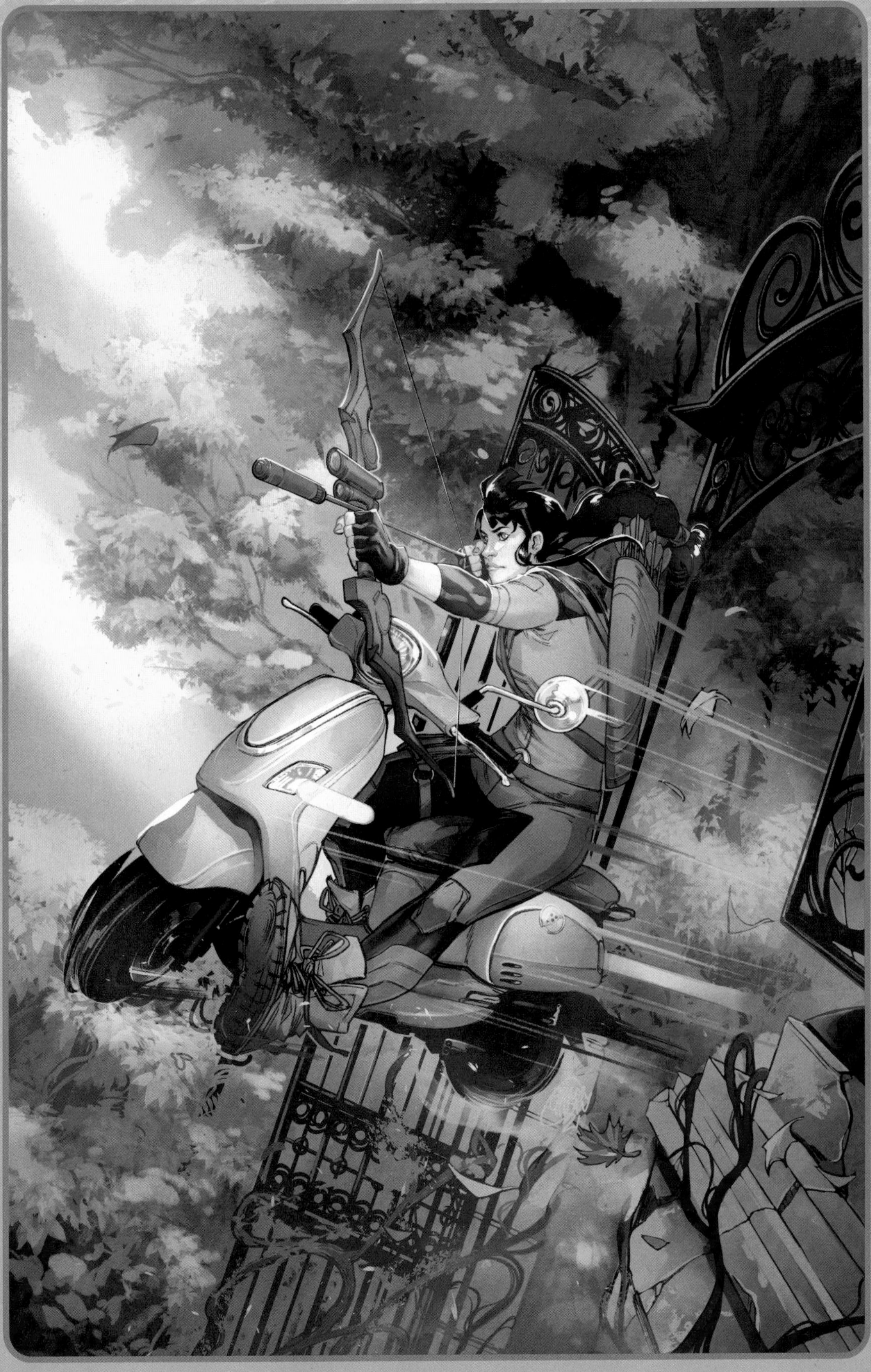

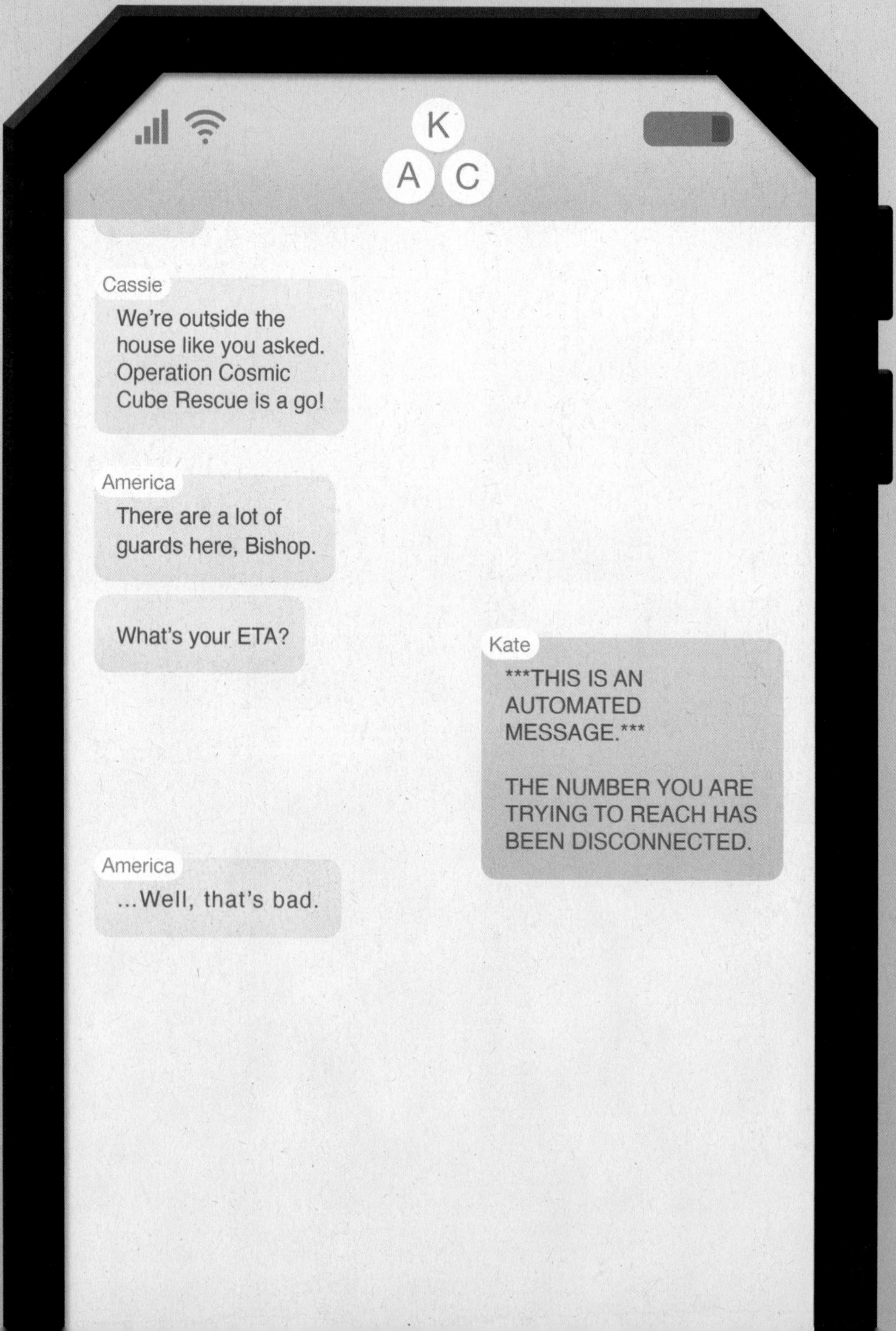
K
A
C
Cassie
We're outside the house like you asked. Operation Cosmic Cube Rescue is a go!
America
There are a lot of guards here, Bishop.
What's your ETA?
Kate
THIS IS AN AUTOMATED MESSAGE.
THE NUMBER YOU ARE TRYING TO REACH HAS BEEN DISCONNECTED.
America
...Well, that's bad.

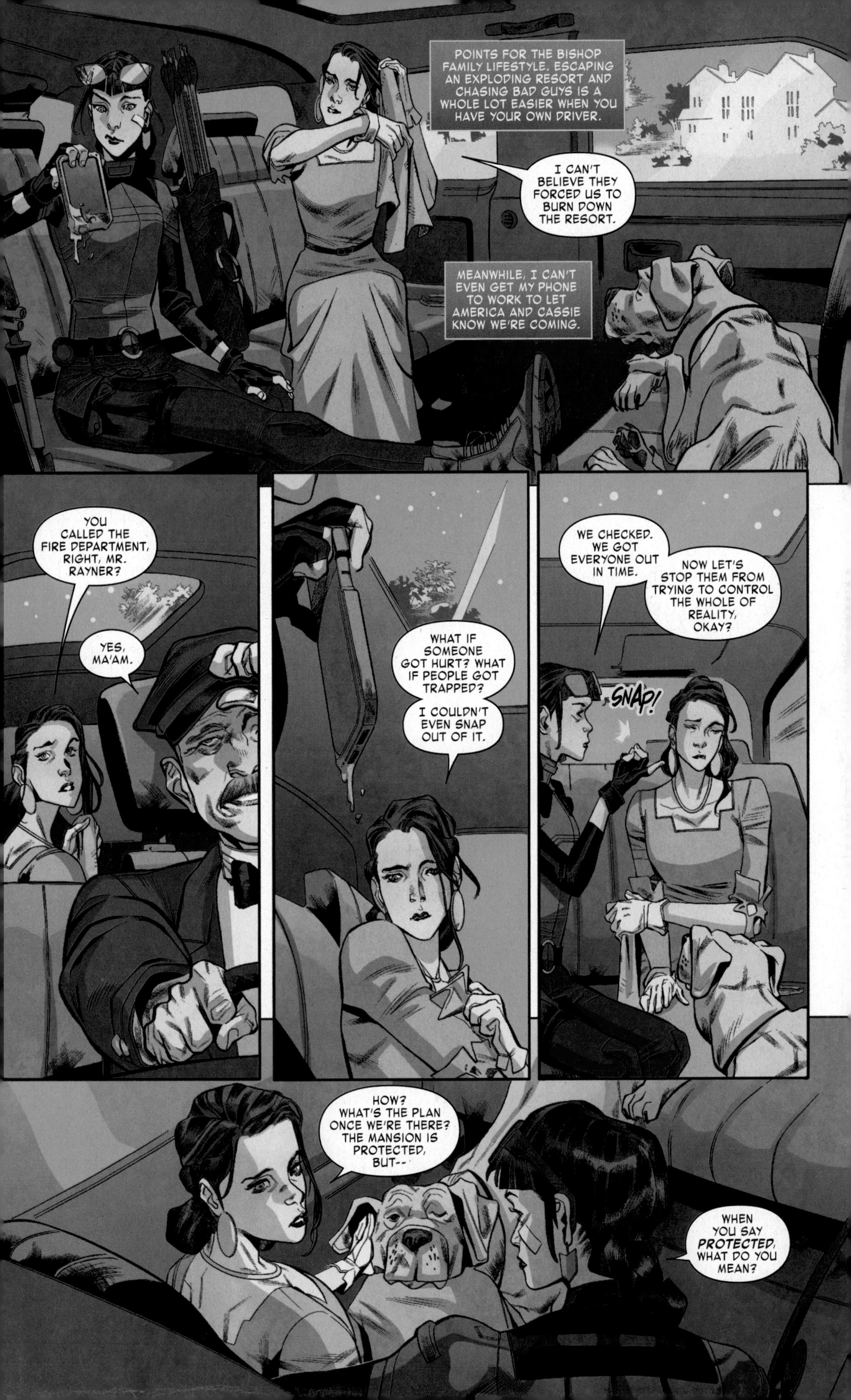
POINTS FOR THE BISHOP FAMILY LIFESTYLE. ESCAPING AN EXPLODING RESORT AND CHASING BAD GUYS IS A WHOLE LOT EASIER WHEN YOU HAVE YOUR OWN DRIVER.
I CAN'T BELIEVE THEY FORCED US TO BURN DOWN THE RESORT.
MEANWHILE, I CAN'T EVEN GET MY PHONE TO WORK TO LET AMERICA AND CASSIE KNOW WE'RE COMING.
YOU CALLED THE FIRE DEPARTMENT, RIGHT, MR. RAYNER?
YES, MA'AM.
WHAT IF SOMEONE GOT HURT? WHAT IF PEOPLE GOT TRAPPED?
I COULDN'T EVEN SNAP OUT OF IT.
WE CHECKED. WE GOT EVERYONE OUT IN TIME.
NOW LET'S STOP THEM FROM TRYING TO CONTROL THE WHOLE OF REALITY, OKAY?
SNAP!
HOW? WHAT'S THE PLAN ONCE WE'RE THERE? THE MANSION IS PROTECTED, BUT--
WHEN YOU SAY *PROTECTED*, WHAT DO YOU MEAN?

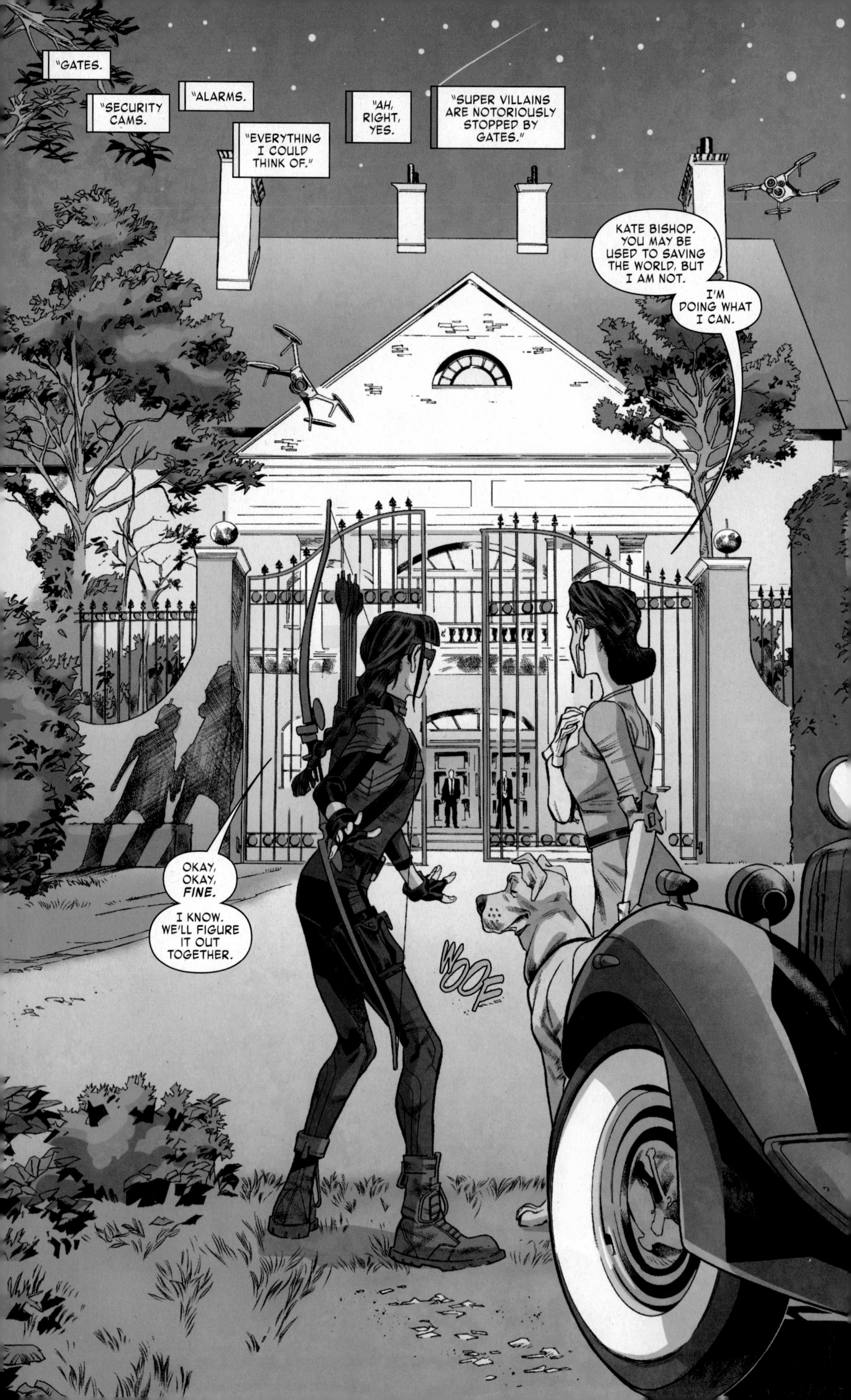
"GATES.
"SECURITY CAMS.
"ALARMS.
"EVERYTHING I COULD THINK OF."
"AH, RIGHT, YES.
"SUPER VILLAINS ARE NOTORIOUSLY STOPPED BY GATES."
KATE BISHOP. YOU MAY BE USED TO SAVING THE WORLD, BUT I AM NOT.
I'M DOING WHAT I CAN.
OKAY, OKAY, *FINE.*
I KNOW. WE'LL FIGURE IT OUT TOGETHER.
WOOF

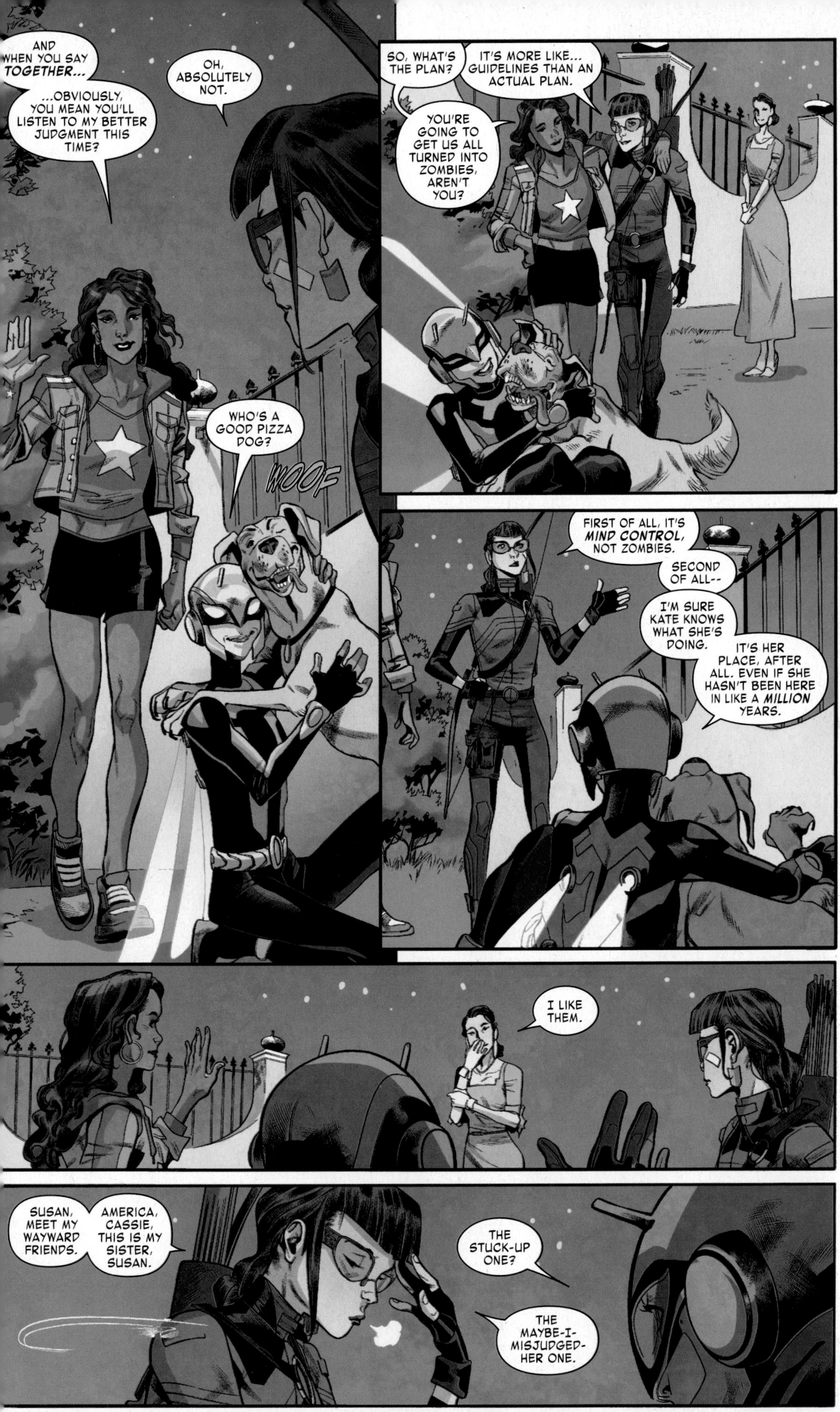
AND WHEN YOU SAY *TOGETHER*...
...OBVIOUSLY, YOU MEAN YOU'LL LISTEN TO MY BETTER JUDGMENT THIS TIME?
OH, ABSOLUTELY NOT.
WHO'S A GOOD PIZZA DOG?
WOOF
SO, WHAT'S THE PLAN?
IT'S MORE LIKE... GUIDELINES THAN AN ACTUAL PLAN.
YOU'RE GOING TO GET US ALL TURNED INTO ZOMBIES, AREN'T YOU?
FIRST OF ALL, IT'S *MIND CONTROL*, NOT ZOMBIES.
SECOND OF ALL--
I'M SURE KATE KNOWS WHAT SHE'S DOING.
IT'S HER PLACE, AFTER ALL. EVEN IF SHE HASN'T BEEN HERE IN LIKE A *MILLION* YEARS.
I LIKE THEM.
SUSAN, MEET MY WAYWARD FRIENDS.
AMERICA, CASSIE, THIS IS MY SISTER, SUSAN.
THE STUCK-UP ONE?
THE MAYBE-I-MISJUDGED-HER ONE.

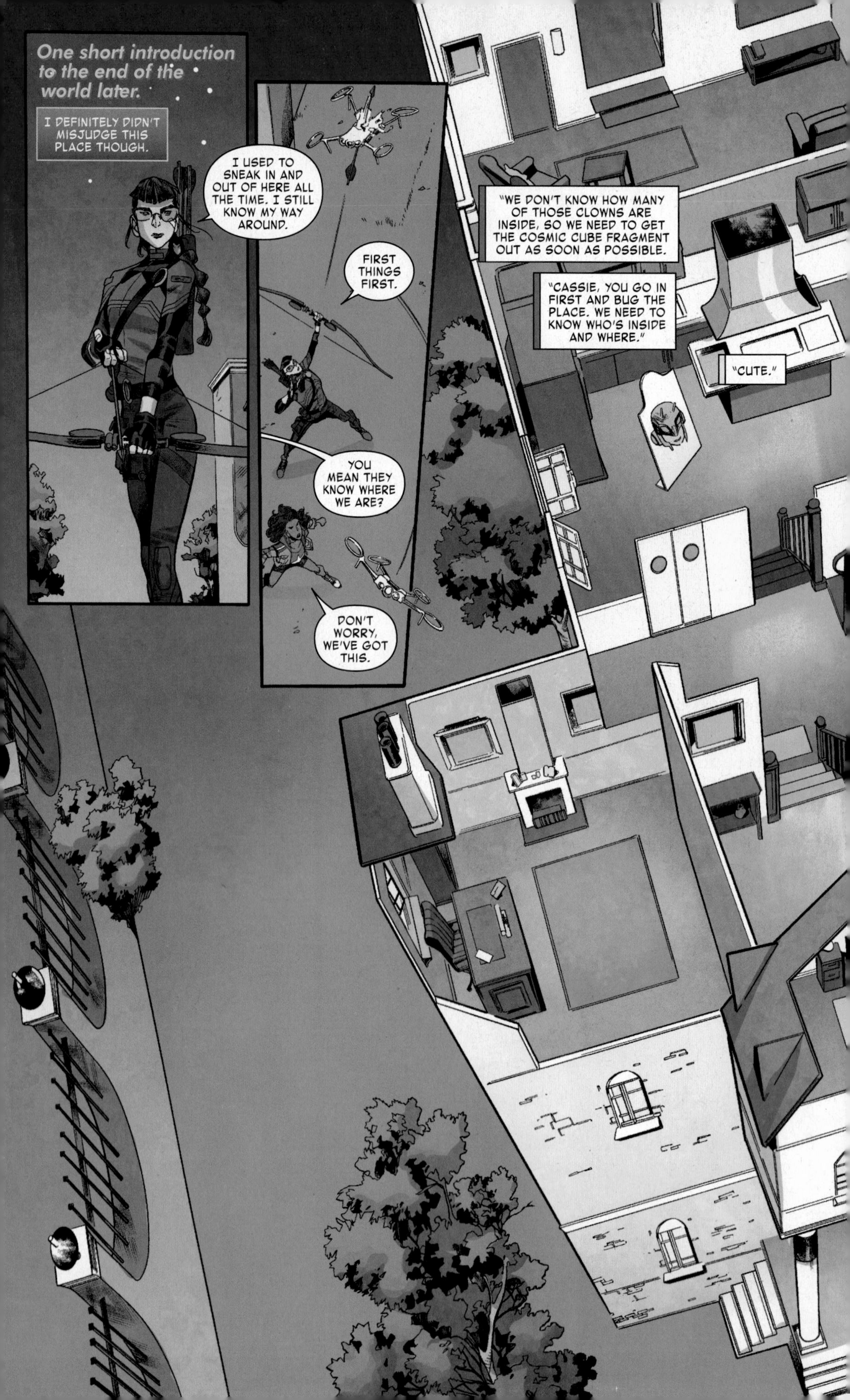
One short introduction to the end of the world later.
I DEFINITELY DIDN'T MISJUDGE THIS PLACE THOUGH.
I USED TO SNEAK IN AND OUT OF HERE ALL THE TIME. I STILL KNOW MY WAY AROUND.
FIRST THINGS FIRST.
YOU MEAN THEY KNOW WHERE WE ARE?
DON'T WORRY, WE'VE GOT THIS.
"WE DON'T KNOW HOW MANY OF THOSE CLOWNS ARE INSIDE, SO WE NEED TO GET THE COSMIC CUBE FRAGMENT OUT AS SOON AS POSSIBLE.
"CASSIE, YOU GO IN FIRST AND BUG THE PLACE. WE NEED TO KNOW WHO'S INSIDE AND WHERE."
"CUTE."

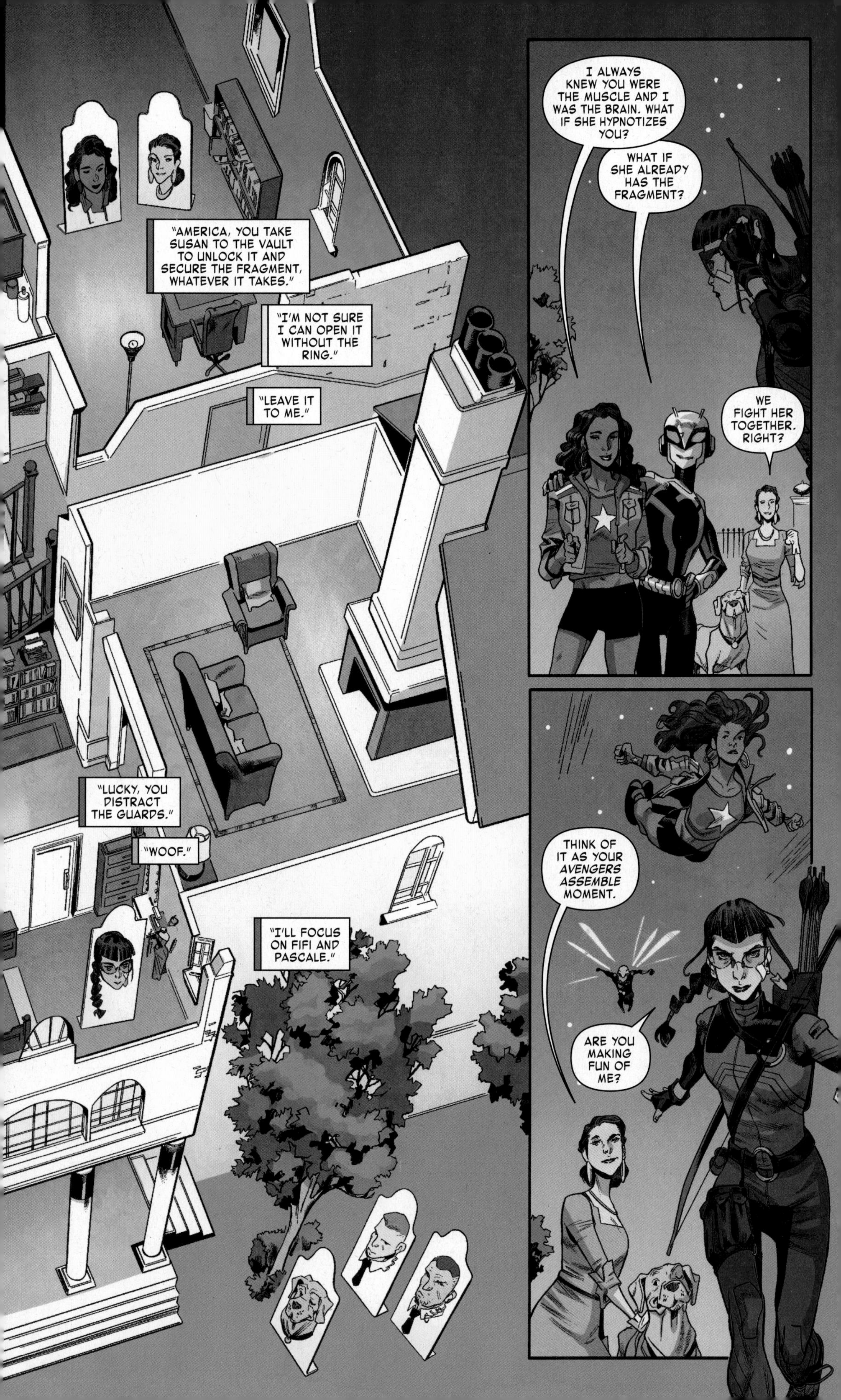

"AMERICA, YOU TAKE SUSAN TO THE VAULT TO UNLOCK IT AND SECURE THE FRAGMENT, WHATEVER IT TAKES."
"I'M NOT SURE I CAN OPEN IT WITHOUT THE RING."
"LEAVE IT TO ME."
"LUCKY, YOU DISTRACT THE GUARDS."
"WOOF."
"I'LL FOCUS ON FIFI AND PASCALE."
I ALWAYS KNEW YOU WERE THE MUSCLE AND I WAS THE BRAIN. WHAT IF SHE HYPNOTIZES YOU?
WHAT IF SHE ALREADY HAS THE FRAGMENT?
WE FIGHT HER TOGETHER. RIGHT?
THINK OF IT AS YOUR *AVENGERS ASSEMBLE* MOMENT.
ARE YOU MAKING FUN OF ME?

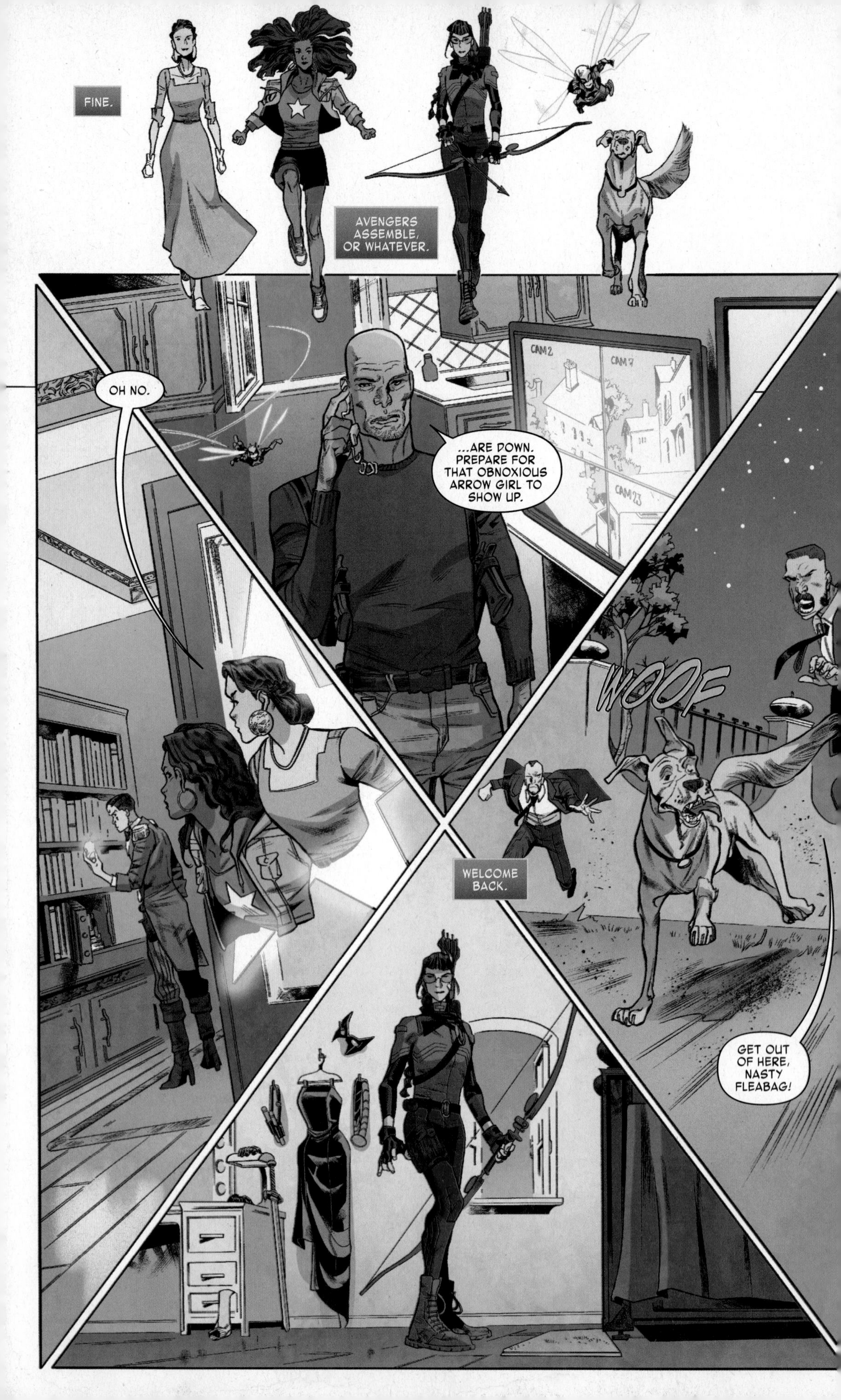
FINE.
AVENGERS ASSEMBLE, OR WHATEVER.
OH NO.
...ARE DOWN. PREPARE FOR THAT OBNOXIOUS ARROW GIRL TO SHOW UP.
CAM 2
CAM 7
CAM 23
WOOF
WELCOME BACK.
GET OUT OF HERE, NASTY FLEABAG!

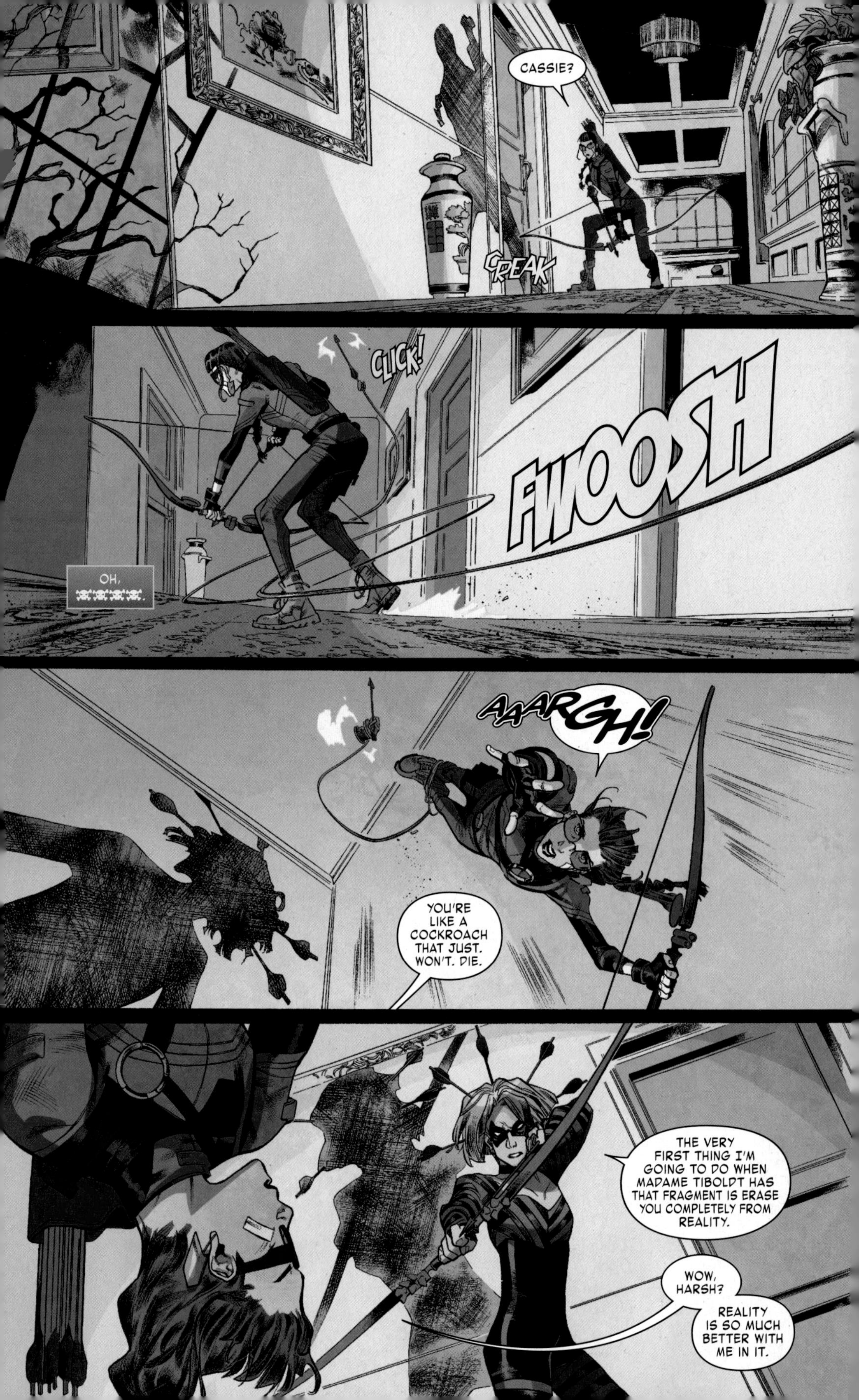
CASSIE?
CREAK
CLICK!
FWOOSH
OH,
☠☠☠☠.
AAARGH!
YOU'RE LIKE A COCKROACH THAT JUST. WON'T. DIE.
THE VERY FIRST THING I'M GOING TO DO WHEN MADAME TIBOLDT HAS THAT FRAGMENT IS ERASE YOU COMPLETELY FROM REALITY.
WOW, HARSH?
REALITY IS SO MUCH BETTER WITH ME IN IT.

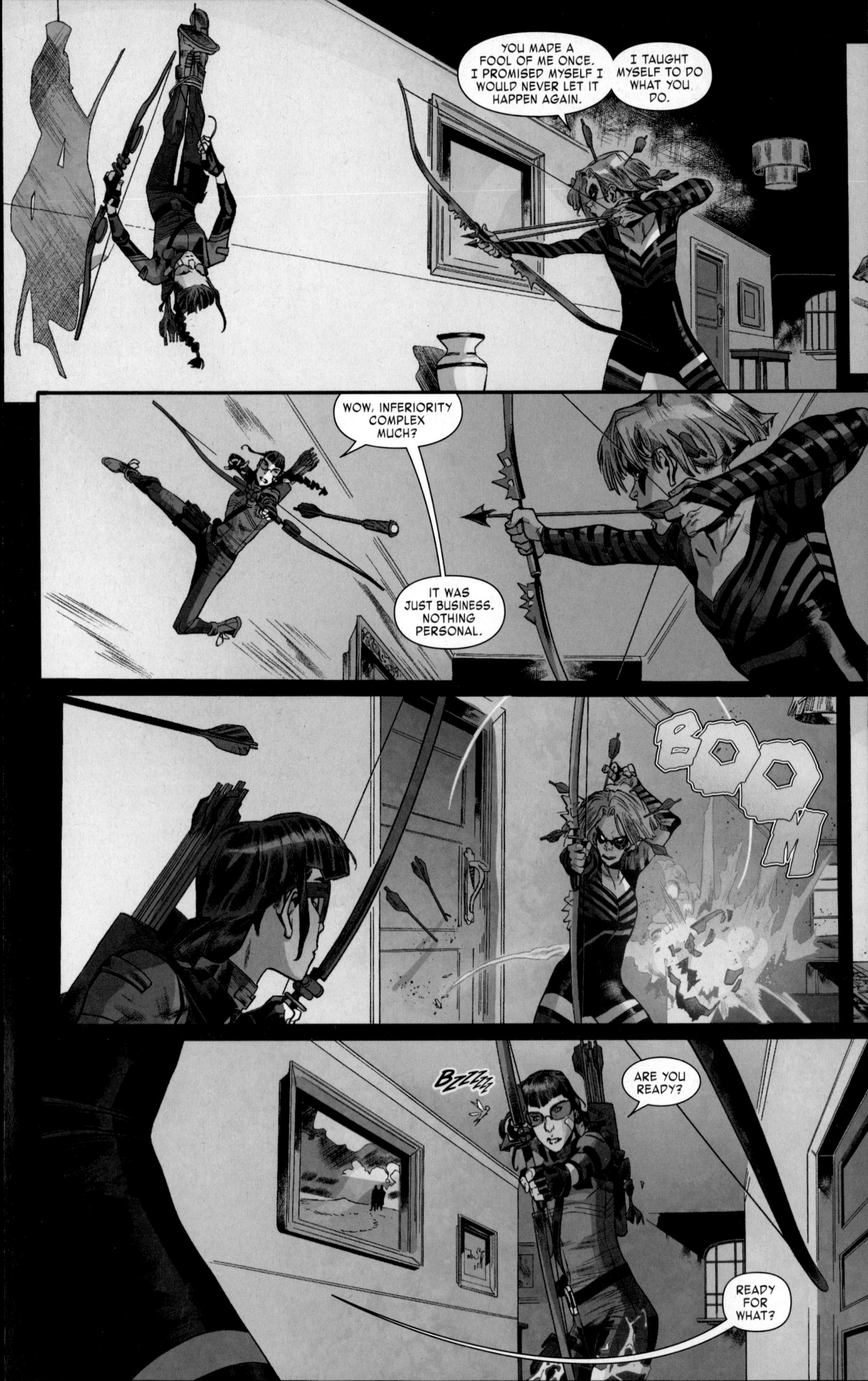

YOU MADE A FOOL OF ME ONCE. I PROMISED MYSELF I WOULD NEVER LET IT HAPPEN AGAIN.
I TAUGHT MYSELF TO DO WHAT YOU DO.
WOW, INFERIORITY COMPLEX MUCH?
IT WAS JUST BUSINESS. NOTHING PERSONAL.
BOOOM
BZZZZZ
ARE YOU READY?
READY FOR WHAT?

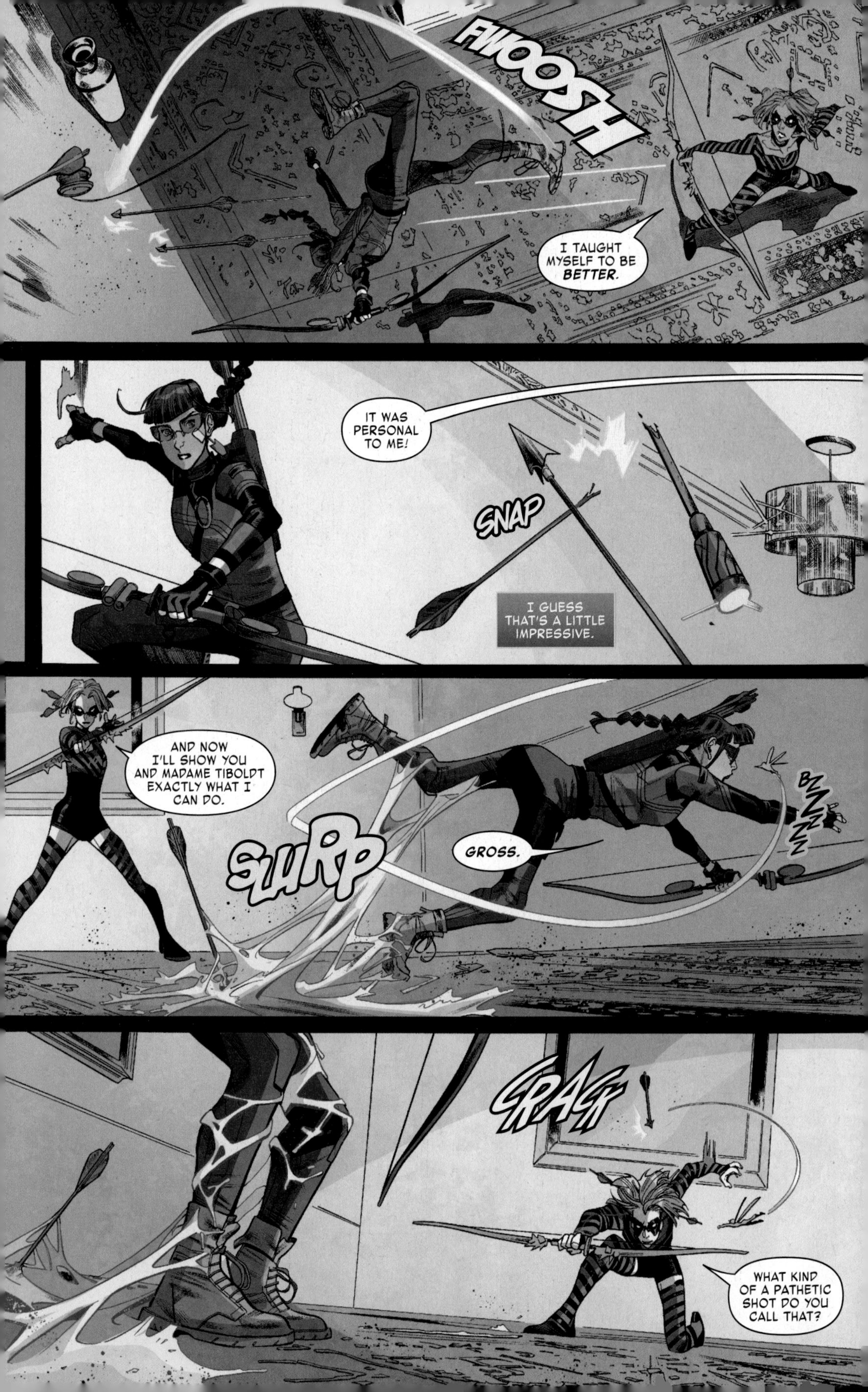
FWOOSH
I TAUGHT MYSELF TO BE BETTER.
IT WAS PERSONAL TO ME!
SNAP
I GUESS THAT'S A LITTLE IMPRESSIVE.
AND NOW I'LL SHOW YOU AND MADAME TIBOLDT EXACTLY WHAT I CAN DO.
SLURP
GROSS.
BZZZZ
CRACK
WHAT KIND OF A PATHETIC SHOT DO YOU CALL THAT?

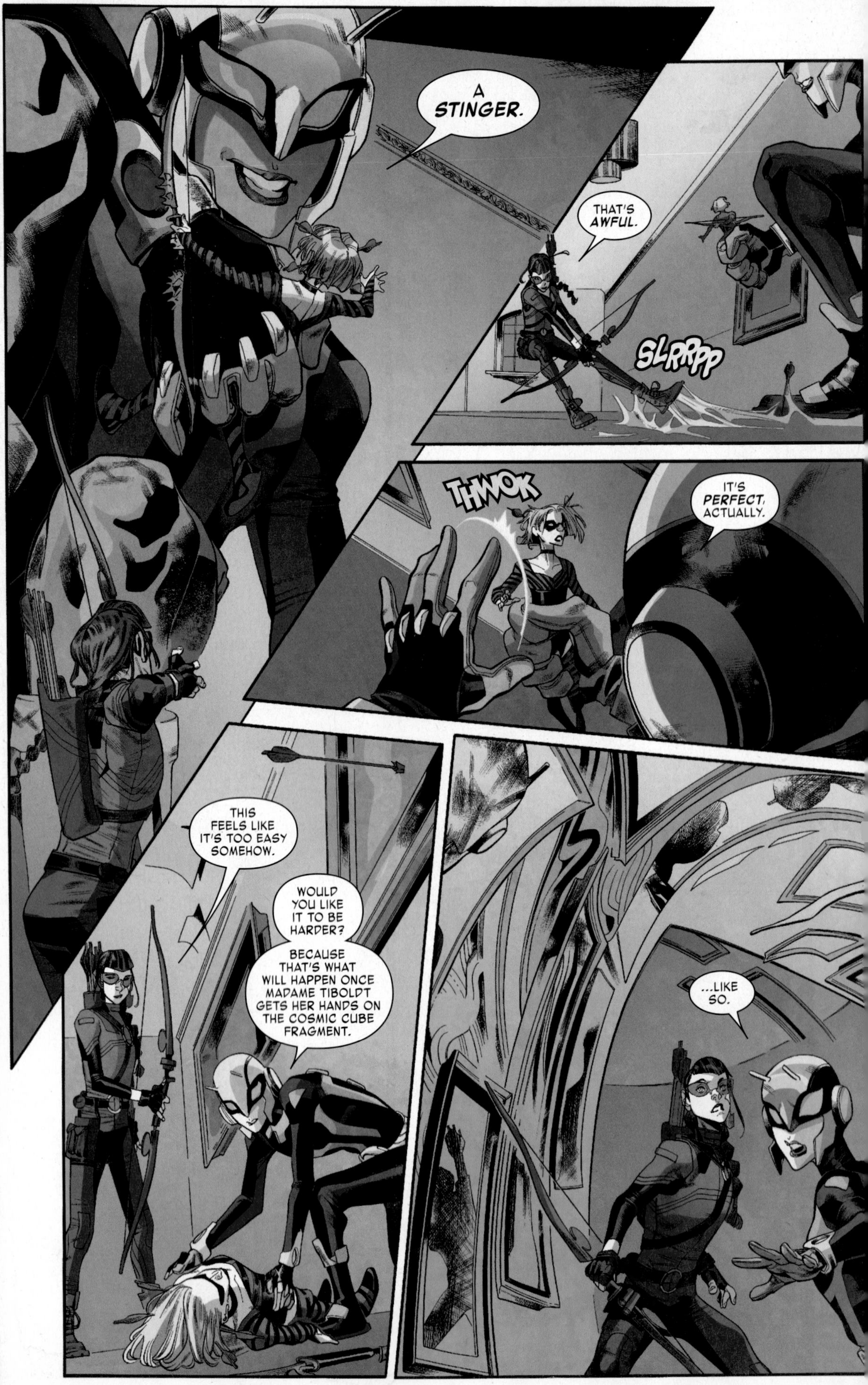
A STINGER.
THAT'S AWFUL.
SLRRPP
THWOK
IT'S PERFECT, ACTUALLY.
THIS FEELS LIKE IT'S TOO EASY SOMEHOW.
WOULD YOU LIKE IT TO BE HARDER?
BECAUSE THAT'S WHAT WILL HAPPEN ONCE MADAME TIBOLDT GETS HER HANDS ON THE COSMIC CUBE FRAGMENT.
...LIKE SO.

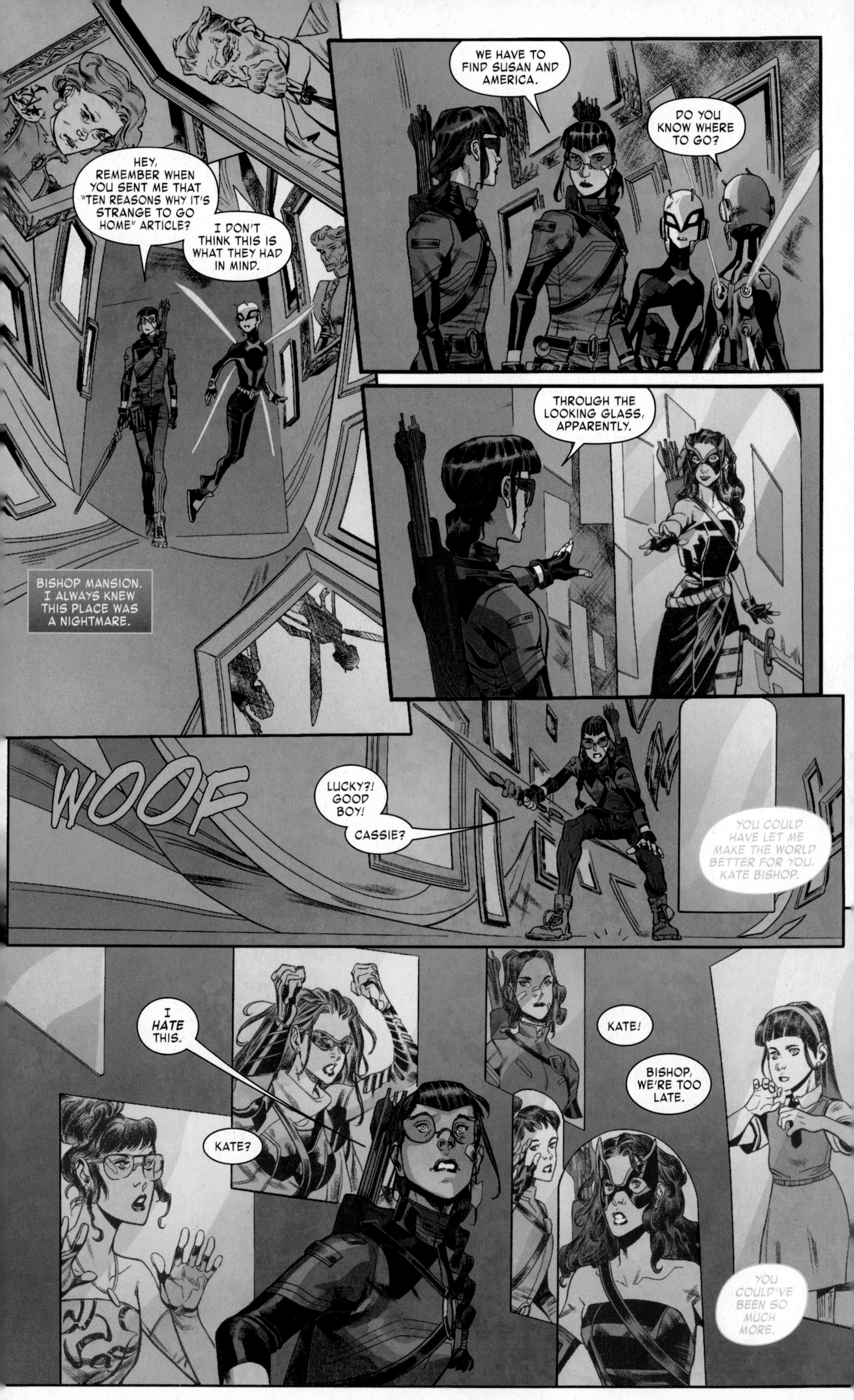
HEY, REMEMBER WHEN YOU SENT ME THAT "TEN REASONS WHY IT'S STRANGE TO GO HOME" ARTICLE?
I DON'T THINK THIS IS WHAT THEY HAD IN MIND.
BISHOP MANSION. I ALWAYS KNEW THIS PLACE WAS A NIGHTMARE.
WE HAVE TO FIND SUSAN AND AMERICA.
DO YOU KNOW WHERE TO GO?
THROUGH THE LOOKING GLASS, APPARENTLY.
WOOF
LUCKY?! GOOD BOY!
CASSIE?
YOU COULD HAVE LET ME MAKE THE WORLD BETTER FOR YOU, KATE BISHOP.
I HATE THIS.
KATE?
KATE!
BISHOP, WE'RE TOO LATE.
YOU COULD'VE BEEN SO MUCH MORE.

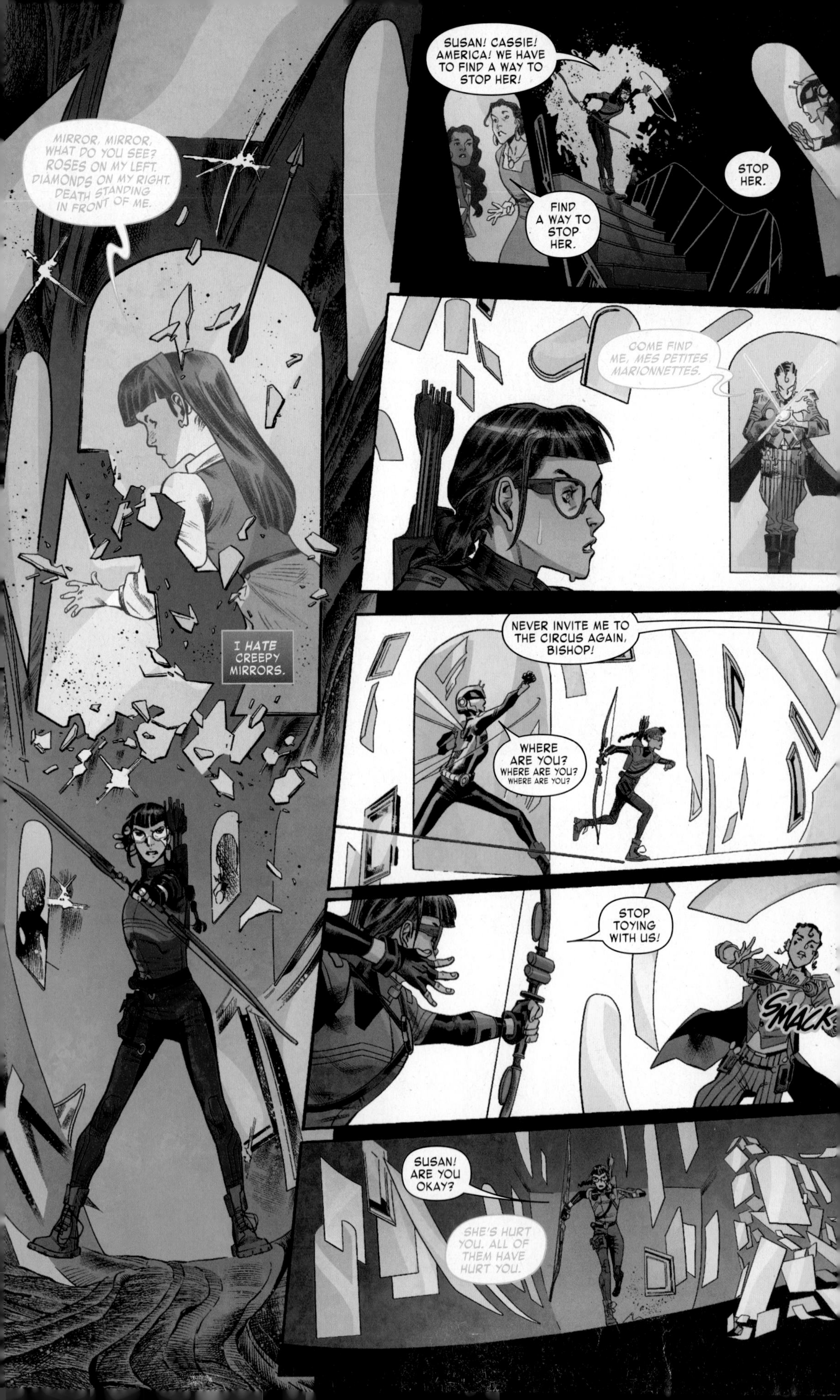
MIRROR, MIRROR, WHAT DO YOU SEE? ROSES ON MY LEFT. DIAMONDS ON MY RIGHT. DEATH STANDING IN FRONT OF ME.
I HATE CREEPY MIRRORS.
SUSAN! CASSIE! AMERICA! WE HAVE TO FIND A WAY TO STOP HER!
FIND A WAY TO STOP HER.
STOP HER.
COME FIND ME, MES PETITES MARIONNETTES.
NEVER INVITE ME TO THE CIRCUS AGAIN, BISHOP!
WHERE ARE YOU? WHERE ARE YOU? WHERE ARE YOU?
STOP TOYING WITH US!
SMACK
SUSAN! ARE YOU OKAY?
SHE'S HURT YOU. ALL OF THEM HAVE HURT YOU.

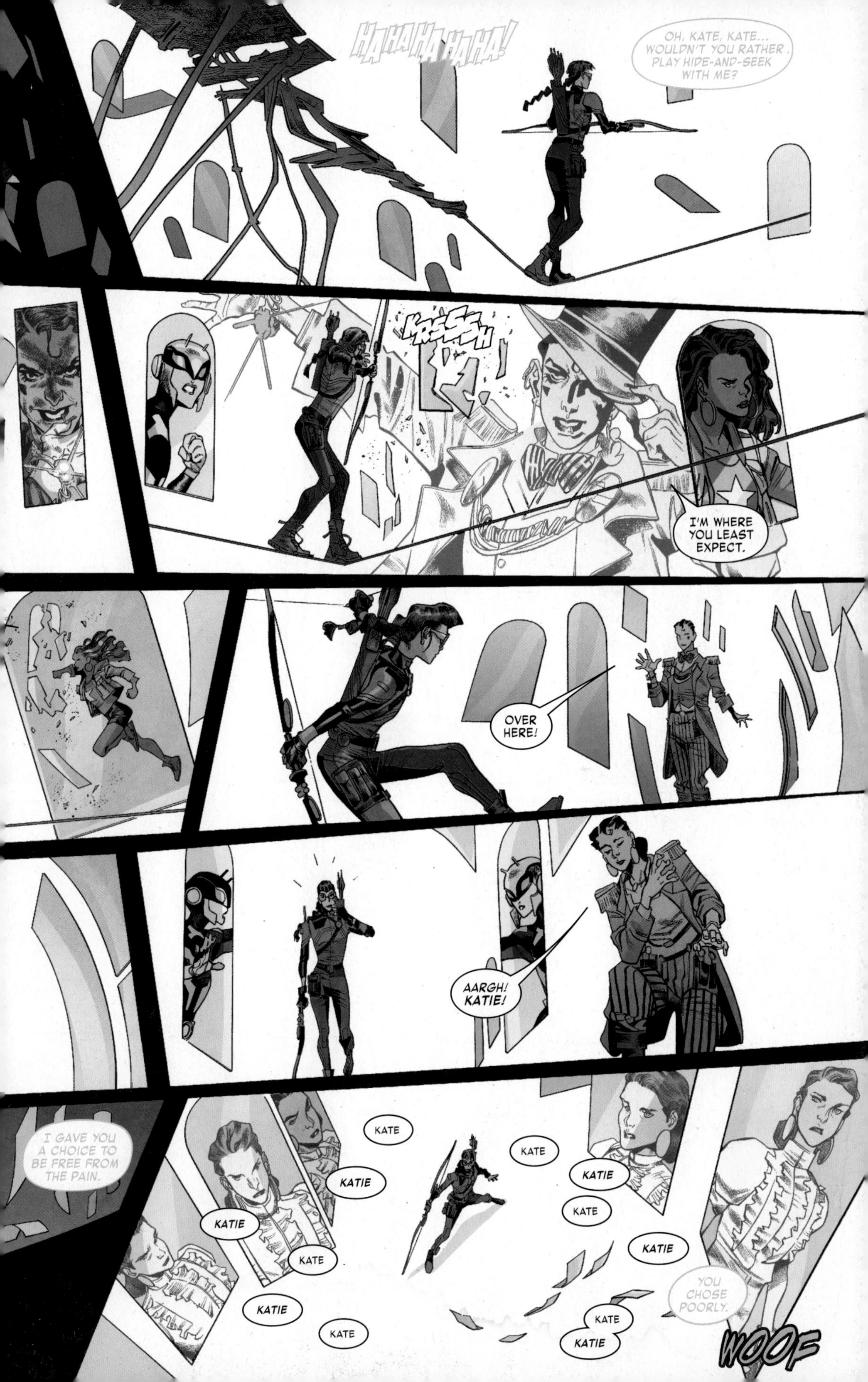
HAHAHAHAHA!
OH, KATE, KATE... WOULDN'T YOU RATHER PLAY HIDE-AND-SEEK WITH ME?
KRSSSH
I'M WHERE YOU LEAST EXPECT.
OVER HERE!
AARGH! KATIE!
I GAVE YOU A CHOICE TO BE FREE FROM THE PAIN.
KATE
KATIE
KATE
KATIE
KATE
KATIE
KATE
KATIE
KATE
KATIE
KATE
KATIE
YOU CHOSE POORLY.
WOOF

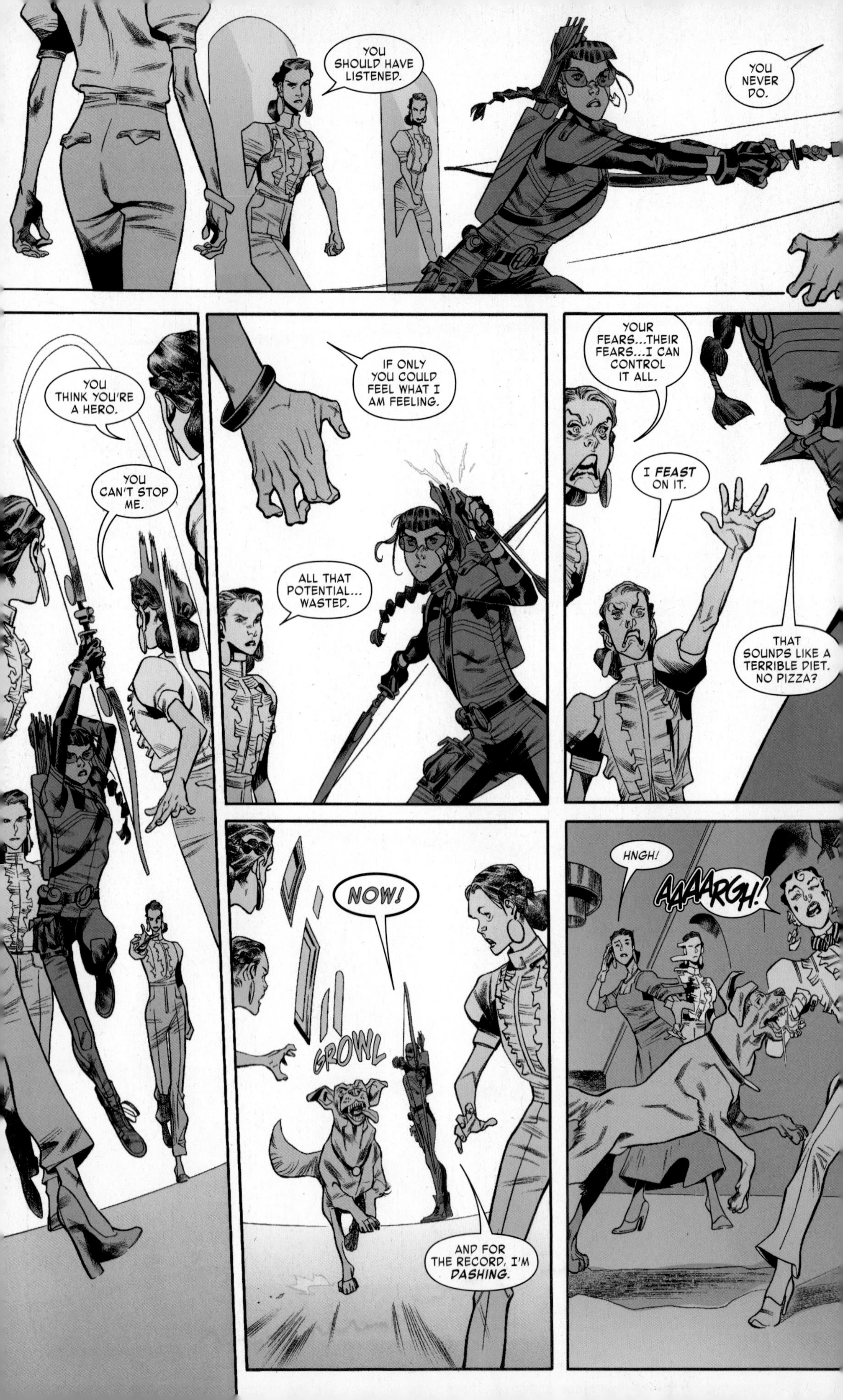
YOU SHOULD HAVE LISTENED.
YOU NEVER DO.
YOU THINK YOU'RE A HERO.
YOU CAN'T STOP ME.
IF ONLY YOU COULD FEEL WHAT I AM FEELING.
ALL THAT POTENTIAL... WASTED.
YOUR FEARS...THEIR FEARS...I CAN CONTROL IT ALL.
I *FEAST* ON IT.
THAT SOUNDS LIKE A TERRIBLE DIET. NO PIZZA?
NOW!
GROWL
AND FOR THE RECORD, I'M *DASHING*.
HNGH!
AAAARGH!

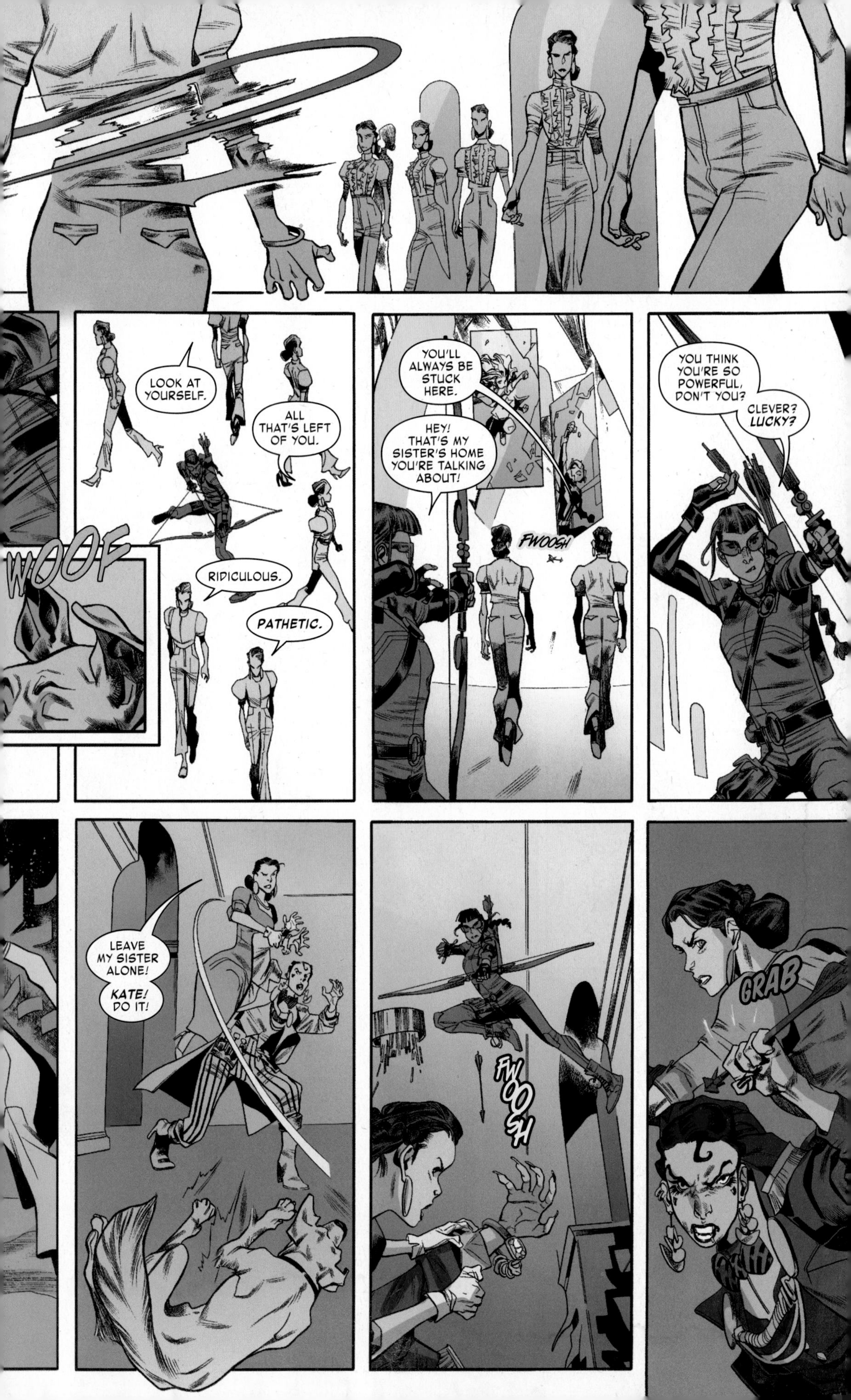

WOOF
LOOK AT YOURSELF.
ALL THAT'S LEFT OF YOU.
RIDICULOUS.
PATHETIC.
YOU'LL ALWAYS BE STUCK HERE.
HEY! THAT'S MY SISTER'S HOME YOU'RE TALKING ABOUT!
FWOOSH
YOU THINK YOU'RE SO POWERFUL, DON'T YOU?
CLEVER? LUCKY?
LEAVE MY SISTER ALONE!
KATE! DO IT!
FWOOSH
GRAB

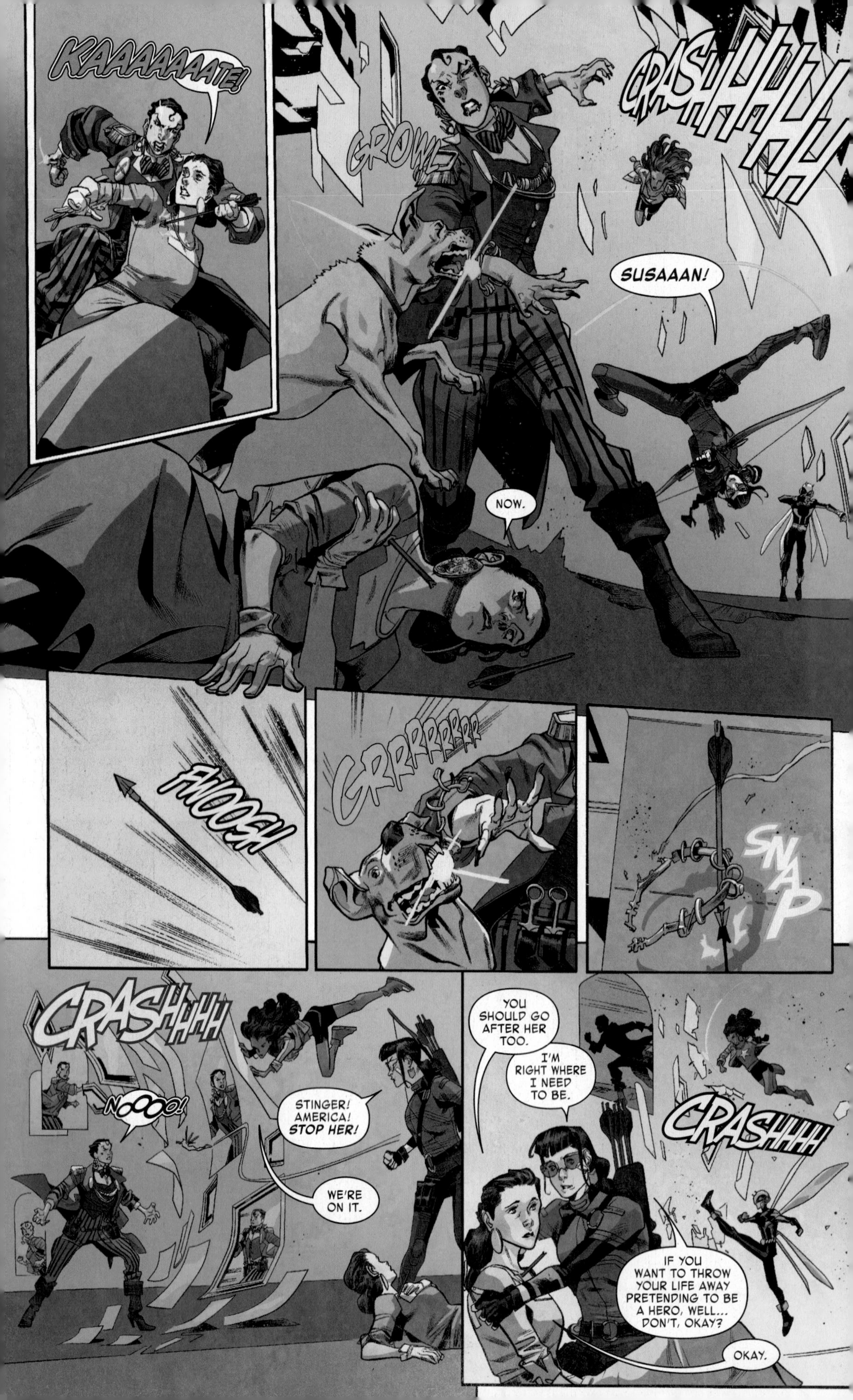
KAAAAAAATE!
GROWL
CRASHHHHH
SUSAAAN!
NOW.
FWOOSH
GRRRRRRR
SNAP
CRASHHHH
NOOOO!
STINGER! AMERICA! STOP HER!
WE'RE ON IT.
YOU SHOULD GO AFTER HER TOO.
I'M RIGHT WHERE I NEED TO BE.
CRASHHH
IF YOU WANT TO THROW YOUR LIFE AWAY PRETENDING TO BE A HERO, WELL... DON'T, OKAY?
OKAY.

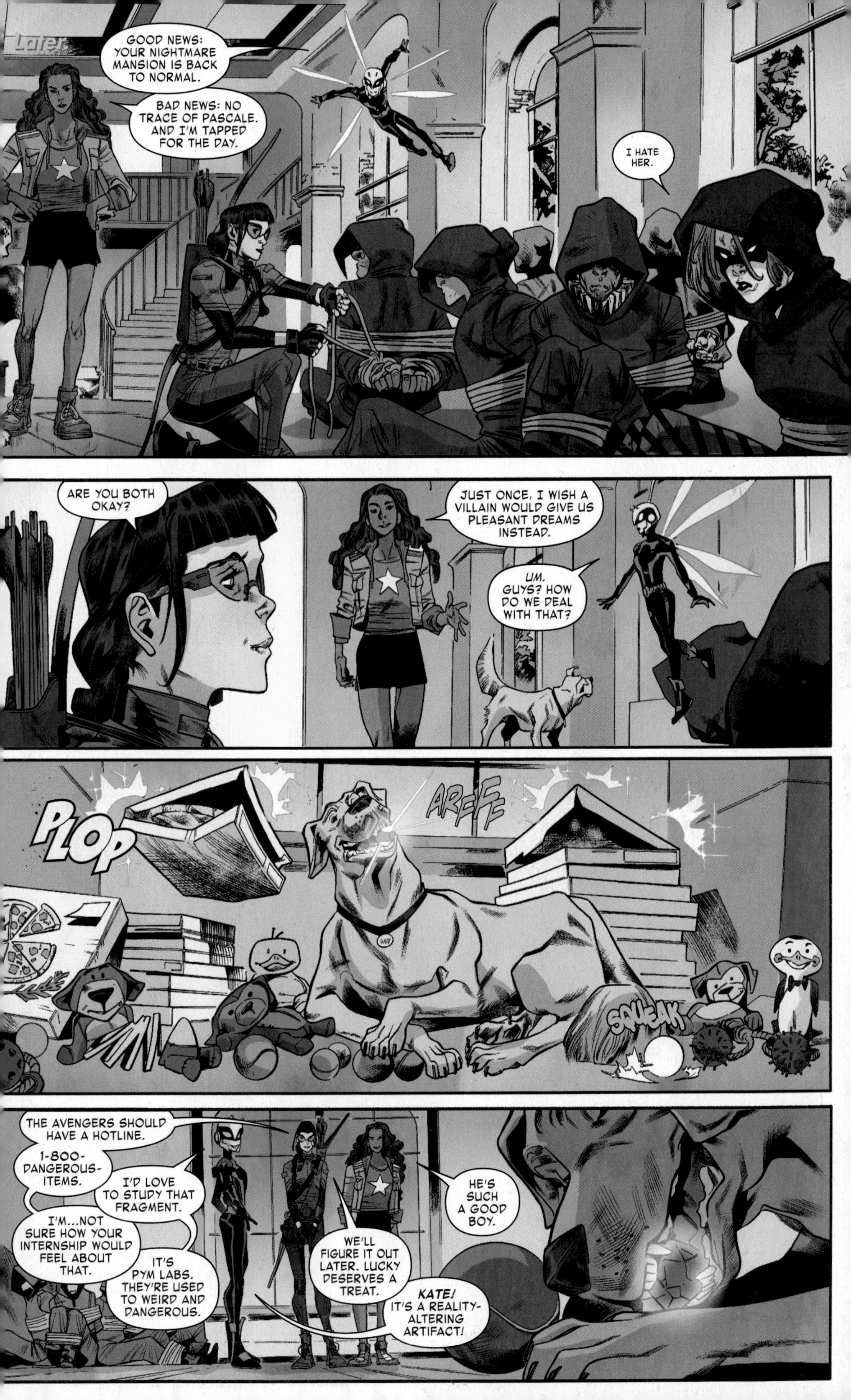
Later
GOOD NEWS: YOUR NIGHTMARE MANSION IS BACK TO NORMAL.
BAD NEWS: NO TRACE OF PASCALE. AND I'M TAPPED FOR THE DAY.
I HATE HER.
ARE YOU BOTH OKAY?
JUST ONCE, I WISH A VILLAIN WOULD GIVE US PLEASANT DREAMS INSTEAD.
UM. GUYS? HOW DO WE DEAL WITH THAT?
PLOP
ARFFF
SQUEAK
THE AVENGERS SHOULD HAVE A HOTLINE.
1-800-DANGEROUS-ITEMS.
I'D LOVE TO STUDY THAT FRAGMENT.
I'M...NOT SURE HOW YOUR INTERNSHIP WOULD FEEL ABOUT THAT.
IT'S PYM LABS. THEY'RE USED TO WEIRD AND DANGEROUS.
HE'S SUCH A GOOD BOY.
WE'LL FIGURE IT OUT LATER. LUCKY DESERVES A TREAT.
KATE! IT'S A REALITY-ALTERING ARTIFACT!

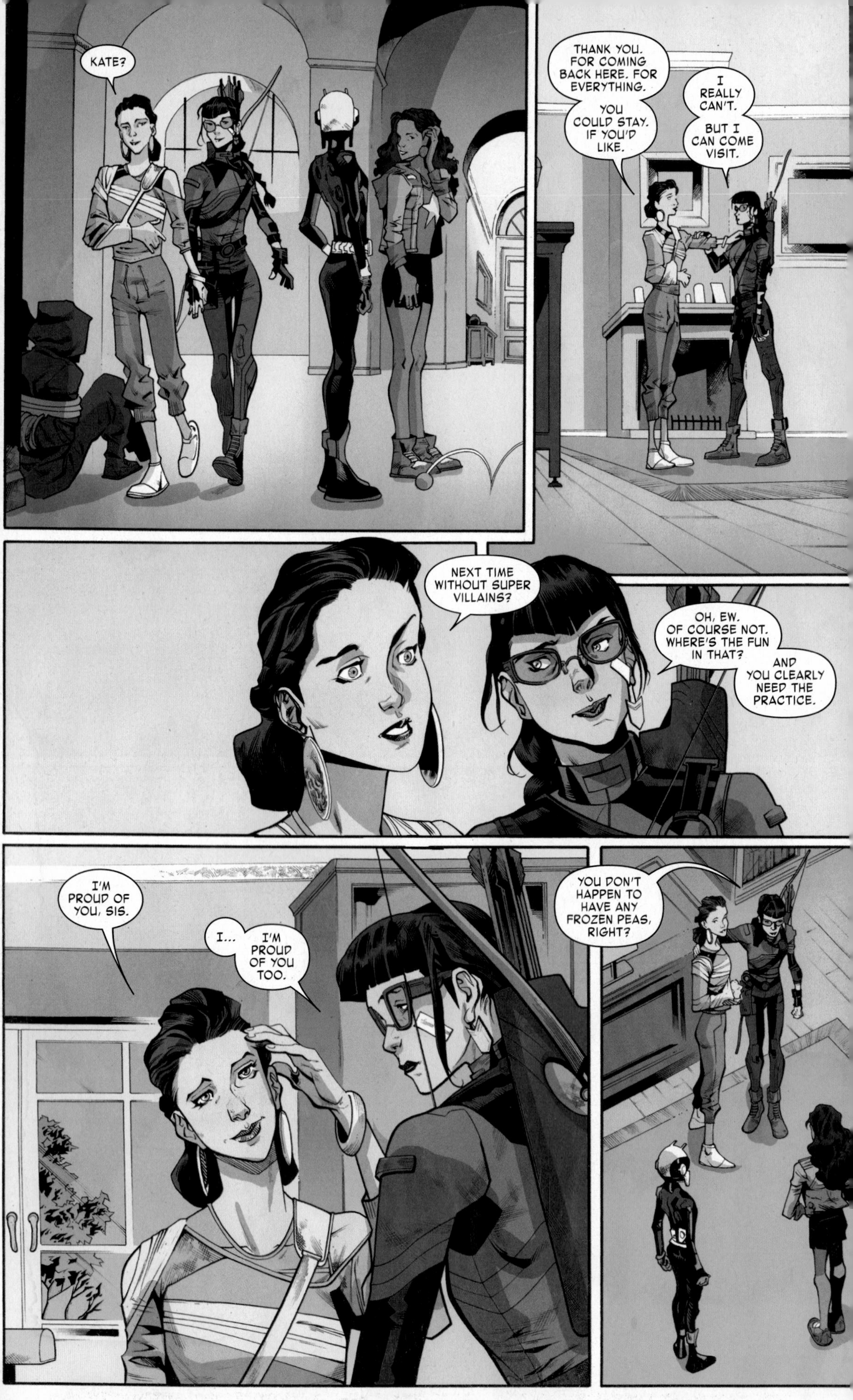
KATE?
THANK YOU. FOR COMING BACK HERE. FOR EVERYTHING.
YOU COULD STAY. IF YOU'D LIKE.
I REALLY CAN'T.
BUT I CAN COME VISIT.
NEXT TIME WITHOUT SUPER VILLAINS?
OH, EW. OF COURSE NOT. WHERE'S THE FUN IN THAT?
AND YOU CLEARLY NEED THE PRACTICE.
I'M PROUD OF YOU, SIS.
I... I'M PROUD OF YOU TOO.
YOU DON'T HAPPEN TO HAVE ANY FROZEN PEAS, RIGHT?

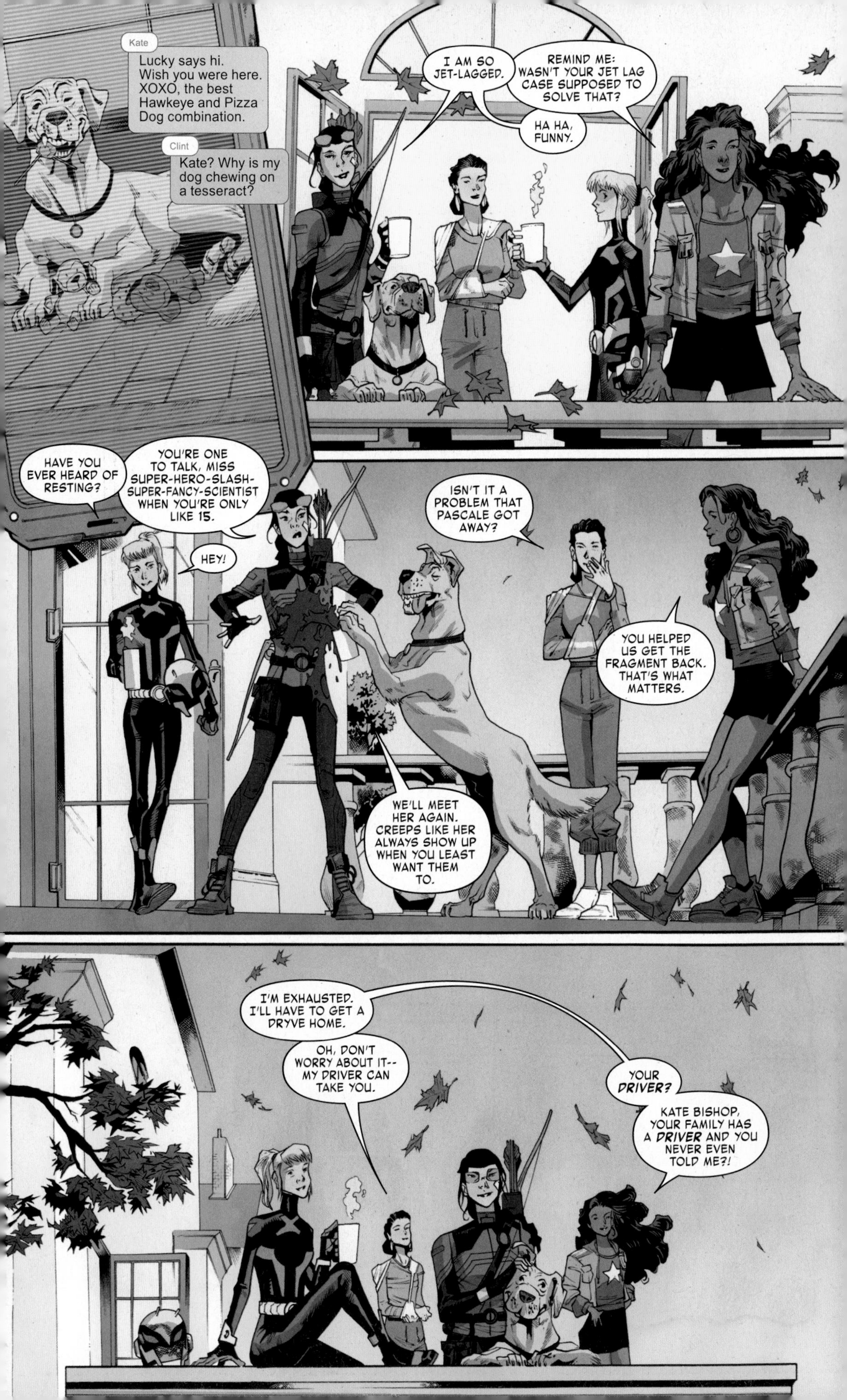
Kate
Lucky says hi. Wish you were here. XOXO, the best Hawkeye and Pizza Dog combination.
Clint
Kate? Why is my dog chewing on a tesseract?
I AM SO JET-LAGGED.
REMIND ME: WASN'T YOUR JET LAG CASE SUPPOSED TO SOLVE THAT?
HA HA, FUNNY.
HAVE YOU EVER HEARD OF RESTING?
YOU'RE ONE TO TALK, MISS SUPER-HERO-SLASH-SUPER-FANCY-SCIENTIST WHEN YOU'RE ONLY LIKE 15.
HEY!
ISN'T IT A PROBLEM THAT PASCALE GOT AWAY?
YOU HELPED US GET THE FRAGMENT BACK. THAT'S WHAT MATTERS.
WE'LL MEET HER AGAIN. CREEPS LIKE HER ALWAYS SHOW UP WHEN YOU LEAST WANT THEM TO.
I'M EXHAUSTED. I'LL HAVE TO GET A DRYVE HOME.
OH, DON'T WORRY ABOUT IT-- MY DRIVER CAN TAKE YOU.
YOUR DRIVER?
KATE BISHOP, YOUR FAMILY HAS A DRIVER AND YOU NEVER EVEN TOLD ME?!

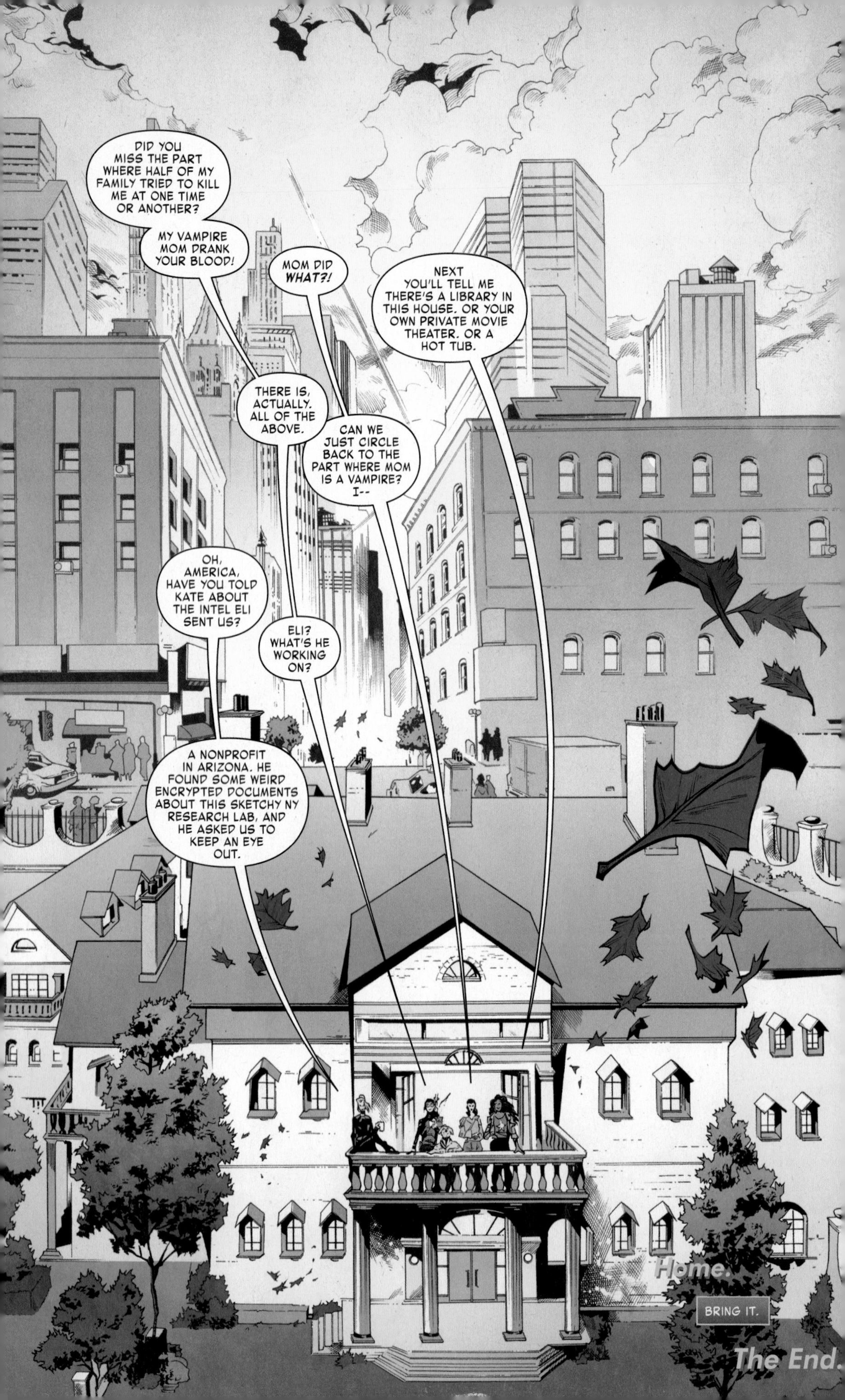

DID YOU MISS THE PART WHERE HALF OF MY FAMILY TRIED TO KILL ME AT ONE TIME OR ANOTHER?
MY VAMPIRE MOM DRANK YOUR BLOOD!
MOM DID *WHAT?!*
NEXT YOU'LL TELL ME THERE'S A LIBRARY IN THIS HOUSE. OR YOUR OWN PRIVATE MOVIE THEATER. OR A HOT TUB.
THERE IS, ACTUALLY. ALL OF THE ABOVE.
CAN WE JUST CIRCLE BACK TO THE PART WHERE MOM IS A VAMPIRE? I--
OH, AMERICA, HAVE YOU TOLD KATE ABOUT THE INTEL ELI SENT US?
ELI? WHAT'S HE WORKING ON?
A NONPROFIT IN ARIZONA. HE FOUND SOME WEIRD ENCRYPTED DOCUMENTS ABOUT THIS SKETCHY NY RESEARCH LAB, AND HE ASKED US TO KEEP AN EYE OUT.
Home.
BRING IT.
The End.

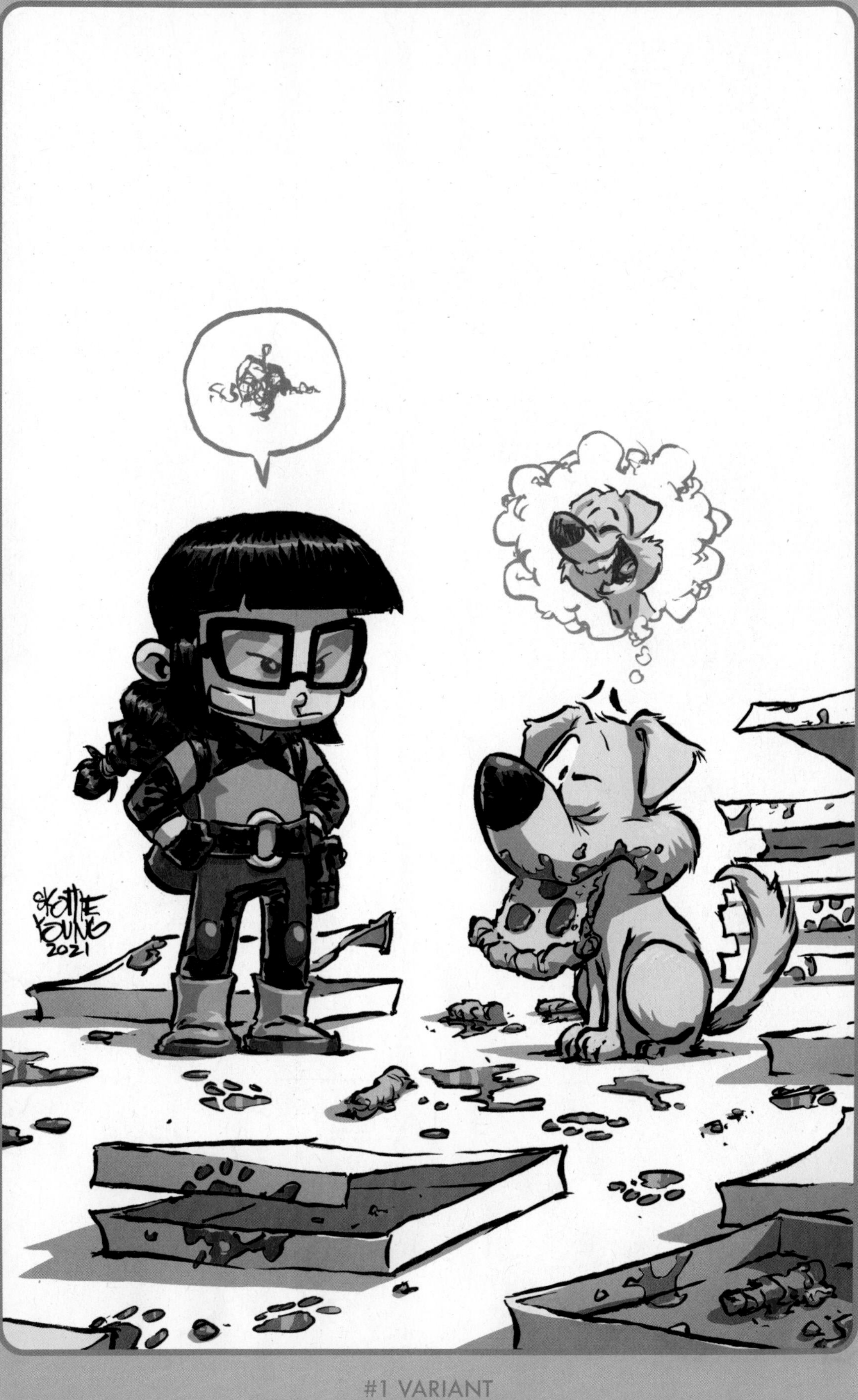
SKOTTIE YOUNG 2021

#1 VARIANT
BY SKOTTIE YOUNG

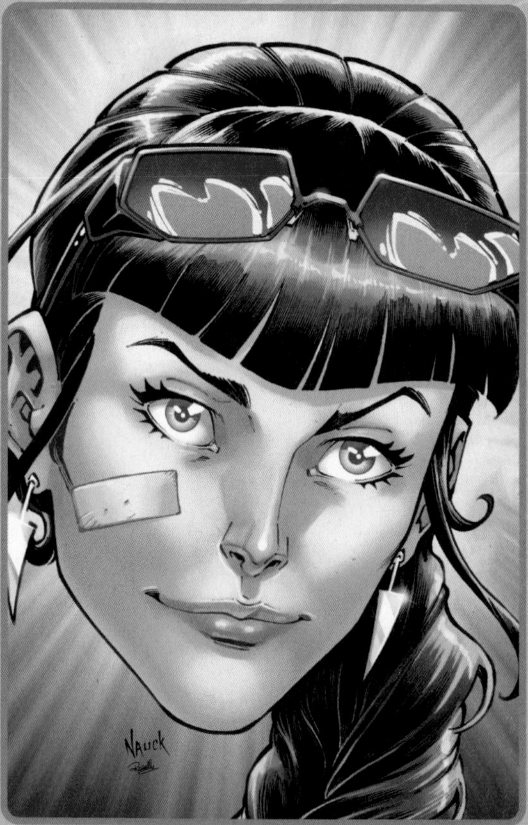
NAUCK

#1 HEADSHOT VARIANT
BY TODD NAUCK & RACHELLE ROSENBERG

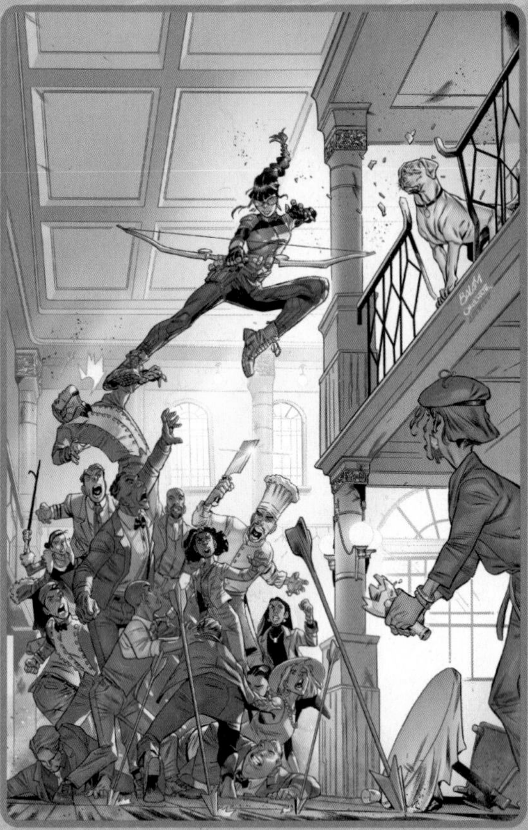

#1 VARIANT
BY ENID BALÁM & JESUS ABURTOV

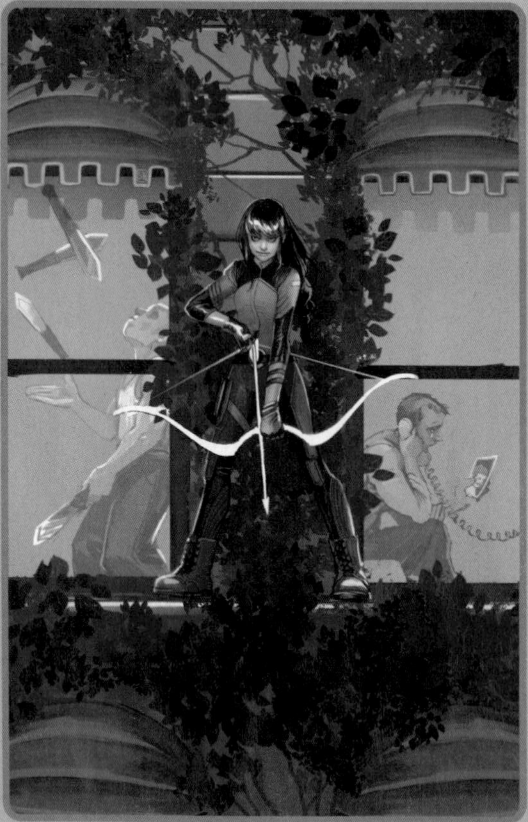

#2 VARIANT
BY STEPHANIE HANS

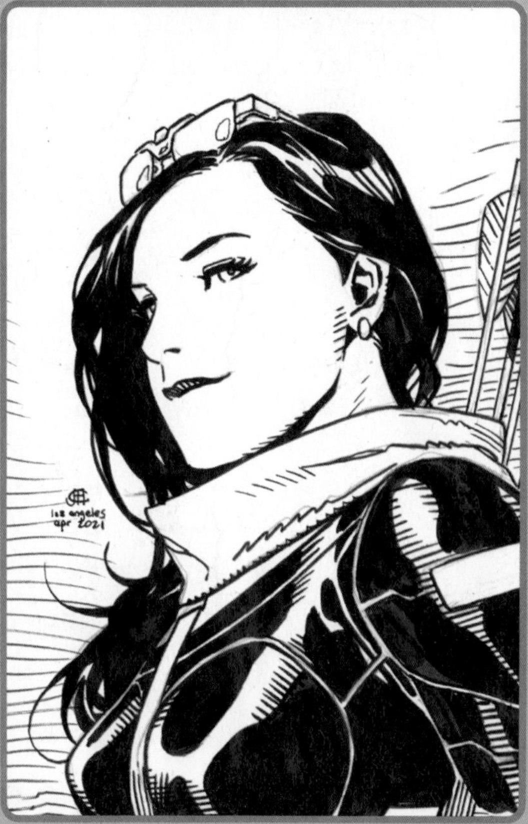
los angeles
apr 2021

#3 HEADSHOT SKETCH VARIANT
BY JIM CHEUNG

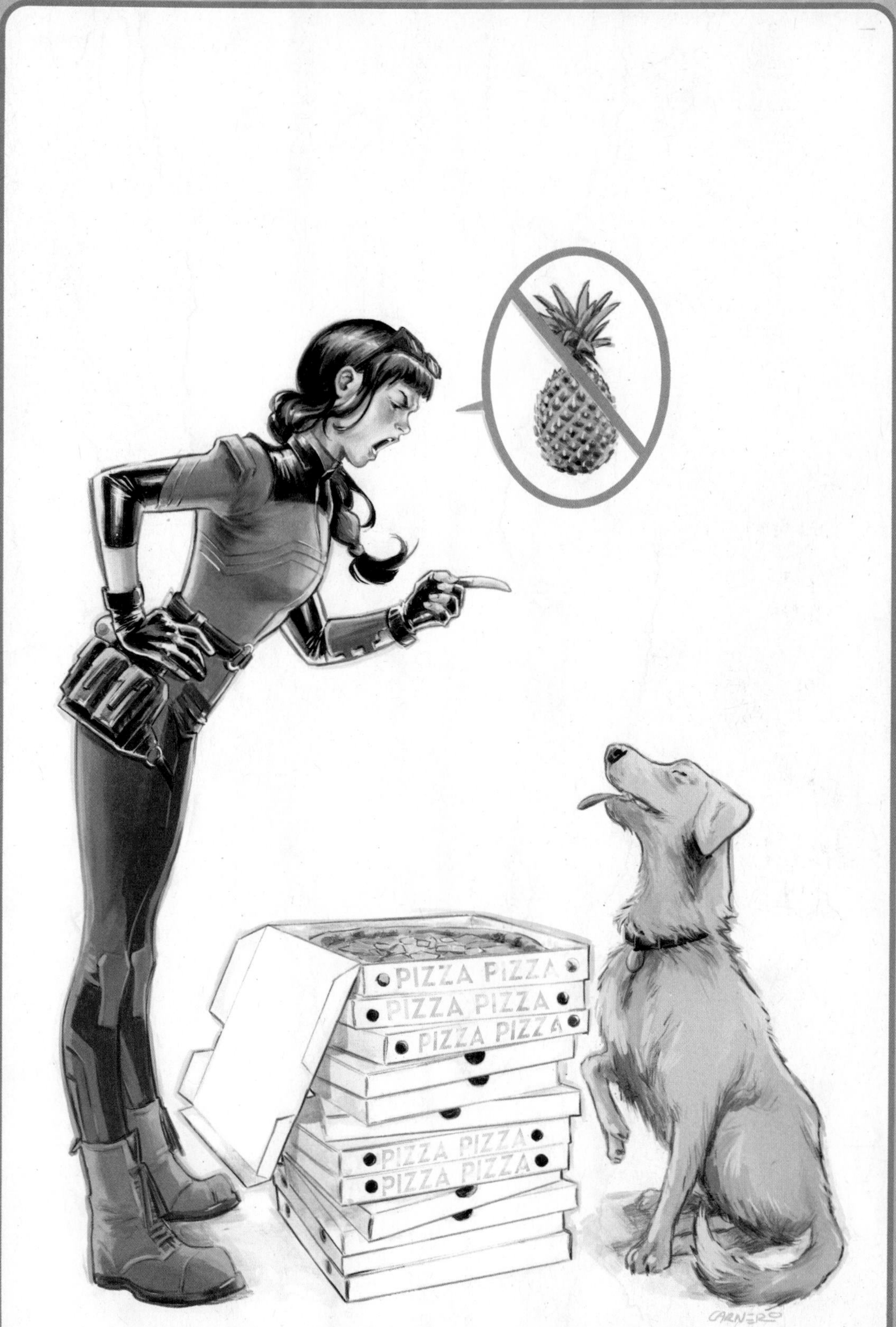
PIZZA PIZZA
PIZZA PIZZA
PIZZA PIZZA
PIZZA PIZZA
PIZZA PIZZA
CARNERO

#4 STORMBREAKERS VARIANT
BY CARMEN CARNERO

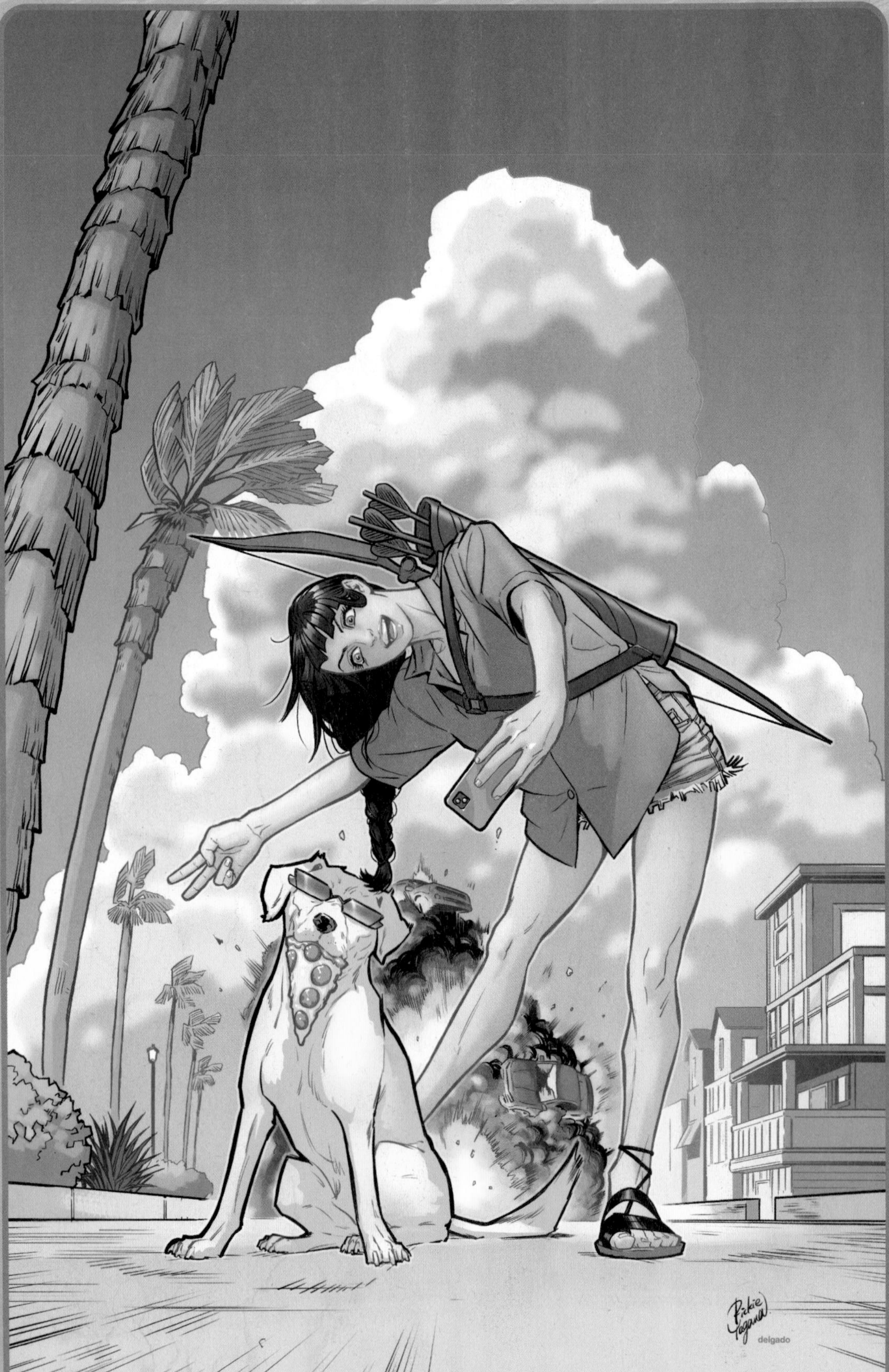
Rickie Yagawa
delgado

#5 VARIANT
BY RICKIE YAGAWA & EDGAR DELGADO

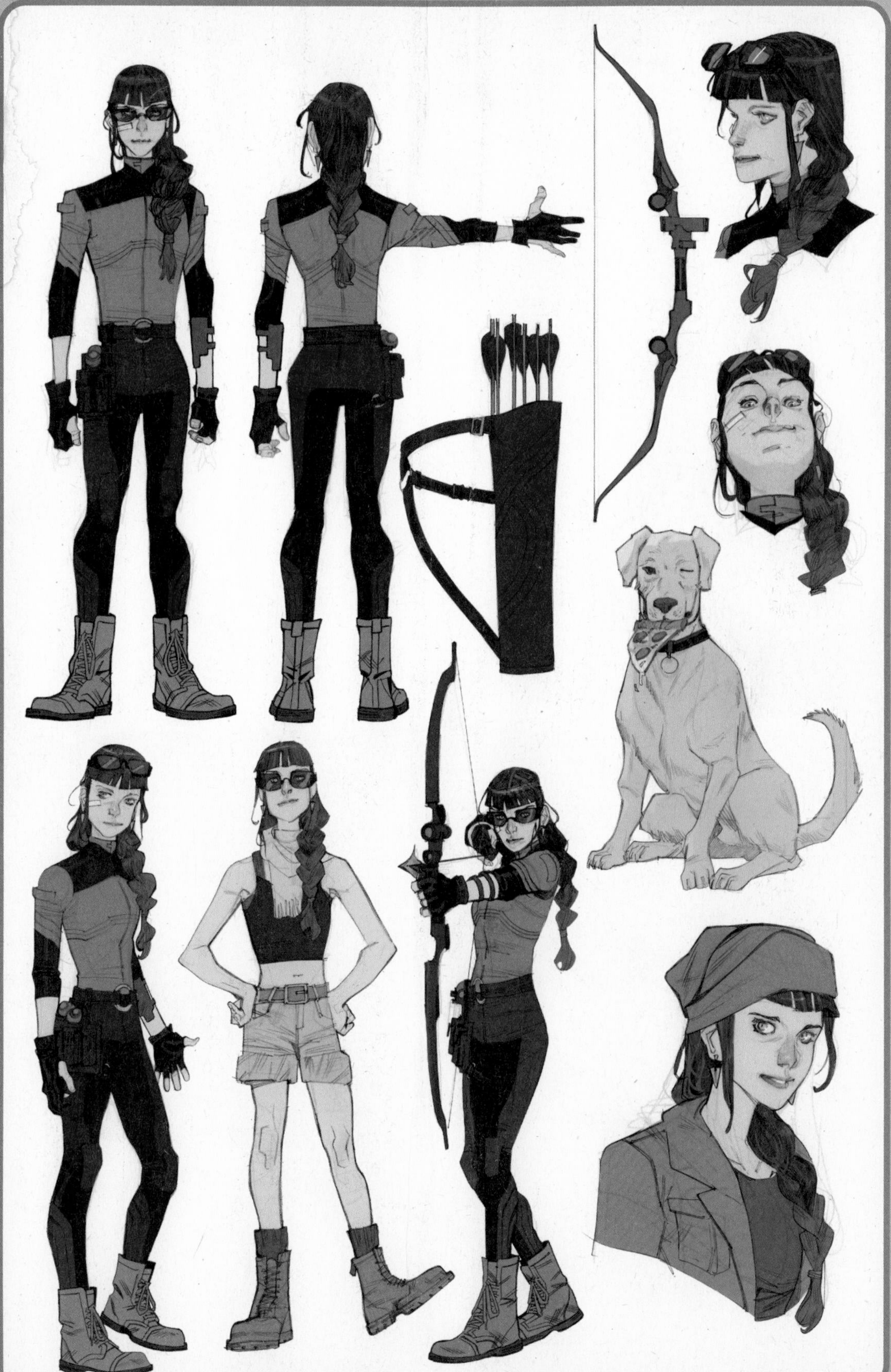

KATE BISHOP DESIGNS
BY **ENID BALÁM**

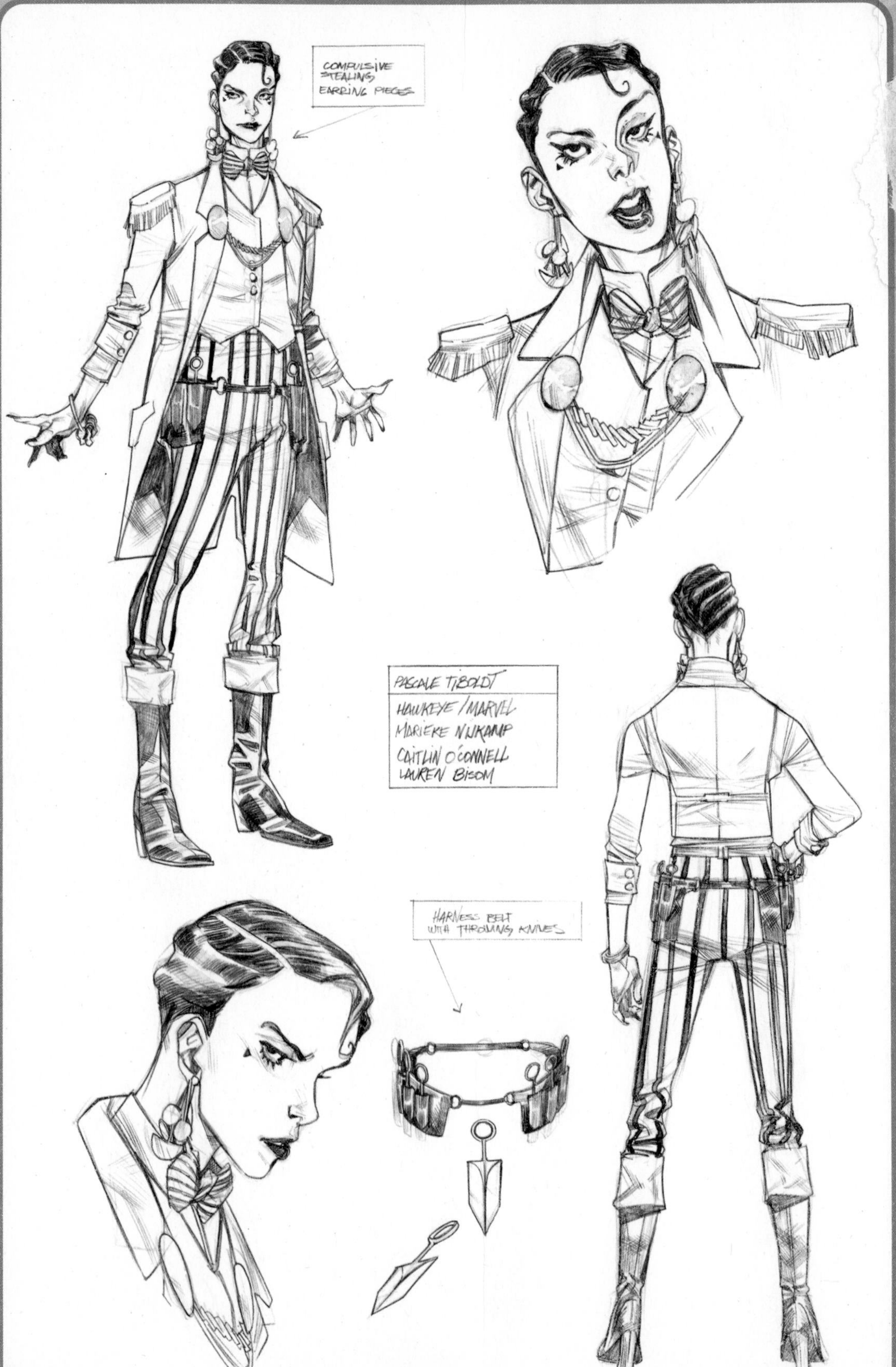
COMPULSIVE STEALING
EARRING PIECES
PASCALE TIBOLDT
HAWKEYE / MARVEL
MARIEKE NIJKAMP
CAITLIN O'CONNELL
LAUREN BISOM
HARNESS BELT WITH THROWING KNIVES

PASCALE TIBOLDT DESIGNS
BY ENID BALÁM